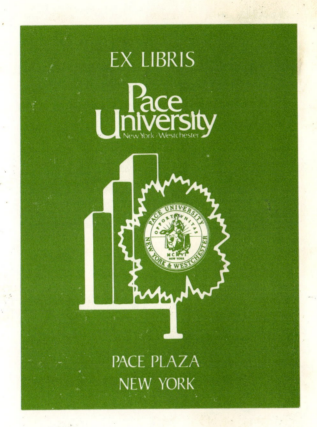

Beowulf to Beatles

Beowulf to Beatles

Approaches to Poetry

Edited by David R. Pichaske

THE FREE PRESS
A Division of Macmillan Publishing Co., Inc.
New York

THE FREE PRESS
A Division of Macmillan Publishing Co., Inc.
866 Third Avenue, New York, N.Y. 10022

Library of Congress Catalog Card Number: 73-160067

Printed in the United States of America

printing number
4 5 6 7 8 9 10

ACKNOWLEDGMENTS

Acknowledgment is gratefully made to the following authors and publishers for permission to reprint copyrighted material:

Tandyn Almer: "Along Comes Mary" copyright © 1965 by Irving Music, Inc. (BMI). Reprinted by permission of Irving Music, Inc. (BMI).

W. H. Auden: "In Memory of W. B. Yeats," "Musée des Beaux Arts," and "The Unknown Citizen" copyright 1940 and renewed 1968 by W. H. Auden; "Paysage Moralisé" copyright 1937 and renewed 1965 by W. H. Auden. Reprinted from *Collected Shorter Poems 1927–1957*, by W. H. Auden, by permission of Random House, Inc.

George Barker: "To My Mother" from *Collected Poems, 1930 to 1965*, copyright © 1957, 1962 and 1965 by George Granville Barker. Reprinted by permission of October House, Inc.

Richard Brautigan: "Discovery" reprinted from *The Pill Versus the Springhill Mine Disaster*, copyright © 1968 by Richard Brautigan. A

Seymour Lawrence Book/Delacorte Press. Used by permission. First published by Four Season Foundation in its Writing series edited by Donald Allen.

Edwin Brock: "Five Ways to Kill a Man" from *With Love from Judas*. Reprinted by permission of Scorpion Press.

Rupert Brooke: "The Soldier" from *The Collected Poems of Rupert Brooke*, copyright 1915 by Dodd, Mead & Company, copyright renewed 1943 by Edward Marsh. Reprinted by permission of Dodd, Mead & Company, Inc.

Gwendolyn Brooks: "love note II: flags" from *Selected Poems*, copyright 1945 by Gwendolyn Brooks Blakely. Reprinted by permission of Harper & Row, Publishers, Inc.

Felice and Boudleaux Bryant: "Bye Bye, Love" reprinted by permission of the authors.

George Chambers: "Deleightful Pie" (story) copyright © 1969 by George Chambers, first published in the *Wisconsin Review* (vol. V, no. 1); "Deleightful Pie" (poem) copyright © 1969 by George Chambers, first published in *The Iowa Review* (vol. I, no. 1). Reprinted by permission of the author.

Sarah N. Cleghorn: "The Golf Links Lie So Near the Mill" from *Portraits and Protests*. All rights reserved. Reprinted by permission of Holt, Rinehart and Winston, Inc.

Leonard Cohen: "Suzanne" reprinted by permission of Project Seven Music, a division of C.T.M.P., Inc. "The Unicorn Tapestries" from *The Spice-box of Earth*, copyright 1961 in all countries of the International Copyright Union by McClelland and Stewart Limited, Toronto. All rights reserved. Reprinted by permission of The Viking Press, Inc.

Judy Collins: "My Father" copyright © 1968 by Rocky Mountain National Park Music Co., Inc. All rights reserved. Used by permission.

Steve Cropper and Otis Redding: "The Dock of the Bay" copyright © 1968, 1969 by East/Memphis Music Corp., Redwal Music Co., Inc. and Time Music Co., Inc. All rights administered by East/Memphis Music Corp., 926 E. McLemore Ave., Memphis, Tenn., 38106. All rights reserved. International copyright secured.

Countee Cullen: "Yet Do I Marvel" from *On These I Stand*, copyright 1925 by Harper & Row, Publishers, Inc., renewed 1953 by Ida M. Cullen. Reprinted by permission of the publishers.

E. E. Cummings: "anyone lived in a pretty how town" copyright 1940 by E. E. Cummings, copyright 1968 by Marion Morehouse Cummings;

303)," *Harvard Journal of Asiatic Studies* 14 (1951) 527–556. Reprinted by permission of the Harvard–Yenching Institute.

Lawrence Ferlinghetti: "Christ climbed down," "I have not lain with beauty," and "Sometime during eternity" from *A Coney Island of the Mind,* copyright © 1958 by Lawrence Ferlinghetti. Reprinted by permission of New Directions Publishing Corporation.

Robert Frost: "Acquainted with the Night," "After Apple-Picking," "Departmental," "Design," "Fire and Ice," "Provide, Provide," and "Stopping by Woods on a Snowy Evening" from *The Poetry of Robert Frost* edited by Edward Connery Lathem. Copyright 1923, 1928, 1930, 1939, © 1969 by Holt, Rinehart and Winston, Inc.; copyright 1936, 1951, © 1956, 1958 by Robert Frost; copyright © 1964, 1967 by Lesley Frost Ballantine. Reprinted by permission of Holt, Rinehart and Winston, Inc.

Tim Hardin: "If I Were a Carpenter" copyright © 1966 by Koppelman–Rubin Enterprises, Inc., 110 East 59th Street, New York, N. Y. 10022. Reprinted by permission of Koppelman–Rubin Enterprises, Inc.

Thomas Hardy: "Channel Firing," "The Division," and "Neutral Tones" from *Collected Poems of Thomas Hardy,* copyright 1925 by The Macmillan Company. Reprinted with permission of The Macmillan Company.

George Harrison: "While My Guitar Gently Weeps" copyright © 1969 by Harrisongs Music, Inc. Written by George Harrison. Used by permission. All rights reserved. International copyright secured. "Within You Without You" copyright © 1967 by Northern Songs Limited. Used by permission. All rights reserved.

Gerard Manley Hopkins: "Carrion Comfort," "God's Grandeur," "Pied Beauty," "Spring and Fall: To a Young Child," "Thou Art Indeed Just, Lord," and "The Windhover" from *The Complete Poems of Gerard Manley Hopkins,* published by Oxford University Press.

A. E. Housman: "1887," "Loveliest of Trees, the Cherry Now," "On Wenlock Edge the Wood's in Trouble," "Terence, This Is Stupid Stuff," "To an Athlete Dying Young," and "The True Lover" from "A Shropshire Lad"—Authorized Edition—from *The Collected Poems of A. E. Housman,* copyright 1939, 1940, © 1959 by Holt, Rinehart and Winston, Inc.; copyright © 1967, 1968 by Robert E. Symons. Reprinted by permission of Holt, Rinehart and Winston, Inc. "Eight O'Clock," "Epitaph on an Army of Mercenaries," and "Shake hands, we shall never be friends, all's over" from *The Collected Poems of*

© 1969 by Don L. Lee. Reprinted by permission of Broadside Press.

John Lennon and Paul McCartney: "A Day in the Life," "Being for the Benefit of Mr. Kite," "Fixing a Hole," "Geting Better," "Good Morning, Good Morning," "I Am the Walrus," "Lovely Rita," "Lucy in the Sky with Diamonds," "Sergeant Pepper's Lonely Hearts Club Band," "She's Leaving Home," "When I'm Sixty-four," and "With a Little Help from My Friends" copyright © 1967 by Northern Songs Limited; "Eleanor Rigby" copyright © 1966 by Northern Songs Limited; "Let It Be" copyright © 1970 by Northern Songs Limited; "Norwegian Wood" copyright © 1965 by Northern Songs Limited. Used by permission. All rights reserved.

Vachel Lindsay: "General William Booth Enters Heaven" from *Collected Poems,* copyright 1913 by The Macmillan Company. Reprinted with permission of The Macmillan Company.

Robert Lowell: "Inauguaration Day: January, 1953" from *Life Studies,* copyright 1953 by Robert Lowell. Reprinted by permission of Farrar, Straus & Giroux, Inc. "Mr. Edwards and the Spider" and "The Quaker Graveyard at Nantucket" from *Lord Weary's Castle,* copyright 1946 by Robert Lowell. Reprinted by permission of Harcourt Brace Jovanovich, Inc.

Claude McKay: "The Outcast" from *Selected Poems of Claude McKay,* copyright 1953 by Bookman Associates, Inc. Reprinted by permission of Twayne Publishers, Inc.

Archibald MacLeish: "Ars Poetica" and "You, Andrew Marvell" from *The Collected Poems of Archibald MacLeish, 1917–1952,* copyright 1952 by Archibald MacLeish. Reprinted by permission of the publisher, Houghton Mifflin Company.

Edna St. Vincent Millay: "My Candle Burns" from *Collected Poems* (Harper & Row), copyright 1922, 1950 by Edna St. Vincent Millay. Reprinted by permission of Norma Millay Ellis.

Howard Nemerov: "Angel and Stone" and "Trees" from *New and Selected Poems,* copyright, The University of Chicago, 1960. Reprinted by permission of the Margot Johnson Agency.

Phil Ochs: "The Flower Lady" copyright © 1966 Barricade Music, Inc.; "Joe Hill," "Pleasures of the Harbor," "The Crucifixion," and "White Boots Marchin' in a Yellow Land" copyright © 1966, 1968 Barricade Music, Inc.; "I Kill Therefore I Am," "The Harder They Fall," "Where Were You In Chicago," and "William Butler Yeats Visits Lincoln Park" copyright © 1968 Barricade Music, Inc. International

Music Pub. Co., Inc. and Irving Music, Inc. (BMI). Reprinted by permission of Irving Music, Inc. (BMI).

Daniel Smythe: "Letter from Maine" from *Strange Element,* copyright © 1966 by The Golden Quill Press. Reprinted by permission of The Golden Quill Press.

Wallace Stevens: "Anecdote of the Jar" and "High Toned Old Christian Woman" copyright 1923 and renewed 1951 by Wallace Stevens; "The Idea of Order at Key West," copyright 1936 by Wallace Stevens and renewed 1964 by Holly Stevens Stephenson. Reprinted from *The Collected Poems of Wallace Stevens* by permission of Alfred A. Knopf, Inc.

Sylvester Stewart: "Thank You (Falletin Me Be Micelf Agin)" copyright © by Stoneflower Music Co. Reprinted by permission of Viva Music–Zapata Music.

Stephen Stills: "For What It's Worth" copyright © 1966, 1967 by Cotillion Music, Inc., Ten East Music & Springalo Toones. Warner-Sevarts Publishing Corp., sole selling agent for the United States and Canada. International copyright secured. All rights reserved. Reprinted by permission of Cotillion Music, Inc.

Dylan Thomas: "Fern Hill" from *Collected Poems,* copyright 1946 by New Directions Publishing Corporation, 1952 by Dylan Thomas. Reprinted by permission of New Directions Publishing Corporation.

Arthur Waley (translator): "The Flower Market" by Po Chu-I from *Translations from the Chinese,* copyright 1919 by Alfred A. Knopf, Inc. and renewed 1947 by Arthur Waley. Reprinted by permission of the publisher.

Richard Wilbur: "Gemini" copyright © 1961 by Richard Wilbur. Reprinted from his volume *Advice to A Prophet and Other Poems* by permission of Harcourt Brace Jovanovich, Inc.

Mason Williams: "You Done Stompt on My Heart" copyright © 1964 by Irving Music, Inc. (BMI). Reprinted by permission of Irving Music, Inc. (BMI).

Peter Yarrow: "The Great Mandella" copyright © 1967 by Pepamar Music Corp.; "Puff (the Magic Dragon)" copyright © 1963 by Pepamar Music Corp. Used by permission of Pepamar Music Corp. All rights reserved.

William Butler Yeats: "Crazy Jane Talks with the Bishop" and "Dialogue of Self and Soul" copyright 1933 by The Macmillan

Company, renewed 1961 by Bertha Georgie Yeats; "Leda and the Swan" and "Sailing to Byzantium" copyright 1928 by The Macmillan Company, renewed 1956 by Georgie Yeats; "The Magi" and "To a Firend Whose Work Has Come to Nothing" copyright 1916 by The Macmillan Company, renewed 1944 by Bertha Georgie Yeats; "The Second Coming" copyright 1924 by The Macmillan Company, renewed 1952 by Bertha Georgie Yeats; "That the Night Come" copyright 1912 by The Macmillan Company, renewed 1940 by Bertha Georgie Yeats; "Upon Being Asked for a War Poem" copyright 1919 by The Macmillan Company, renewed 1947 by Bertha Georgie Yeats; "When You Are Old" copyright 1906 by The Macmillan Company, renewed 1934 by William Butler Yeats. From the *Collected Poems of William Butler Yeats.* Reprinted by permission of The Macmillan Company.

Yevgeny Yevtushenko: "Babiy Yar" and "The Knights" from *Selected Poems by Yevgeny Yevtushenko,* translated with an Introduction by Robin Milner-Gulland and Peter Levi, S. J., copyright © 1962 by Robin Milner-Gulland and Peter Levi. Reprinted by permission of Penguin Books, Ltd.

This book is for

Miss Esther Ann Schisa

and

Dr. G. Herbert Moffses,

who have laid a lot of love on this world.

Since the time of Socrates, at the very
least, it has been a truism that a teacher
must start with where his students are
if he is to take them somewhere else.

Charles E. Silberman,
Crisis in the Classroom

Contents

7. A Selection of Poems 336

Love 336

War 347

Preface

Laughter and unqualified ridicule are the usual reactions within the halls of academia to any mention of rock and roll lyrics as poetry, although it would appear that such reactions are no longer entirely justified. Over the past few years there has indeed emerged something we can call "the poetry of rock," something that can at times be quite good. The beginnings, of course, were far from promising. Despite the fertile sources on which rock music of the 1950's drew, it was musically innovative and vibrant but lyrically almost unrelievedly banal and trivial. If it contained any poetry at all, that poetry was pedestrian, adolescent doggerel full of unrefined slang and trite neoromantic convention. But in the early 1960's there burst upon the scene a number of exceptionally talented artists, perhaps even poets, who managed to bring together in various degrees all the many elements of what we now call rock and to make of them something of quality. It is true that Bob Dylan and Paul Simon and John Lennon in their early years were not much of an improvement over Buddy Holly or Elvis Presley, but they grew rapidly, sorting and mixing and improvising until things like "Sad-Eyed Lady of the Lowlands" and "Bleecker Street" and the lyrics of *Sergeant Pepper's Lonely Hearts Club Band* demonstrated that rock musicians could be poets too; that there could be and in fact was a poetry of rock as deserving of respect as the poetry of the English Renaissance or of the early Romantic period. Suddenly rock has become respectable—as respectable as rock can be—and it is fashionable to quote rock, to "study" rock, to criticize rock as one would criticize new volumes of poetry or new symphonic performances. There now exists a substantial and growing body of what we might call rock criticism, and one expects—or fears—that it will not be too many years before critics and criticians will be crawling over the still-living bodies of Bob Dylan and John Lennon, just as they now crawl over the still-warm corpses of Eliot and Frost. Rock poetry has arrived, although many are still unaware of its arrival. Perhaps it is already departing.

This book accepts the idea of a poetry of rock and uses that poetry in conjunction with the poetry traditionally taught in poetry courses. It accepts the fact that most rock is bad poetry; but so also is 50 per cent of all published poetry, and so too was most of what was written during that incredibly productive decade of English literature between 1590 and 1600. And as we know only too well from experience, even bad poetry can serve a pedagogical purpose. Those who are unwilling to accept the idea of a poetry of rock may still find it useful to use rock as a vehicle into more traditional material, which is also contained in this volume. Whatever we wish to discuss about poetry, be it imagery and metaphor, alliteration and euphony, dramatic monologue and complaint, or simply the careful use of language in all its many aspects, we can find that in rock. What is more important, the idea of poetry becomes more immediate when it is demonstrated that everything we designate as "poetic" is to be found in rock lyrics, because the college generation is most obviously "into" rock. To approach poetry through rock has the advantage of demonstrating the relevance of poetry and poetic criticism to a generation that is highly skeptical about everything its fathers and grandfathers found worth studying. Poetry suddenly becomes not a thing far removed from the ordinary sphere of human experience, but a thing at the center of our lives, a thing with which we are all familiar —which is, of course, what poetry always was and still is (despite the opinions of the majority of Americans to the contrary).

Some will agree with Robert Christgau's dictum that "poems are read or said. Songs are sung," and go on to argue that this fundamental distinction between music and poetry ought to be made, and that this distinction invalidates the entire idea of a poetry of rock. But such an attitude is narrow and historically inaccurate. Virtually all early poetry was sung, or at least chanted to some kind of musical accompaniment. Many medieval poems were written to be sung, including that most treasured lyric, "Summer is icumen in." Those lyrics in Shakespeare's plays were songs before they were poems, as were the ballads we read in poetry anthologies. The fact is that lyrics make good poems, just as poems make good lyrics for musical compositions, and the distinction is not as easily drawn as Cristgau would have us believe. Hearing Vachel

Lindsay perform his poems on records, one would begin to doubt that any distinction at all exists.

Others will quarrel with the organization of this anthology, arguing that it is impossible to find good poetry that relies exclusively on, say, alliteration or metaphor; that poetry really cannot be dissociated into component parts; that some method of structuring an anthology that does not break poetry into pieces would better fit the purposes of a college course. There is a certain amount of truth to that argument, of course, but the alternatives are not at all attractive. Either we must forget about some very useful critical terminology entirely, or we must use it haphazardly, as the individual poems demand. Neither of these approaches is pedagogically useful or sound, and I have accepted the structure I use as the most useful of all possibilities, even with its limitations. This structure allows the student to discuss poets and poetry in general, examine words as symbols and as sounds, engage in generic criticism, develop the ability to read poems in aggregations, and, finally, to form some qualitative judgments about individual poems.

The nature of the organizational apparatus changes as the text proceeds and the student presumably develops in his capability to "handle" criticism. The first chapter relies almost entirely on analysis presented in the text (except, of course, in the closing selection of poems, which is where the student is concerned more with poetic content than technique), on the theory that the student has the right to examine examples of the sort of critical writing and thought he will be expected to produce before he is actually asked to produce it. The following four chapters—"Words as Meaning," "Words as Sound," "Genres," and "Sustained Performances"—move gradually from author analysis to reader analysis as the student develops his ability to think critically when stimulated by the right kind of questions. Analysis diminishes and questions become more frequent and more complicated: in the early chapters distinctions are usually drawn between questions that are easily answered and questions that are not (with a preponderance of the former); late in the text the questioning becomes more open-ended. Poems begin to appear without either analysis or questions. Over these pages the student should develop the ability to distinguish between a good question and a bad question, between a question that will take him somewhere and one that will not, between a question that can be answered and one that will produce informative discussion but no definite answers. He should also develop the ability to formulate questions on his own—the sort of questions that will take him into a poem on his own, without the aid of his text or teacher. (The real function of a teacher is, after all, to teach his students to do without him.) As the student develops this ability to frame questions for himself and to distinguish between useful, fruitful, productive questions and sterile, dead-end issues, the questions in the text disappear, leaving the student to confront poetry with nothing more than a few textual notes and the aid of his instructor—and ultimately, without even the aid of the instructor. Ideally, the organization of this book will, by a carefully controlled process, enable students to produce thoughtful, sensitive criticism of poetry *without* the aid of an instructor. The students' performance in dealing with the poems of the final chapter—"A Selection of Poems"— should provide the measure of the text's success or lack of success.

Still, some who use this text may wish to reorganize the contents to suit their own bent—to move from narrative to dramatic to lyric poetry, for example—or to replace the apparatus here presented with some other of their own devising, or even to discard all critical apparatus. The lyrics and poems contained here are not wholly dependent on the apparatus and structure I have given them; the selection is good and various, and will support a variety of other pedagogical and critical approaches.

Some people will argue that if poetry is at all like music, then it ought to be heard, not read. I agree entirely, and for that reason have provided an Appendix of recordings of the songs *and poems* contained in this volume. At a relatively modest cost, a department can build a substantial library of recorded poetry—students are usually more than willing to loan rock albums—which can be used either in a listening room of the library or on tape in a language lab to supplement the printed words that appear in this book. Frequently I have referred to recorded versions of both poems and songs in the discussions of this book; on such occasions tapes or records might with considerable profit be brought into the classroom to provide the basis for discussion.

A brief note on the texts of the rock lyrics. Only one who has dealt with these lyrics as poems can fully understand the textual problems they present—problems complicated beyond all telling by the fact that they, like medieval lyrics and ballads, seem invariably to have been sung before or as they were written; by the fact that those who compose them in a recording studio seem to take only the most casual interest in their publication in printed form; by the fact that music indicates no line lengths and frequently no punctuation; by the fact that transcription from recording to printed version (as on the jacket of *Sergeant Pepper*) is done in the most careless manner imaginable; by the fact that manuscript versions of some lyrics (Bob Dylan's "All Along the Watchtower," for example) serve to confuse rather than clarify problems; and by the fact that every time a lyric is printed somewhere it appears in a slightly different version. It is also apparent that rock singers have a distressing tendency to forget lyrics (sometimes their own) or to improvise upon the spot, so that what is sung on a record is not necessarily what appears on the lead sheet, and vice versa (Judy Collins' "Story of Isaac" and Leonard Cohen's lyric are virtually two different poems). This is not to chastise the composers and the singers; it is merely to observe some of the difficulties involved when one attempts to set an oral culture in print. Suffice it to say that when the variorum Bob Dylan appears, it will be a very sizeable volume. Meanwhile, we all labor in a cloud of unknowing.

And a final note concerning the selections. I have tried to strike a reasonable balance between the contemporary and the traditional, the fresh and the familiar, the sacred and the profane, in both rock and poetry. If that balance seems to favor the contemporary, the fresh, and the profane, it is because I believe that such a proportion is necessary to correct an imbalance other textbooks have created in favor of the traditional, the familiar (even stale), and the sacred—an imbalance that I believe has contributed greatly to the current American distaste for poetry of all kinds.

For their help in preparing this volume I owe special thanks to Tom Kent, Charles Clancy, Jack Carey, David Isaacson, and Robert C. Albrecht, who read the original manuscript and offered many valuable and insightful suggestions; Suzie Gordon and Cindy Newman, who did a great deal of typing; Bradley University, which provided a grant that paid for much of the typing and Xerox work; Dick Stewart of Irving Music, who has been most helpful and civil in all things; Byerly Music of Peoria, Illinois, which helped me with both sheet music and recordings; RCA, Vanguard, and Caedmon Records, who donated or loaned many records; Free Press editors Pat Vitacco and Tom Gay, whose assistance was invaluable; and Elaine, my wife, for spending many nights alone while I worked in my office. And of course to Bob Dylan, Phil Ochs, The Beatles, Leonard Cohen, and Peter, Paul, and Mary—all brothers and sisters of mercy, bringers of comfort and song.

1

Poetry:
What It Is and
What It Does

Most academic disciplines, especially the sciences and social sciences, begin with some kind of working definition of what it is they mean to study, some well-defined notions about what they expect their study to reveal, and the assumption that the subject is to be studied not because it is fun or pleasurable, but because it is useful or inherently worth knowing about. The study of literature begins with none of these. The problems of constructing a definition of poetry broad enough to cover all those things we usually call poetic, but narrow enough to be at all meaningful, staggers the imagination. It is only infrequently attempted, and then with consistent failure. Poetry is a game with words; poetry is a mystical, nearly religious experience. Poetry sometimes reads like prose; some prose reads like poetry. Wordsworth tells us that poetry is a "spontaneous overflow of powerful feelings"; Pope tells us that poetry is "thought to admiration dressed." To one man the essence of poetry is tension, to another ambiguity, to a third the sound of words, to a fourth word pictures. Poets of the Middle Ages and the Renaissance had a special vocabulary reserved for poetry; the Romantics refused to recognize any difference between the language of poetry and that of ordinary speech. And yet the work of Pope, Swinburne, e. e. cummings, T. S. Eliot, Wordsworth, Milton, Jonson, Whitman, and hundreds of other writers is indeed poetry. Clearly, then, definition is difficult, and the best way to learn what is meant by poetry is to hang around poets for a while listening to what they have to say and observing how they say it. For the present, we can say a thing or two about the varieties of poetry, and make some general observations about the art of poetry, but formal definition must wait.

Nor can we say exactly why poets ought to be studied. Unlike most other disciplines, literature proposes to study that which was written primarily to be enjoyed, and only secondarily—if at all—to teach; and there is something of a paradox in studying what was meant to entertain. Does one study poetry to learn how to appreciate it? It could not have been very entertaining in the first place if we have to learn how to appreciate it now. And if we read for enjoyment, why trouble the brain with intellectualizing the whole business? Why all the bothersome terminology? Why not just sit down and read some poems and enjoy them?

There is an increasingly strong tendency among teachers of literature to do just this: to admit candidly that poems mean different things to different people, to assume that technique cannot be taught or even discussed in the abstract, and simply to read poems and read poems and read poems. Such an approach to poetry can be fun. It does not teach much, though, either about poetry itself or about the criticism of poetry. If we want to read "groovy poetry," let us all go home and read groovy poetry; if we want to learn something about poetry and how it goes about entertaining us and—perhaps more important—how we can talk about how it entertains us, then let us get on with the business of studying and quit trying to have a good time about it. This is not to say, of course, that we cannot choose for study poems that interest us and are relevant to the world of the 1970's; it is only to say that once we have chosen, we will study rather than simply experience them. Although our subject and perhaps even our study may accidently be entertaining, we will still study primarily to learn.

What, then, do we expect to learn? Why study what was meant to entertain? From a historical point of view, of course, there are any number of reasons, the most compelling of which is the fact that the poetry of an age or a country or even an individual poet tells us quite a bit about what that age or country or poet thought about human existence as it was experienced. Think, for example, of how much the poetry of rock tells us about the values and attitudes toward sex, drugs, and protest held by those who write the songs, or how much the poetry of Yeats or Milton or Donne tell us about both the individuals and the ages in which they lived. Certainly we can study poems as cultural documents and be well rewarded for our efforts.

There are other, quite compelling reasons. If poetry is anything, it is a communication between the poet and his audience—sometimes very subtle and sophisticated communication of a thought, or a feeling, or a mood (something laid between the lines, as Peter, Paul, and Mary would put it), but communication nevertheless. In studying poetry we are actually studying the process of communication developed into an art. Of course, there is manifest absurdity in the statement, "If people would read more poetry there would be less trouble in the world today"; but insofar as poetry is communication and this world of ours has some very real communication problems, we might well profit by an increased awareness of language, the prime medium of communication, that a study of poetry can give us.

But most important, poetry is an art, an art that is practiced—usually in hiding—by very many people, even in the 1970's. Art invites qualitative judgements, whether one is judging his own work or the work of someone else, and when one begins to make qualitative judgements about anything, vague statements like "I like it" or "It interests me," simply won't do. The study of poetry can give us some terminology to use when we discuss poetry, it can help us understand how certain poems came to be as they are, it can give us a better understanding of what makes a poem good or bad, and it can give us some practice in making aesthetic judgements that may do much for our taste in poetry and in rock lyrics. And if there is one thing America needs, it is a little taste.

SENSITIVITY TO LANGUAGE

So we shall study poetry for one reason or another, perhaps only because it is required of us. Where shall we begin? One thing that is certain about all poetry is that it uses words, so let us begin with the words to a poem, a good poem, that achieved widespread popularity just a few years ago.

Twentieth Century Fox

Well, she's fashionably lean
And she's fashionably late.
She'll never wreck a scene,

She'll never break a date;
But she's no drag   5
Just watch the way she walks,
She's a twentieth century fox.

She's a twentieth century fox;
No tears, no fears,
No ruined years,   10
No clocks;
She's a twentieth century fox.

She's the queen of cool,
And she's the lady who waits,
Since her mind left school,   15
It never hesitates;
She won't waste time
On elementary talk,
She's a twentieth century fox.

She's a twentieth century fox.   20
Got the world
Locked up
Inside a plastic box;
She's a twentieth century fox.

—*Jim Morrison*

At first glance the song appears to be something of a love poem to a girl of the twentieth century. Morrison appears to compliment her in the opening lines: "She'll never wreck a scene,/She'll never break a date;/ But she's no drag/Just watch the way she walks." But some very important words undercut that first impression and turn this love song into one of the most scathing satires yet written on modern women. "Plastic," for instance: what are the connotations of plastic? Could the word ever be used in a complimentary manner in reference to a woman? Or "fashionably." All we know of Morrison's attitude toward what is fashionable in morals, dress, and behavior makes it clear that this word is used pejoratively. The title phrase calls to mind a Hollywood film company and plays on the associations of false glamour that any mention of Hollywood and filmdom is bound to carry. The "fox" may suggest the modern American woman-as-predator, source of all kinds of sexual and psychological problems in both men and woman resulting from this reversal of traditional male-female roles. It does not take very long before the connotation of the language of this song makes us very much aware that this is certainly no love lyric to the modern American woman. In fact, the connotation of the language makes it exactly the opposite.

Listen to The Doors' performance of this song. To what extent does the music—the two drum beats before "twentieth century fox," the insistence on that phrase achieved by the regularity of its rhythm contrasted to the rhythm of the initial four lines, the tone of Morrison's voice, his pronunciation—supplement the connotative meaning of the lyrics?

Loveliest of Trees, the Cherry Now

Loveliest of trees, the cherry now
Is hung with bloom along the bough,
And stands about the woodland ride
Wearing white for Eastertide.

Now, of my threescore years and ten,   5
Twenty will not come again,
And take from seventy springs a score,
It only leaves me fifty more.

And since to look at things in bloom
Fifty springs are little room,   10
About the woodlands I will go
To see the cherry hung with snow.

—*A. E. Housman*

> 5. *threescore years and ten:* the biblical life-span of man.

This is one of the most well-known of all A. E. Housman's lyrics—perhaps known to the point of being worn out. The subject is not complicated: a young man of twenty contemplates the freshness of spring, calculates that he has but fifty or so more years left in his life, and concludes that this time is "little room" to absorb "things in bloom." The thought is not profound; it might be even a bit maudlin and sentimental, but it strikes a responsive chord in even the most jaded of us. What makes the poem memorable, however, is the single word "snow," and the wealth of conflicting connotative meanings it is made to carry. On one level the poet is comparing the white of the cherry blossoms to the white of snow—an apt if trite comparison. On another level, "snow" echoes the thought of death in the second stanza, and carries connotations of mortality and death at the very moment it is being used to connote the life and rebirth of spring blossoms. We had nearly forgotten the unpleasant business of line 7 in the descriptions of the final stanza, but the last word of the poem brings it startlingly back into our minds in a fashion we simply cannot forget.

It is important, then, to be aware of connotative as well as denotative values of words in the poems we hear; some, like the two we've been discussing, simply do not make any sense without this awareness. The sensitive poet is very much aware of the connotations of words, and he chooses his language carefully when writing his poems. What makes things difficult for a reader is that a word may have some connotations for the poet that are not common to the rest of the population—that is, a word may have private rather than public connotative meaning. Of course, familiarity with the poet's other work and the way in which he uses language will help clarify troublesome usages, but a good poet will be careful not to use words that confuse rather than enhance his clarity.

Another problem with connotations is that they change. Such changes are out of the poet's control, and they often present problems for readers. T. S. Eliot, in his play *Murder in the Cathedral,* used the phrases, "Old Tom, gay Tom, Becket of London," and "The strain on the brain of the small folk. . . ." Unfortunately for the poet and his play, these now sound a trifle humorous because of the current usage of "gay" and the abuse of the expression "strain on the brain" a few years ago. It is difficult if not impossible for modern readers to put current connotations out of their minds when they read the play. Sometimes words lose the connotations they once had, and it becomes necessary to reconstruct meaning. Imagine, for example, a reader one hundred years from now trying to reconstruct the connotations Canada has in war literature today; or the different meaning "Twentieth Century Fox" would have if plastic one day came to be valued as we now value pewter or brass or wood. There is no doubt that being this careful about connotation is something of a bother, but it is a very necessary bother, especially for readers of poetry.

Words have qualities other than connotative and denotative meanings, of course, and a good poet makes use of them. In the first place, words have sounds, and poetry makes considerable use of words as sounds. Everyone knows what Poe did in adjusting sound combinations of the words of "The Bells" to make his verse imitate the sounds of the various bells he described, and we can all think of a number of other lines of poetry that are memorable more for the way they sound than for what they actually say. Some of the lines in "Twentieth Century Fox," for example, are memorable in this manner: "No tears,/No fears,/No ruined years." The phrase "wearing white" sticks in our minds long after we have put down Housman's poem because of the repetition of the "w" sound is "wearing" and "white." The very successful advertisement "Pepsi pours it on" owed its appeal as much to the repetition of the "p" sound in "Pepsi pours" as to the pun in "pours it on." We are used to listening to rock songs and television advertisements, so we may be aware of the sound value of words in a Doors lyric or a soft drink commercial, but poetry has become in modern times too much a thing of the printed page for us to be fully attuned to the sound of words in a poem. But poetry should not—perhaps it cannot—be read silently, like a textbook or a newspaper—just as we would never dream of reading a song silently to ourselves. Poetry should be read aloud or, if possible, listened to, because in poetry as in rock songs, the music of the lines is important.

And finally, words acquire another dimension when they are printed: they are shape and form, ink on a page. *Playboy* magazine exploits this aspect of words when it prints wordplays like B☉S☉m or TALL. Advertising uses words as shapes when it prints something like *The* HOMESTEAD in an attempt to sell readers a piece of real estate. Notice how the large block letters of *homestead* emphasize connotations of solidarity and tradition already implicit in the meaning of the word itself. How does the type face of *The* compliment or supplement those connotations?

A few poets have experimented with visual, or concrete, poetry, making designs out of the words on the page, or twisting letters or typography into strange shapes. Some of this concrete poetry is even quite literally cast in concrete, or etched into glass, or painted on canvas. The poet e. e. cummings is famous for disarraying the typography of his poems intentionally, either to convey meaning or to catch the reader's attention. Sometimes the arrangement of words and letters is so important that it becomes the whole poem, as in the following example.

r-p-o-p-h-e-s-s-a-g-r

<pre>
                    r-p-o-p-h-e-s-s-a-g-r
               who
     a) s w (e loo) k
     upnowgath
               PPEGORHRASS   5
                         eringint(o-
     aThe):l
            eA
               !p:
     S   a   10
                (r
       rIvInG   .gRrEaPsPhOs)
                         to
     rea(be)rran(com)gi(e)ngly
     ,grasshopper;   15
</pre>

—e. e. cummings

The poet is trying to capture on paper that instant when you have been walking along thinking of nothing in particular and looking at nothing in particular, and suddenly out of nowhere something springs up by you. At first you are not sure of what this thing is—only that it is indeed something, and that it has leapt up with great energy. It is not until it lands, "rearranges itself" as cummings puts it, that we actually discover that it's a grasshopper. The successive rearrangements of the word "grasshopper" are clearly attempts by cummings to show this process of gradual recognition, and the typography of "leaps" is meant to suggest an actual leap. Is this merely clever, or is the poet doing something significant? Are the clever and the significant necessarily different? Whether we consider this selection to be poetry or not depends, as do so many other things, on how far we are willing to extend our concept of poetry. In the twentieth century, especially, there has been a tendency for distinctions to break down between prose and poetry, visual and auditory arts, even art and reality; we are confronted with visual poetry, or pieces of sculpture that make noise or destroy themselves, or "happenings" that are neither stage drama nor real life. All the old distinctions lose their force in the face of these productions, and we are forced to invent new terms like "visual poetry" or "happening" to describe what we experience. Whether "prose-poetry" or "visual poetry" or "concrete poetry" is "real poetry" is almost an academic question.

THEME

So poets use words as denotation and connotation, as sounds, as shapes—to what end? Is a poem simply an art object, a thing, an arrangement of sounds and forms, or do those sounds and forms have further significance? We have suggested that the poet uses words to communicate a thought or a feeling or an attitude, and it would be safe to assume that because a poet uses words, and words mean things, poems are going to mean things too. In actual fact, it is very difficult to come up with an assortment of words that has no meaning at all, even when one makes up words of one's own. Humpty Dumpty showed in his enormously lucid and perceptive analysis of "Jabberwocky" that even nonsense verse has meaning, although in some cases the meaning of a piece of nonsense verse may be only that the world as the poet sees it is meaningless and absurd. All this is not to say that a poem is only meaning—if you want that, go read an essay. It is to argue, however, that all poems have an identifiable theme, a meaning that we can pin down within wider or narrower boundaries. A poem does not mean anything any reader happens to get out of it, although its exact meaning may vary somewhat from individual to individual. "D-O-G" may mean many things to many people: to one person a puppy, to another a full-grown dog, to a third a beagle, to a fourth a St. Bernard —but "D-O-G" does not mean a two-legged creature with wings and feathers. By the same token, even a very vague poem like "I Am the Walrus" or "The Sick Rose" can mean several different things to

different individuals but still have a general meaning upon which
everyone agrees. Neither, for example, could be read as a poem on
racism or the 4-H Club. The problem of drawing the line between
possible legitimate interpretations of a poem and utter absurdities is a
matter of practice, careful reading of the poem itself, an awareness of
the poet and his age, and—perhaps most important—sound judgment.
In some cases there is little room for argument; in others, a couple of
different interpretations may appear equally valid; in still others, we
may admit a wide variety of possible meanings. In the following two
poems, for example, there is little room for doubt. They yield to a first
reading.

If I Were a Carpenter

If I were a carpenter
And you were a lady
Would you marry me anyway,
Would you have my baby?

If a tinker were my trade   5
Would you still love me?
Carrying the pots I made,
Following behind me.

Save my love through loneliness,
Save my love for sorrow.   10
I've given you my ownliness
Come and give me your tomorrow.

If I worked my hands in wood
Would you still love me?
Answer me, Baby, "Yes I would,   15
I'd put you above me."

If I were a miller
At a mill wheel grinding,
Would you miss your colored box,
Your soft shoes shining?   20

Save my love through loneliness
Save my love for sorrow.
I've given you my ownliness,
Come and give me your tomorrow.

—Tim Hardin

We Wear the Mask

We wear the mask that grins and lies,
It hides our cheeks and shades our eyes—
This debt we pay to human guile;
With torn and bleeding hearts we smile,
And mouth with myriad subtleties.   5
Why should the world be otherwise,
In counting all our tears and sighs?

Nay, let them only see us while
   We wear the mask.

We smile, but, O great Christ, our cries   10
To thee from tortured souls arise.
We sing, but oh the clay is vile
Beneath our feet, and long the mile;
But let the world dream otherwise,
   We wear the mask.   15

—Paul Laurence Dunbar

There can be little argument that "If I Were a Carpenter" and "We Wear the Mask" make definite statements; nor, once we learn that Dunbar is a black poet, can there be much doubt as to what those statements are. You can, no doubt, easily work out the circumstances with which each concerns itself. In fact, there is little to the poems apart from their statements: no flowery language, no figures of speech, only overt and undisguised statement. There is a good deal of this "poetry of statement" both in English literature and in contemporary rock music. One thinks immediately of The Beatles' song "Why Don't We Do It in the Road," and the two lyrics by Bob Dylan and by

Lennon–McCartney, both entitled unambiguously "I Want You." This poetry is not bad poetry or inferior poetry, although one might get that impression from its conspicuous absence from poetry courses and the fact that it is not much discussed in criticism. It simply leaves little to say; it offers the teacher and critic no opportunity to exercise their ingenuity. And it may not wear well, since it lacks the attractive ambiguity and subtlety that come from complex indirection in poetry. But although it is not pretentious, it is still poetry; as these examples demonstrate, it can be good poetry.

Frost's well-known "After Apple-Picking" is more complicated. The poet is more than a bit unclear as to the nature of his impending sleep.

After Apple-Picking

My long two-pointed ladder's sticking through a tree
Toward heaven still,
And there's a barrel that I didn't fill
Beside it, and there may be two or three
Apples I didn't pick upon some bough.   5
But I am done with apple-picking now.
Essence of winter sleep is on the night,
The scent of apples: I am drowsing off.
I cannot rub the strangeness from my sight
I got from looking through a pane of glass   10
I skimmed this morning from the drinking trough
And held against the world of hoary grass.
It melted, and I let it fall and break.
But I was well
Upon my way to sleep before it fell,   15
And I could tell
What form my dreaming was about to take.
Magnified apples appear and disappear,
Stem end and blossom end,
And every fleck of russet showing clear.   20
My instep arch not only keeps the ache,
It keeps the pressure of a ladder-round.
I feel the ladder sway as the boughs bend.
And I keep hearing from the cellar bin

The rumbling sound   25
Of load on load of apples coming in.
For I have had too much
Of apple-picking: I am overtired
Of the great harvest I myself desired.
There were ten thousand thousand fruit to touch,   30
Cherish in hand, lift down, and not let fall.
For all
That struck the earth,
No matter if not bruised or spiked with stubble,
Went surely to the cider-apple heap   35
As of no worth.
One can see what will trouble
This sleep of mine, whatever sleep it is.
Were he not gone,
The woodchuck could say whether it's like his   40
Long sleep, as I describe its coming on,
Or just some human sleep.

                                                                        —*Robert Frost*

In one sense the poet is tired after strenuous work, and looks forward
to rest; his sleep will be the kind of sleep that follows any day of hard
work. But in another sense sleep is associated with winter, heightening
the connotations of death that already surround sleep; it may be that
apple picking represents the labor of living, and sleep the rest of
death. Frost himself seems unsure as to whether this is "just some
human sleep" or a "long [final?] sleep" like the hibernation of the
woodchuck; or it may be that sleep represents only escape or relaxation
after work. There is little in the poem to help us decide among the
three possibilities, and the poem can be interpreted any way.

Some poems are less definite yet. "Morning, Morning" is so simple
that we look for something deeper—and the combination of time, the
poet, his love, and his grief suggests a vague something, although it is
impossible to put one's finger on just what that something might be.

Morning, Morning

Morning, morning,
Feel so lonesome in the morning
Morning, morning,
Morning brings me grief.

Sunshine, sunshine,   5
Sunshine laughs upon my face
And the glory of the growing
Puts me in my rotting place.

Evening, evening,
Feel so lonesome in the evening   10
Evening, evening,
Evening brings me grief.

Moonshine, moonshine,
Moonshine drugs the hills with grace
And the secret of the shining   15
Seeks to break my simple face.

Nighttime, nighttime,
Kills the blood upon my cheek
Nighttime, nighttime,
Does not bring me to relief.   20

Starshine, starshine,
Feel so loving in the starshine
Starshine, starshine,
Darling kiss me as I weep.

—*Tuli Kupferberg*

Given a choice between this song and "If I Were a Carpenter," which do you think you would rather hear ten or twelve times in succession? Why? Is there anything about Richie Haven's recording of this song that makes it capture especially well the sense of the lyrics?

Some of the lyrics of The Beatles, Bob Dylan, Jefferson Airplane, and Leonard Cohen are the vaguest of all pop songs except, of course, for those that degenerate into utter absurdity. They are not different from much of contemporary poetry, which has also become so subtle and indirect as to admit to a wide variety of possible interpretations. "All Along the Watchtower" suggests all sorts of interpretations. Very little can definitely be said about the theme of "I Am the Walrus," except that it is an exceptionally unpleasant song about death or ugliness or perversion or a combination of the three and even more. "Norwegian Wood" is a hauntingly beautiful lyric on a more pleasant but equally vague theme.

Norwegian Wood

I once had a girl,
Or should I say
She once had me;

She showed me her room,
Isn't it good   5
Norwegian Wood?

She asked me to stay
And she told me to sit anywhere
So I looked around
And I noticed there wasn't a chair.   10

I sat on a rug
Biding my time,
Drinking her wine.

We talked until two
And then she said   15
"It's time for bed."

She told me she worked in the morning
And started to laugh,
I told her I didn't
And crawled off to sleep in the bath.   20

And when I awoke
I was alone,
This bird had flown,

So I built a fire,
Isn't it good,   25
Norwegian Wood?

—John Lennon–Paul McCartney

More than one individual has suggested that this is a narrative about a drug trip and that "Norwegian Wood" is yet another slang term for marijuana. But apart from the surrealism of the action and perhaps the exotic instrumental accompaniment, a result of the use of the sitar for the first time in rock music, there is little to support such an argument. The girl suggests a sexual relationship and perhaps even love, although it is certainly casual and impermanent; in an interview in *Rolling Stone* Lennon claimed the song was about an affair he had had. The woman is intriguing, even intoxicating, as many women are, but the poet does not seem to miss her when she leaves. Their relationship is pleasant while it lasts, but not mourned when it is over. Most importantly and most perplexingly, we are not sure whether this is a real woman or whether she represents something else—like marijuana. On the other hand, for all its ambiguities, the song does have a reasonably definite subject and theme: it is about an enjoyable, transient experience, and it suggests that pleasant experiences may all be temporary and should be accepted as such and not mourned excessively when they end. Within these limits, the individual reader is free to set up his own definite interpretation, provided that it is supported by evidence within the poem.

Lennon's "Norwegian Wood" has been puzzling people for nearly a decade; Blake's "The Sick Rose" has been haunting readers for the better part of two centuries.

The Sick Rose

O rose, thou art sick!
The invisible worm

That flies in the night,
In the howling storm,

Has found out thy bed   5
Of crimson joy,
And his dark secret love
Does thy life destroy.

—*William Blake*

One meaning of the poem is obvious: a cutworm or slug or some other creature has been devouring the rose in Blake's garden until there is nothing much left of it. It is sick, nearly destroyed. But the poem suggests a lot more. The worm flies in the night like a dragon. Dragons suggest evil and deformity, just as the rose suggests goodness and beauty. Is the poem about the conflict between the good and the bad, between the beautiful and the ugly? Words like "love" and "bed" and "crimson joy" suggest something sexual, and the worm may be phallic; is the poem about the loss of virginity? Or are there other possible meanings to the poem? Or does it mean all of these together? How would you interpret the poem? What evidence would you cite to support your interpretation?

Lennon is alive; Blake is dead. Neither is saying much about either "Norwegian Wood" or "The Sick Rose." The absence of extensive critical exposition by either poet allows each poem to carry all interpretations supported by the words themselves. The spectrum of possible interpretations of these poems is very broad indeed.

POETRY, ROUGH AND POLISHED

A poem, then, does not mean "whatever I get out of it." We must lay that fallacy to rest at the outset if our study is to be at all fruitful. Another commonly held notion with which we must deal is the idea that poems which are highly regular in their rhythm and use of rhyme and poems that make excessive use of flowery language or patterns of rhetorical organization are inherently superior to poems that are looser in their rhythm and rhyme and have less rigid organization. We have already observed that poetry of statement is not really inferior to more ornate poetry; let us now note that poetry that is highly polished is not necessarily superior to poetry that is relatively rough. There is art that calls attention to itself by showing off, and there is art that conceals art. If anything, we tire of the former before we tire of the latter. It is true that rough poetry tends to be sloppy: freedom from restriction frequently becomes a license for carelessness that would never be tolerated in more polished verse. Such poetry is indeed inferior. But just because a poet chooses to write loose rather than tight poetry does not mean that he is opting for the easy way out, or that his poetry is ipso facto inferior. There are many degrees between the monotony of perfect regularity and the prosiness of undisciplined irregularity, and the good reader is eclectic enough in his tastes to appreciate everything in between. Consider the following two songs:

Horse Latitudes

When the still sea conspires an armor
And her sullen and aborted
Currents breed tiny monsters,
True sailing is dead.

Awkward instant   5
And the first animal is jettisoned,
Legs furiously pumping
Their stiff green gallop,
And heads bob up
Poise   10
Delicate
Pause
Consent
In mute nostril agony
Carefully refined   15
And sealed over.

—Jim Morrison

I Pity the Poor Immigrant

I pity the poor immigrant
Who wishes he would've stayed home,
Who uses all his power to do evil
And in the end is always left alone.
That man who with his fingers cheats   5
And who lies with ev'ry breath,
Who passionately hates his life
And likewise fears his death.

I pity the poor immigrant
Whose strength is all in vain,   10
Whose heaven is like Ironsides,
Whose tears are like rain;
Who eats but is not satisfied,
Who hears but does not see,
Who falls in love with wealth itself,   15
And turns his back on me.

I pity the poor immigrant
Who tramples through the mud,
Who fills his mouth with laughing
And who builds his town with blood;   20
Whose visions in their final end
Must shatter like the glass,
I pity the poor immigrant
When his gladness comes to pass.

—Bob Dylan

There is no rhyme in Morrison's poem, and the lines are of various lengths; but the line lengths and the lack of unifying rhyme are not capricious whims of the poet. The first three lines are all one clause, long and uninterrupted by the pauses that inevitably result from regular perfect rhyme. The free flow of the verse is entirely consistent with the meaning of the lines, and contrasts sharply with the fourth line, which has a static quality to its sound and its sense. Then there is a break in the verse, which signals a break in time as the sailors make the decision to jettison their cargo of horses in order to lighten the ship caught in the dead calm of the doldrums. The poet captures in the next several lines the awkward instant, in reality only a half a minute or so even though it seems an eternity both to the horse and the poet watching this agony, during which the horse struggles, bobs up for the last time, and finally drowns. The length of that moment is conveyed by breaking "Poise/ Delicate/ Pause/ Consent" into four one-word lines. And then the horse is gone and the poem and sea move quietly on, as if nothing had happened. The poem ends on the very final and highly effective "over." The form of the poem, then, is an adjunct to conveying the meaning, which is the poet's description of one horrifying, fascinating moment. On the record the poem is read to an eerie, atonal cacophony that builds to a deafening crescendo of feedback, approximating the terror felt by horse and poet—and audience.

In contrast, the Dylan song is a highly polished, regular, carefully rhymed piece of work that should certainly muzzle those critics who claim Dylan cannot write anything but loose and jangling verse. The poem divides into three stanzas, and these divide further into four and even two-line units. There is considerable parallelism and balance of phrases: "Who eats but is not satisfied,/Who hears but does not see." The rhyme, on alternate lines, is always perfect. The lines are of regular length. In short, the song is as regular and polished as we could wish.

Songs, because they are set to music that is itself usually regular, are only infrequently as rough as "Horse Latitudes." But because the regularity of music makes no distinction between, say, two eighth notes and one quarter note (which may mean either two syllables or one syllable, respectively), when poetry is polished it tends to be much more regular than even the most polished song. Here are a couple of poems from opposite ends of the poetic spectrum.

Come, My Celia

Come, my Celia, let us prove,
While we can, the sports of love;
Time will not be ours forever:

He at length our good will sever.
Spend not, then, his gifts in vain;   5
Suns that set may rise again,
But if once we lose this light,
'Tis with us perpetual night.
Why should we defer our joys?
Fame and rumor are but toys.   10
Cannot we delude the eyes
Of a few poor household spies?
Or his easier ears beguile,
Thus removèd by our wile?
'Tis no sin love's fruits to steal;   15
But the sweet thefts to reveal,
To be taken, to be seen,
These have crimes accounted been.

—Ben Jonson

1. *prove*: test by experiencing. 13. *his*: Celia's husband in *Volpone*, Corvino. 18. *been*: in seventeenth century England, "been" would have rhymed perfectly with "seen."

The Creation
A Negro Sermon

And God stepped out on space,
And He looked around and said,
"I'm lonely—
I'll make me a world."

And far as the eye of God could see   5
Darkness covered everything,
Blacker than a hundred midnights
Down in a cypress swamp.

Then God smiled,
And the light broke,   10
And the darkness rolled up on one side,
And the light stood shining on the other,
And God said, "That's good!"

Then God reached out and took the light in His hands,
And God rolled the light around in His hands,   15
Until He made the sun;
And He set that sun a-blazing in the heavens.
And the light that was left from making the sun
God gathered up in a shining ball
And flung against the darkness,   20
Spangling the night with the moon and stars.

Then down between
The darkness and the light
He hurled the world:
And God said, "That's good!"   25

Then God himself stepped down—
And the sun was on His right hand,
And the moon was on His left;
The stars were clustered about His head,
And the earth was under His feet.   30
And God walked, and where He trod
His footsteps hollowed the valleys out
And bulged the mountains up.

Then He stopped and looked and saw
That the earth was hot and barren.   35
So God stepped over to the edge of the world
And He spat out the seven seas;
He batted His eyes, and the lightnings flashed;
He clapped His hands, and the thunders rolled;
And the waters above the earth came down,   40
The cooling waters came down.

Then the green grass sprouted,
And the little red flowers blossomed,
The pine-tree pointed his finger to the sky,
And the oak spread out his arms;   45
The lakes cuddled down in the hollows of the ground,
And the rivers ran down to the sea;
And God smiled again,

And the rainbow appeared,
And curled itself around His shoulder.   50

Then God raised His arm and He waved His hand
Over the sea and over the land,
And He said, "Bring forth! Bring forth!"
And quicker than God could drop His hand,
Fishes and fowls   55
And beast and birds
Swam the rivers and the seas,
Roamed the forests and the woods,
And split the air with their wings,
And God said, "That's good!"   60

Then God walked around
And God looked around
On all that He had made.
He looked at His sun,
And He looked at His moon,   65
And He looked at His little stars;
He looked on His world
With all its living things,
And God said, "I'm lonely still."

Then God sat down   70
On the side of a hill where He could think;
By a deep, wide river He sat down;
With His head in His hands,
God thought and thought,
Till He thought, "I'll make me a man!"   75

Up from the bed of the river
God scooped the clay;
And by the bank of the river
He kneeled Him down;
And there the great God Almighty,   80
Who lit the sun and fixed it in the sky,
Who flung the stars to the most far corner of the night,
Who rounded the earth in the middle of His hand—

This Great God,
Like a mammy bending over her baby,   85
Kneeled down in the dust
Toiling over a lump of clay
Till He shaped his own image;
Then into it He blew the breath of life,
And man became a living soul.   90
Amen. Amen.

                            —*James Weldon Johnson*

"Come, My Celia" is a seduction song from Ben Jonson's play *Volpone*.
Volpone, a lecherous and somewhat deluded old Venetian nobleman,
has cornered the virtuous but empty-headed Celia in his bedroom, and
attempts to win her favors by this exceptionally polished, carefully
reasoned argument. In the context of the play, it provides a measure
of Volpone's distorted judgment: not only will virtuous Celia probably
resist his seduction, she will most certainly be unimpressed by the
lyric through which he intends to accomplish it. To the reader, however,
the poem is impressive: it breaks neatly into three separate arguments
(lines 1–8, 9–14, and 15–18), rhymes regularly, and contains lines of
length regular to the last syllable. Each line pauses at its end, usually
with a mark of punctuation. In its content and form, this poem of
Jonson's is very tight, very polished.

Contrast it to "The Creation." Johnson subtitles his poem "A Negro
Sermon," which explains the looseness of the verse in the same way that
the use of "Come, My Celia" in *Volpone* explains its polish. Several
rhetorical devices do, however, give "The Creation" some structure
and organization, as a comparison of this poem and the biblical account
of creation will demonstrate. "Come, My Celia" involves the distortion
of normal English syntactical patterns for the sake of rhyme: "He at
length our good will sever," "Or his easier ears beguile." The freer
"Creation" does not distort syntax in this manner, but this type of
verse has defects of its own. Using the two poems and the two songs
we have discussed as models, work out for yourself the advantages and
disadvantages inherent in "free verse" and in the more traditional,
regular poetry.

POETRY, PUBLIC AND PRIVATE

One more illusion we ought to dispel is the idea of the poet far removed from the world of reality, a man all wrapped up in himself, a man living in a world of illusion and make-believe—and of poetry as therefore almost entirely irrelevant to and divorced from normal human experience. Historically, of course, this is nonsense, and even today's poets are as much public figures as private individuals. Spenser and Sidney were both courtiers at the court of Elizabeth I. Shakespeare and his company found themselves hauled in front of the Privy Council to explain the performance of one of his dramas on the eve of the Essex rebellion—the crown thought he was involved in the conspiracy! Milton was Latin secretary to Oliver Cromwell and very much involved in the political and social life of the seventeenth century. Lord Byron, Keats, and Shelley were all involved in the Greek struggle for independence. William Butler Yeats was similarly committed to the cause of Irish nationalism. Robert Frost read at the inauguration of President Kennedy. Poets are public men, very aware of and involved in the social, political, and intellectual ferment of "the real world," and this involvement is reflected in their poetry. They often write poems about that "real world," public poems, poems about a war or a social movement or a political issue. Phil Ochs, Bob Dylan, Paul Simon, The Beatles, Joni Mitchell, Jim Morrison all comment on public matters: the Vietnamese War, political and social revolution, alienation in the modern world, the new American woman. So too do Frost and Yeats and Ferlinghetti and cummings.

Woodstock

I came upon a child of God,
He was walking along the road.
And I asked him, "Where are you going?"
And this he told me:
"I'm going down to Yasgur's farm,   5

"Woodstock"—words and music by Joni Mitchell. Copyright © 1969, reprinted by permission of the publisher, Siquomb Publishing Corp.

I'm going to join in a rock-n-roll band,
I'm going to camp out on the land
And try an' get my soul free."
  We are stardust,
  We are golden,   10
  And we've got to get ourselves
  Back to the garden.
"Then can I walk beside you?
I have come here to lose the smog,
And I feel to be a cog in something turning.   15
Well maybe it is just the time of year,
Or maybe it's the time of man,
I don't know who I am
But life is for learning."
  We are stardust,
  We are golden,   20
  And we've got to get ourselves
  Back to the garden.
By the time we got to Woodstock
We were half a million strong,   25
And everywhere there was song and celebration.
And I dreamed I saw the bombers
Riding shotgun in the sky,
And they were turning into butterflies
Above our nation.   30
  We are stardust,
  We are golden,
  And we've got to get ourselves
  Back to the garden.

                                   —Joni Mitchell

    5. *Yasgur's farm*: the farm near Woodstock where the rock festival was held.
12. *garden*: the Garden of Eden?

The rock festival at Woodstock was an event that 500,000 of us shared in person, and in which millions of Americans participated vicariously via television and the movie *Woodstock*. It is not an experience Joni Mitchell had about which the rest of us know nothing at all. The song is about one aspect of life in the real world. But the public event *is* colored by the poet: judging from the connotations of some of the language she uses, what would you take to be her attitude toward the rock festival? Do you know some people who take a somewhat different view? Is her evaluation the same as your own? While the subject of the song is public, then, the point of view contained in the lyrics is that of Joni Mitchell: we receive a public experience filtered through the poet's own special vision.

As we have mentioned, most poetry, like most rock lyrics, is public and deals with subjects familiar to us all: the creation, a grasshopper, picking apples, the position of the black man in white society. Here is a poem by Robert Lowell, one of modern America's more traditional poets.

Inauguration Day: January, 1953

The snow had buried Stuyvesant.
The subways drummed the vaults. I heard
the El's green girders charge on Third,
Manhattan's truss of adamant,
that groaned in ermine, slummed on want   5
Cyclonic zero of the word,
God of our armies, who interred
Cold Harbor's blue immortals, Grant!
Horseman, your sword is in the groove!

Ice, ice. Our wheels no longer move.   10
Look, the fixed stars, all just alike
as lack-land atoms, split apart,
and the Republic summons Ike,
the mausoleum in her heart.

—*Robert Lowell*

title: President Eisenhower's first inauguration. 1. *Stuyvesant*: a housing project in New York. 8. *Cold Harbor*: the site of two Civil War battles involving General (later President) Grant; also a pun on New York harbor locked with ice. Grant is buried in a large mausoleum in Manhattan.

Although not everyone felt what Lowell felt in 1953, just as the majority of Americans today would still not agree with his opinion of General Eisenhower, this is a poem about the public world. It describes a city we all know, an event we all experienced, weather we all felt. Even though the poet has filtered the inauguration through his own mind, thereby casting it in his own special light, his poem is certainly not something irrelevant or private, just as Joni Mitchell's song about Woodstock was not private, just as Johnson's poem on creation, Frost's poem on apple-picking, and Dunbar's poem on the black man were not private poems.

But poets *do* write about their own private lives, especially in the twentieth century, someone objects. They write about their own personal loves, their own successes and failures, their own feelings and emotions. And these are private affairs about which we as an audience know very little. Even Yeats, the Yeats of the Irish Rebellion, constructed for himself a whole new world in *The Vision,* then wrote poems like "The Second Coming" about his private construct. And look at some of the songs of poet-composer Leonard Cohen. Is not "Suzanne" a private thing? Or "Sisters of Mercy?"

Certainly poets write about their own experiences, about their private lives, and it would be foolish indeed to call a song like "Suzanne" or Dylan's "Visions of Johanna," or some of Donne's religious meditations or Dickinson's wrestlings with faith and doubt anything but private poetry. But private poetry is not nearly so private as we would at first suppose, because the poet is a human being just as we are human beings, and in the commonality of our humanity there exists a bridge between his experience and our understanding. His love affair is not really that much different from our love affairs; we have experienced highs and lows just like his; we ourselves have wrestled with problems of justice and good and evil just as he has. And even when the poet is being most personal, we can respond to some of his personal experiences because in our own lives we have had similar experiences ourselves. Take, as an example, "Sisters of Mercy."

Sisters of Mercy

Oh, the Sisters of Mercy
They are not departed or gone

They were waiting for me
When I thought that I just can't go on
And they brought me their comfort 5
And later they brought me their song
O, I hope you run into them
You who've been traveling so long.

Yes, you who must leave everything
That you cannot control 10
It begins with your family
But soon it comes round to your soul.
Well, I've been where you're hanging
I think I can see how you're pinned
When you're not feeling holy 15
Your loneliness says that you've sinned.

They lay down beside me
I made my confession to them
They touched both my eyes
And I touched the dew on their hem. 20
If your life is a leaf
That the seasons tear off and condemn
They will bind you with love
That is graceful and green as a stem.

When I left they were sleeping 25
I hope you run into them soon.
Don't turn on the lights,
You can read their address by the moon;
And you won't make me jealous
If I hear that they sweetened your night 30
We weren't lovers like that
And besides it would still be all right
We weren't lovers like that
And besides it would still be all right.

—*Leonard Cohen*

It is difficult to say anything definite about this song without running the risk of becoming too clever, but certain things are obvious. The poet has experienced a period of deep depression, from which he was rescued by the "Sisters of Mercy," literally a religious order but here probably merely an agent of comfort and grace. The renewing experience is couched in religious terms ("confession," "soul," "holy," "sinned,") but may or may not be religious in any traditional sense. The exact nature of his trouble and the exact identity of his rescuers are unclear. What is definite, though, is that he was at one time very down, and that he is now up again. And he commends the sisters to us. The exact experience in Cohen's life that produced this poem is so personal that we have no way of relating it to any of our own, but we have all experienced moods of depression, real downs, and in one of these moods this poem has considerable appeal. It communicates so well that some people are actually ready to follow after the band that marches in one speaker and out of the other during Cohen's own performance of this song, and go searching for the sisters wherever the poet left them sleeping.

This poem by Yeats speaks to us in exactly the same way.

To a Friend Whose Work Has Come to Nothing

Now all the truth is out,
Be secret and take defeat
From any brazen throat,
For how can you compete,
Being honour bred, with one   5
Who, were it proved he lies,
Were neither shamed in his own
Nor in his neighbors' eyes?
Bred to a harder thing
Than Triumph, turn away   10
And like a laughing string
Whereon mad fingers play
Amid a place of stone,
Be secret and exult,
Because of all things known   15
That is most difficult.

—*William Butler Yeats*

Even though we do not know exactly what happened to Yeats' friend, the poem says things to all of us: somewhere we have all failed because of our human nature, and we have all stood in need of the consolation this poem offers. In this sense it is a public poem, although it focuses on an experience shared only by the poet, his friend, and those who knew and still remember what the whole business was about. Even poems that are born of very intimate experiences, then, are made public by the common bonds that link the poet and his audience.

POETRY: WHAT IT IS AND WHAT IT DOES

So the poet is not off in another world. What does he do? Just what is poetry? Perhaps Wordsworth best answered these questions a century and a half ago in the Preface to his first collection of poems, *The Lyrical Ballads*.

> Taking up the subject, then, upon general grounds, let me ask, what is meant by the word poet? What is a poet? To whom does he address himself? And what language is to be expected from him?—He is a man speaking to men: a man, it is true, endowed with more lively sensibility, more enthusiasm and tenderness, who has a greater knowledge of human nature, and a more comprehensive soul, than are supposed to be common among mankind; a man pleased with his passions and volitions, and who rejoices more than other men in the spirit of life that is in him; delighting to contemplate similar volitions and passions as manifested in the goings-on of the universe, and habitually impelled to create them where he does not find them. To these qualities he has added a disposition to be affected more than other men by absent things as if they were present; an ability of conjuring up in himself passions, which are indeed far from being the same as those produced by real events, yet (especially in those parts of the general sympathy which are pleasing and delightful) do more nearly resemble the passions produced by real events, than anything which, from the motions of their own minds merely, other men are ac-

customed to feel in themselves:—whence, and from practice, he has acquired a greater readiness and power in expressing what he thinks and feels, and especially those thoughts and feelings which, by his own choice, or from the structure of his own mind, arise in him without immediate external excitement.

The poet is a man speaking to men: a black man, a white man, an intellectual, an aristocrat, a proletarian, an artist, a worker speaking to us all about all the serious, funny, lovely, ugly, holy, obscene ideas, emotions, experiences, feelings that we all have. His subject is the totality of human experience, his medium words, his audience the whole human community. Sometimes, to be sure, his audience is not listening. Sometimes it takes real sensitivity to language and perhaps even a little cultural acclimatization before we can catch what he's saying. Sometimes the poet succumbs to the constant temptation to escape his confining world or his inattentive audience and writes some poetry that is actually irrelevant and removed. But these are the exceptional, problematical cases. Perhaps they are even poetic failures, for when the poem does not communicate it ceases to be a poem and we are confronted with the mutterings of an old man, once a poet.

The poet's subjects and the process of poetic creation were described some centuries ago by Lu Chi, a Chinese poet, in his *Wen-fu* in terms of which Wordsworth would have approved.

Wen-fu

Taking his position at the hub of things, [the writer] contemplates the mystery of the universe; he feeds his emotions and his mind on the great works of the past.

Moving along with the four seasons, he sighs at the passing of time; gazing at the myriad objects, he thinks of the complexity of the world.

He sorrows over the falling leaves in virile autumn; he takes joy in the delicate bud of fragrant spring.

With awe at heart, he experiences chill; his spirit solemn, he turns his gaze to the clouds.

He declaims the superb works of his predecessors; he croons the clean fragrance of past worthies.   5

He roams in the Forest of Literature, and praises the symmetry of great art.

Moved, he pushes his books away and takes the writing-brush, that he may express himself in letters.

At first he withholds his sight and turns his hearing inward; he is lost in thought, questioning everywhere.

His spirit gallops to the eight ends of the universe; his mind wanders along vast distances.

In the end, as his mood dawns clearer and clearer, objects, clean-cut now in outline, shove one another forward.

He sips the essence of letters; he rinses his mouth with the extract of the Six Arts.

Floating on the heavenly lake, he swims along; plunging into the nether spring, he immerses himself.

Thereupon, submerged words wriggle up, as when a darting fish, with the hook in its gills, leaps from a deep lake; floating beauties flutter down, as when a high-flying bird, with the harpoon-string around its wings, drops from a crest of cloud.

He gathers words never used in a hundred generations; he picks rhythms never sung in a thousand years.

He spurns the morning blossom, now full blown; he plucks the evening bud, which has yet to open.

He sees past and present in a moment; he touches the four seas in a twinkling of an eye.

Now he selects ideas and fixes them in order; he examines words and puts them in their places.

He taps at the door of all that is colorful; he chooses from among everything that rings.

Now he shakes the foliage by tugging the twig; now he follows back along the waves to the fountainhead of the stream.

Sometimes he brings out what was hidden; sometimes, looking for an easy prey, he bags a hard one.

Now, the tiger puts on new stripes, to the consternation of other beasts; now, the dragon emerges, and terrifies all the birds.

Sometimes things fit together, are easy to manage; sometimes they jar each other, are awkward to manipulate.

He empties his mind completely, to concentrate his thoughts; he collects his wits before he puts words together.

He traps heaven and earth in the cage of form; he crushes the myriad objects against the tip of his brush.

At first they hesitate upon his parched lips; finally they flow   25
   through the well-moistened brush.
Reason, supporting the matter [of the poem], stiffens the trunk;
   style, depending from it, spreads luxuriance around.
Emotion and expression never disagree: all changes [in his mood]
   are betrayed on his face.
If the thought touches on joy, a smile is inevitable; no sooner is
   sorrow spoken of than a sigh escapes. . . .

—*Lu Chi*
(translated by *Achilles Fang*)

11. *Six Arts*: ceremonial observances, music, archery, writing, mathematics, and charioteering.

"Taking his position at the hub of things," Lu Chi writes, a poet "feeds his emotions and his mind." After experiencing and contemplating all things, the poet writes his poem. Sometimes composition is difficult, sometimes the words come easily; but always the subject is human experience and the medium is words, words of communication. The words of a man talking to men.

What then, distinguishes the words of the poet from the words of the novelist? It is clear that both artists concern themselves with experience, both use words, both communicate a meaning to their readers; what is special about the poet's communication? Perhaps if we examine poetic and prose treatments of the same subject, we can find some of them. Here is a poem, not a great poem but a good poem, called "Deleightful Pie"; it is followed by a short story by the same title on the same subject by the same author. What are the differences between the two?

Deleightful Pie

the fat man eats pie. he eats pie this way
first he takes a small bite with his fork
then he takes a larger piece and smells it
with his nose. then he places nose and mouth
close to the plate and he eats deleightful   5
pie quick quick quick someone is watching

Deleightful Pie

Once upon a time, once upon a time there was a man, who must have been a magic man, there was a man who ate pie. He ate custard pie and lemon pie and apple pie and coconut pie and mince pie and pumpkin pie and rhubarb pie and cherry pie and whatever other kind of pie a person can think of. Now, you might ask, what is so special about a man who eats pie, what is so magical about a man who eats ordinary pie? Now, that's an altogether fair question. It is also a question which is answerable. And the answer is this tale, for it isn't, of course, WHAT one eats that is important, but what IS important is HOW one eats what one eats.

Now this man, this marvellous pie eater, this magical special man, was also, as we say, an important-man-in-the-world. He was important not because he ate pie of course, for anyone can eat pie, even, after all, a person without teeth can eat pie after all. So eating pie in itself is not that special. He was an important-man-in-the-world because he WAS that way, a natural characteristic, like the size of one's nose. He just was, this pie eater, an important-man-in-the-world. So.

One day, it was mid-afternoon of a bright clear blue high cloud and light wind from the southwest day, typical of the kind of day we have in the midwest in late August, well, on this day, the man was in a building by the river where food was served. He took a piece of pie from the counter and placed it carefully on his tray. Now this act alone took some time. For first the man watched each piece of pie for a good long solid time. Looked at each piece closely and attentively, the way kids look at weeds and things to see if they can actually see them grow. He watched the pies that way. He stared, for example, at the pecan pie, almost as long as a worm stares at the full moon. (And you know how long that is!) When he had stared at each possible piece of pie that way, he drew back from the counter, heaved a great sigh, threw his eyes into the air, and then, quite suddenly, his fat chop of a hand leaped out of his body and siezed a piece of

coconut cream pie. Siezed, that is, the plate on which the
pie sat. When the pie in its plate was on the man's tray he
watched it again for a while, almost unhappily. One can
never know another person completely, so that we can only
guess just exactly why the magic pie eater MAY have been
slightly unhappy at this point. All one can safely say is that
our important man seemed unhappy, at least for the moment.

Then the man walked to the milk dispenser, drew himself a glass, a tall chalky white glass, of good pure whole
100% milk from an all-American cow. He drew it
PROUDLY, as an American salutes the flag proudly, or
thinks proudly of all the wars we have won as a nation. He
held the glass before him as a proud soldier holds his rifle
before him for the inspecting officer to inspect. Then he put
it carefully on his tray beside the pie and walked to the
cashier. He payed for the milk and pie, holding his head
down, as if he didn't want the cashier to recognise him, as
if he wanted to be the incognito pie-eater, the one who
traveled fartherest Mexico in his mini-bus, eating pie all over
the Yucatan Penninsula in dark glasses and no name. So that
when the cashier said thank you, he didn't even want her to
hear his voice. And so he took his change and glided, or
glid, like a spoon-snake, to his familiar table by the tall pillar
overlooking the moving waters of the ribber.

There he placed his tray on the table and sat down. Now
he put both hands on the table and stared for just a bit at
the moving waters, just as long as it takes to run through a
prayer, or count from one to ten, if one counts quickly.
Then he took a fork and poised it over the pie. Then, scoop-
ing a small piece he raised it to his nose, just a second or
two off his thick dragondroopy mustachios, and inhaled, as
if the pie were or was some heavenly scented flower. Satisfied with whatever he smelled, he returned the piece of pie
to the plate and commenced to look furtively about to see if
he was being watched. He looked left and right and up and
down. After all, what kind of pie eater is it that could eat
pie while being watched? I ask you. What, I want to know,
is your answer, eh? Well, feeling all safe and secure, our
important man patted his mustache with his right forefinger,

adjusted his glasses with his left thumb and index finger, gazed furtively and secretively about once again, then took, slowly, a bit of a drink of that 100% milk. Next he took both hands and pulled his sweater down over his belly. It was a large capacious wonderful sort of clown belly. It was, in a word, important.

Then, eyes shifting left and right and up and down, he drew his mouth close to the plate and quick quick quick he shovelled and scooped and forked the pie into the opening below his nose that we usually call the mouth. Ah, ah! quick quick quick, someone is watching! Ah! Such deleightful pie!

Now the pie was gone. Our man sat back in his chair and stared at the moving waters while drinking the rest of his milk. Again there was a sadness on his face, as if someone he loved very much had left for Dubuque, or Wappello. Or as if he was expecting something very strange to happen. The waters moved and rushed and churned before his eyes. Then a tear came to his eye, perhaps a tear for all the lost pies, er that is, lost people, I mean peeple, all those lost in the floods and so forth. Well, we can never know. Then our man rose, placed his two hands on his belly, and was gone.

—George Chambers

One thing is certain: the poem is considerably shorter than the prose version, which might even be too lengthy a treatment of so trivial a subject. The poem comes to the core of the subject right away as it focuses on the man, his pie, the haste with which he ate it, and most importantly the delight with which he ate and the delight with which the poet watched him eat. Supporting detail that appears in the story is left out of the poem: buying the pie, drinking the milk, leaving the restaurant. Perhaps this detail would enhance our understanding of the events of the poem, but it might also destroy the poem's compression, which is very important to its success. Like most good poetry, "Deleightful Pie" is condensed: it gives only the details we need to know. Even the lines of long poems that are apparently diffuse and loose— Whitman's "Song of Myself," or Milton's "Paradise Lost"—are in reality quite compacted, as readers who try to paraphrase them always discover.

The poem is immediate. Even though the short story gives us a clear enough picture of the man eating his pie, the poem seems more immediate. In part this immediacy is a result of the present tense, but there is nothing especially poetic in that: the story might have been cast in the present rather than the past. Some of the immediacy of the poem comes from the last line (the absence of punctuation giving it added speed). But the same line appears (with punctuation) near the end of the short story: "quick quick quick, someone is watching." The major difference between the poem and the story is that the poem ends on this line and the story moves anticlimatically on. The immediacy of the poem is a result of its condensation: the poet strips away extraneous detail, focuses on a few central, concrete items—the fat man, a small bite, a fork, a larger piece, a nose, a mouth, a plate and someone—and lets these concrete details create the scene and tell the story. Whatever is lost because of this condensation is more than made up for in the immediacy created by the sparse, concrete details.

Poetry is structured. Lu Chi talks about a "cage of form"; this is the structure of poetry. Polished poetry has the form of regular line length and rhyme but, as we saw in James Weldon Johnson's poem, rhetorical devices of balance and repetition can be used to create structure. Chambers' poem has a rhetorical organization that makes it much tighter than the prose version: line 1 balances one "eats pie" against another "eats pie"; lines 2–4 create a tripartite series ("first . . ./then . . . , then . . ."). Appropriately, the stasis of the rhetorical balance breaks apart in the haste of the final two lines, as the poet describes the alacrity of the actual pie-eating. The short story has nothing of the poem's form, just as it lacks the poem's compression.

Condensation, immediacy, structure: these are qualities of all poetry. Other, more specific qualities are shared by many but not by all poems; we shall be talking about them shortly. Much else remains to be said about poetry in general, for poets have had much to say about their art —in fact, it is probably their favorite theme. "Wen Fu" encompasses, or tries to encompass, all dimensions of poetry; other poets have limited themselves to less ambitious statements. Paul Simon, for example, concerns himself with the religious aspect of poetry and the priest-like role the poet plays in a modern, essentially secular society.

Bleecker Street

Fog's rollin' in off the East River bank—
Like a shroud it covers Bleecker Street,
Fills the alleys where men sleep,
Hides the shepherd from the sheep.

Voices leaking from a sad cafe,   5
Smiling faces try to understand,
I saw a shadow touch a shadow's hand
On Bleecker Street.

The poet reads his crooked rhyme,
"Holy, holy" is his sacrament.   10
Thirty dollars pays your rent
On Bleecker Street.

Heard a churchbell softly chime
In a melody softly strainin'
It's a long road to Canaan   15
On Bleecker Street.

—*Paul Simon*

    2. *Bleecker Street*: a street in the Greenwich Village section of New York, long the center of protest and folk music. 15. *Canaan*: the biblical promised land.

Art Garfunkel, commenting on the song, had this to say.

> I confess that "Bleecker Street" (finished in October 1963) was too much for me at first. The song is highly intellectual, the symbolism extremely challenging. The opening line in which the fog comes in like a "shroud" over the city introduces the theme of "creative sterility." But it is the second verse which I find particularly significant. . . . The first line is a purely poetic image. The second line touches poignantly on human conditions of our time. To me, it shows

the same perceptive psychological characterization as "Sparrow". . . . The third line marks the first appearance of a
theme that is to occupy great attention in later work—"lack
of communication."

The author says that the poets have "sold out" ("the poet
writes [sic] his crooked rhyme"). The line "Thirty dollars
pays your rent" reminds one of Judas Iscariot's betrayal of
Christ for thirty pieces of silver.

The song and Garfunkel's analysis of it are both diffuse, but it is interesting and significant that Simon links poetry, religion, and communication. How does the poet see these apparently diverse areas relating to each other?

Ferlinghetti implies that poetry is not quite as pure and holy as
Simon would make it, although he admits that—at least for some people—art might be a thing of "the choicest of/ Church seats/ up there
where art directors meet." In very sexual language we are informed
that this poet has made a scene with beauty in his own weird way, and
"spilled out" his own profane poems. What different areas of human
experience does the poet bring together? How do they relate?

I have not lain with beauty

> I have not lain with beauty all my life
>   telling over to myself
>   its most rife charms
>
> I have not lain with beauty all my life
>   and lied with it as well   5
>   telling over to myself
>   how beauty never dies
>   but lies apart
>   among the aborigines
>   of art   10
>   and far above the battlefields
>   of love
>   It is above all that
>   oh yes

It sits upon the choicest of   15
                              Church seats
        up there where art directors meet
to choose the things for immortality
                                        And they have lain with beauty
                all their lives   20
                              And they have fed on honeydew
        and drunk the wines of Paradise
                                        so that they know exactly how
        a thing of beauty is a joy
                forever and forever   25
                              and how it never never
                quite can fade
                        into a money-losing nothingness

        Oh no I have not lain
                        on Beauty Rests like this   30
                afraid to rise at night
                              for fear that I might somehow miss
        some movement beauty might have made

        Yet I have slept with beauty
                              in my own weird way   35
        and I have made a hungry scene or two
                              with beauty in my bed
        and so spilled out another poem or two
          and so spilled out another poem or two
                              upon the Bosch-like world   40
                              —*Lawrence Ferlinghetti*

21. The line echoes "Kubla Khan," line 54. 24. The line echoes the first line
of Keats' "Endymion": "A thing of beauty is a joy forever." 40. *Bosch*: a Renaissance painter whose landscapes are unusually grotesque and surrealistic.

In an extremely significant statement on the art of poetry, a statement
that might serve as a guide to the selection of poems and songs for this
book, Wallace Stevens joined the sacred and the profane, arguing that
art can be created out of either. Might these apparent contraries be in-
terdependant as well as interrelated?

A High-Toned Old Christian Woman

Poetry is the supreme fiction, madame.
Take the moral law and make a nave of it
And from the nave build haunted heaven. Thus,
The conscience is converted into palms,
Like windy citherns hankering for hymns.   5
We agree in principle. That's clear. But take
The opposing law and make a peristyle,
And from the peristyle project a masque
Beyond the planets. Thus, our bawdiness,
Unpurged by epitaph, indulged at last,   10
Is equally converted into palms,
Squiggling like saxophones. And palm for palm,
Madame, we are where we began. Allow,
Therefore, that in the planetary scene
Your disaffected flagellants, well-stuffed,   15
Smacking their muzzy bellies in parade,
Proud of such novelties of the sublime,
Such tink and tank and tunk-a-tunk-tunk,
May, merely may, madame, whip from themselves
A jovial hullabaloo among the spheres.   20
This will make widows wince. But fictive things
Wink as they will. Wink most when widows wince.

                                             —*Wallace Stevens*

3. *nave*: the main part of a church. 5. *cithern*: an old, guitar-like instrument.
7. *peristyle*: a court enclosed by columns. 8. *masque*: a lavish, stylized, artificial,
quasi-dramatic entertainment popular during the Renaissance. 15. *flagellants*:
medieval European religious fanatics who beat themselves publicly. The practice
smacks of sexual perversion.

Bob Dylan had this to say about the artist and his mistress the muse;
what does the song tell us about poetry?

She Belongs to Me

She's got ev'rything she needs,
She's an artist,
She don't look back.
She's got ev'rything she needs,
She's an artist,   5
She don't look back.
She can take the dark out of the night-time
And paint the day-time black.

You will start out standing,
Proud to steal her anything she sees.   10
You will start out standing,
Proud to steal her anything she sees.
But you will wind up peeking through her keyhole
Down upon your knees.

She never stumbles,   15
She's got no place to fall.
She never stumbles,
She's got no place to fall.
She's nobody's child,
The law can't touch her at all.   20

She wears an Egyptian ring,
That sparkles before she speaks.
She wears an Egyptian ring
That sparkles before she speaks.
She is a hypnotist collector,   25
You are a walking antique.

Bow down to her on Sunday,
Salute her when her birthday comes.
Bow down to her on Sunday,
Salute her when her birthday comes.   30

For Halloween give her a trumpet
And for Christmas, buy her a drum.

—*Bob Dylan*

Dylan's statements are relatively oblique, even though he wrote this
song during a period when his statements were usually very direct. Art
has the power to transform: it can make the dark appear light and vice
versa. Art is independent, above the law of conventional justice and
morality. And art attracts us, in spite of the fact that satisfying our
desire involves a certain amount of self-abasement on our part. The
relationship between artist and audience implied in the last stanza is
particularly interesting. In what ways do the themes treated in this
lyric compare with those in Wallace Stevens' "A High-Toned Old
Christian Woman"? In Stevens' "The Idea of Order at Key West"?

Shakespeare concerns himself with the permanence of poetry; Jeffers
with the impermanence of all artistic effort. The survival of Shakespeare's poem after three centuries argues persuasively for his position;
the fragmentary nature of our knowledge of Anglo-Saxon or classical
Greek poetry suggests that in the last analysis Jeffers is probably right.

Sonnet 55

Not marble, nor the gilded monuments
Of princes, shall outlive this powerful rhyme;
But you shall shine more bright in these contents
Than unswept stone, besmeared with sluttish time.
When wasteful war shall statues overturn,   5
And broils root out the work of masonry,
Nor Mars his sword nor war's quick fire shall burn
The living record of your memory.
'Gainst death and all oblivious enmity
Shall you pace forth; your praise shall still find room   10
Even in the eyes of all posterity
That wear this world out to the ending doom.
So, till the judgment that yourself arise,
You live in this, and dwell in lovers' eyes.

—*William Shakespeare*

6. *broils*: quarrels, tumults. 7. *Mars his*: Mars'. 13. *that*: when.

To the Stone-Cutters

Stone-cutters fighting time with marble, you foredefeated
Challengers of oblivion
Eat cynical earnings, knowing rock splits, records fall down,
The square-limbed Roman letters
Scale in the thaws, wear in the rain. The poet as well   5
Builds his monument mockingly;
For man will be blotted out, the blithe earth die, the brave sun
Die blind, his heart blackening:
Yet stones have stood for a thousand years, and pained thoughts
    found
The honey peace in old poems.   10
                                        —*Robinson Jeffers*

One of the most important statements by a twentieth-century poet is
that of W. H. Auden in his elegy for William Butler Yeats, a fellow
poet. Part 1 describes the events of the day in 1939 on which the poet
died, and makes only implicit commentary on poetry: "The words of
the dead man/ Are modified in the guts of the living." Section 2 says
some very important things about poetry, however, especially in the
light of the dead poet's revolutionary work, which he combined with a
poetic career. Section 3 contains an echo of Shakespeare's sonnet: time,
which ignores physical beauty, worships language and honors poets.
What other statements does Auden make or imply about poetry? Are
they consistent with what other poets have said, or with what you have
read in poems?

In Memory of W. B. Yeats

1

He disappeared in the dead of winter:
The brooks were frozen, the airports almost deserted,
And snow disfigured the public statues;
The mercury sank in the mouth of the dying day.
O all the instruments agree   5
The day of his death was a dark cold day.

Far from his illness
The wolves ran on through the evergreen forests,
The peasant river was untempted by the fashionable quays;
By mourning tongues   10
The death of the poet was kept from his poems.

But for him it was his last afternoon as himself,
An afternoon of nurses and rumours;
The provinces of his body revolted,
The squares of his mind were empty,   15
Silence invaded the suburbs,
The current of his feeling failed: he became his admirers.

Now he is scattered among a hundred cities
And wholly given over to unfamiliar affections;
To find his happiness in another kind of wood   20
And be punished under a foreign code of conscience.
The words of a dead man
Are modified in the guts of the living.

But in the importance and noise of tomorrow
When the brokers are roaring like beasts on the floor of the Bourse,   25
And the poor have the sufferings to which they are fairly ac-
    customed,
And each in the cell of himself is almost convinced of his freedom;
A few thousand will think of this day
As one thinks of a day when one did something slightly unusual.
O all the instruments agree   30
The day of his death was a dark cold day.

        2
You were silly like us: your gift survived it all;
The parish of rich women, physical decay,
Yourself; mad Ireland hurt you into poetry.
Now Ireland has her madness and her weather still,   35
For poetry makes nothing happen: it survives
In the valley of its saying where executives
Would never want to tamper; it flows south
From ranches of isolation and the busy griefs,

Raw towns that we believe and die in; it survives,   40
A way of happening, a mouth.

   3
Earth, receive an honoured guest;
William Yeats is laid to rest:
Let the Irish vessel lie
Emptied of its poetry.   45

Time that is intolerant
Of the brave and innocent,
And indifferent in a week
To a beautiful physique,

Worships language and forgives   50
Everyone by whom it lives;
Pardons cowardice, conceit,
Lays its honours at their feet.

Time that with this strange excuse
Pardoned Kipling and his views,   55
And will pardon Paul Claudel,
Pardons him for writing well.

In the nightmare of the dark
All the dogs of Europe bark,
And the living nations wait,   60
Each sequestered in its hate;

Intellectual disgrace
Stares from every human face,
And the seas of pity lie
Locked and frozen in each eye.   65

Follow, poet, follow right
To the bottom of the night,
With your unconstraining voice
Still persuade us to rejoice;

With the farming of a verse   70
Make a vineyard of the curse,
Sing of human unsuccess
In a rapture of distress;

In the deserts of the heart
Let the healing fountain start,   75
In the prison of his days
Teach the free man how to praise.

                                        —*W. H. Auden*

   9. *quay*: pier, wharf. 25. *Bourse*: the stock exchange in Paris. 55. *Kipling*:
British writer and poet. His views included the benign imperialism of "the white
man's burden." 56. *Claudel* (Paul): French diplomat, writer, poet; his writing is
strongly colored by an ascetic Christianity.

   In "The Idea of Order at Key West," Wallace Stevens returns to the
subject of poetry and art, this time with more concern for what the poet
does with his subject than the sources from which he derives it.

The Idea of Order at Key West

She sang beyond the genius of the sea.
The water never formed to mind or voice,
Like a body wholly body, fluttering
Its empty sleeves; and yet its mimic motion
Made constant cry, caused constantly a cry,   5
That was not ours although we understood,
Inhuman, of the veritable ocean.

The sea was not a mask. No more was she.
The song and water were not medleyed sound
Even if what she sang was what she heard,   10
Since what she sang was uttered word by word.
It may be that in all her phrases stirred
The grinding water and the gasping wind;
But it was she and not the sea we heard.

For she was the maker of the song she sang.   15
The ever-hooded, tragic-gestured sea
Was merely a place by which she walked to sing.
Whose spirit is this? we said, because we knew
It was the spirit that we sought and knew
That we should ask this often as she sang.   20

If it was only the dark voice of the sea
That rose, or even colored by many waves;
If it was only the outer voice of sky
And cloud, of the sunken coral water-walled,
However clear, it would have been deep air,   25
The heaving speech of air, a summer sound
Repeated in a summer without end
And sound alone. But it was more than that,
More even than her voice, and ours, among
The meaningless plungings of water and the wind,   30
Theatrical distances, bronze shadows heaped
On high horizons, mountainous atmospheres
Of sky and sea.
              It was her voice that made
The sky acutest at its vanishing.
She measured to the hour its solitude.   35
She was the single artificer of the world
In which she sang. And when she sang, the sea,
Whatever self it had, became the self
That was her song, for she was the maker. Then we,
As we beheld her striding there alone,   40
Knew that there never was a world for her
Except the one she sang and, singing, made.

Ramon Fernandez, tell me, if you know,
Why, when the singing ended and we turned
Toward the town, tell why the glassy lights,   45
The lights in the fishing boats at anchor there,
As the night descended, tilting in the air,
Mastered the night and portioned out the sea,
Fixing emblazoned zones and fiery poles,
Arranging, deepening, enchanting night.   50

Oh! Blessed rage for order, pale Ramon,
The maker's rage to order words of the sea,
Words of the fragrant portals, dimly-starred,
And of ourselves and of our origins,
In ghostlier demarcations, keener sounds.   55

                                                —*Wallace Stevens*

43. *Ramon Fernandez*: a Spanish critic and aesthetician.

Stevens presents us with two seas: one surrounding Key West, and
one created in the song of the female singer. The relationship between
the two is somewhat unclear in the first four sections of the poem, but
begins to emerge in the fifth: "And when she sang, the sea,/Whatever
self it had, became the self/That was her song." The artist, according
to Stevens, takes natural phenomena and transforms them into something different. And when the audience turns from the sea of the
song to the sea in the harbor, it finds that latter sea transformed: "The
lights . . ./Mastered the night and portioned out the sea." The natural
sea is magically ordered after the production of the poem, apparently
as a result of the process of poetic creation. So too, Stevens implies,
the artist orders experience for his audience, first in his poem and
afterwards in the arrangement the artistic construct imposes on natural
phenomena. How is what Stevens says here about poetry similar to
what he said in "A High-Toned Old Christian Woman?"

2
Critical Terminology: Words as Meaning

Every discipline and every occupation, from engineering to cab driving to medicine, has its own special language. Although those familiar with jargon sometimes take great delight in using it to confuse and impress the novice, and although it may appear at times unnecessary and an end in itself, jargon is created by the necessities of the job and is really a useful means to the end of efficient performance of a particular set of tasks. True, one is not likely to know what an EEG is unless one is involved with medicine, or what a stress study involves unless one is an engineer, or what a cross body block is unless one plays football; but these terms are not made up by insiders merely to mystify outsiders. They are designations for specific things, and allow doctors and football coaches to talk intelligently about their respective subjects. They serve an end beyond themselves. If we want to begin a study of football or medicine, we begin with a study of terminology, a study that may at first seem like an exercise in pedantry, but that we soon realize to be quite necessary to an understanding of what goes on in these areas.

Like any other discipline, English has its own jargon; and like any other people, teachers of English are sometimes prone to wave terms like "dangling modifier," "split infinitive," or "assonance and alliteration" in front of students in an attempt to impress them with the mystery of language and literature and how much they as students must learn (and, by implication, how much the teacher already knows) in order to "understand" the subject. This is a patently false idea, though: one need not be able to define "prose" to be able to write it, or be able to define "alliteration" to know that a phrase like "commie creeps" has a certain ring to it. Terminology does not make us understand poetry any more than being able to define "cross body block" will automatically make us good football players. But it can and does help us understand other people when they talk about poetry, and it can help us talk and write intelligently ourselves. Critical terminology is not to be learned as an end in itself, but as a means to another end: the sensitive and intelligent discussion of poetry. And for our purposes, it provides a convenient device for structuring a discussion of the rather unwieldly subject, poetry.

DICTION

Diction is one of the loosest of all critical terms. In its dictionary sense, it means simply the words a writer uses, but since people in all ages have had some strange ideas about what words are and are not appropriate for use in poems, poetic diction is a more complex matter. Connotation and denotation play a considerable role in the formulation of poetic diction, as do a poet's own taste and the taste of the age in which he lives. In the Middle Ages, and again in the eighteenth century, poetic diction meant "high," elegant language for "high," important subjects, and "low" language for "low" subjects. The poet used two different dictions, depending on his subject. Because he usually considered his subject important, however, the high style predominated and the language of poetry during those periods was a pretty high-flown thing. The Romantics, writing at the beginning of the nineteenth century, refused to recognize any difference between the language of poetry and that of "common men," so they ignored high and low styles and wrote in what they considered common language—but what sounds to us more like a rough approximation of the King James version of the Bible. Victorian diction was consciously genteel, and used only words that would not offend the ear of a well-bred lady.

Modern ideas of poetic diction are less precise and vary widely from poet to poet. Usually we allow poets their choice of language from any of the four levels of diction: formal, informal, colloquial, and slang. We do not hold them to the use of formal language for important subjects and colloquial diction or slang for low subjects. We ask only that their words be appropriate to what they are trying to communicate, that they be honest in their use of language. Poets are then free to achieve impressive effects by suddenly changing their level of diction, or by using incongruous diction to comment ironically on their subject.

A. E. Housman used a deliberately informal, colloquial diction in this poem. In what ways is it appropriate to the subject and the situation?

Shake Hands, We Shall Never Be Friends

Shake hands, we shall never be friends, all's over;
   I only vex you the more I try.
All's wrong that ever I've done or said,
And nought to help it in this dull head:
   Shake hands, here's luck, good-bye.   5

But if you come to a road where danger
   Or guilt or anguish or shame's to share,
Be good to the lad that loves you true
And the soul that was born to die for you,
   And whistle and I'll be there.   10

                      —*A. E. Housman*

Ferlinghetti's use of slang in a poem on a religious subject startles many people.

Sometime during eternity

          Sometime during eternity
                    some guys show up
and one of them
          who shows up real late
                is a kind of carpenter   5
   from some square-type place
              like Galilee
    and he starts wailing
            and claiming he is hip
   to who made heaven   10

                              and earth
                                    and that the cat
                    who really laid it on us
                                    is his Dad

      And moreover   15
         he adds
                    It's all writ down
                              on some scroll-type parchments
            which some henchmen
                          leave lying around the Dead Sea somewheres   20
               a long time ago
                              and which you won't even find
      for a coupla thousand years ago or so
                                    or at least for
      nineteen hundred and fortyseven   25
                              of them
                    to be exact
                              and even then
            nobody really believes them
                                    or me   30
                                    for that matter

      You're hot
                    they tell him

      And they cool him

      They stretch him on the Tree to cool   35

      And everybody after that
                              is always making models
                    of this Tree
                              with Him hung up
      and always crooning His name   40
                              and calling Him to come down
                    and sit in
                              on their combo
               as if he is *the* king cat

                              who's got to blow   45
        or they can't quite make it

        Only he don't come down
                              from His Tree

Him just hang there
                        on His Tree   50
                              looking real Petered out
                        and real cool
                                    and also
                according to a roundup
                              of late world news   55
        from the usual unreliable sources
                              real dead
                                    —Lawrence Ferlinghetti

18. *scroll-type parchments*: the Dead Sea scrolls.

The effect here is achieved by the disparity between what many people
would consider the proper level of diction for a religious poem and the
kind of language Ferlinghetti actually uses. We simply aren't used to
hearing Christ referred to as *"the* king cat." Some readers find this
sort of diction offensive, but Ferlinghetti has a point to make, which
he suggests almost overtly in his final lines. If the sources are unreliable, there is some doubt as to the actual demise of Christ. Those
circles in which he is considered dead, the poet implies, are those
circles that have codified religion into some "scroll-type parchments,"
that have refined Christ to sterility (as Och's puts it in "The Crucifixion"), that are offended at hearing Christ discussed in the living, immediate language Ferlinghetti uses. As the poem demonstrates, one's
attitude toward religious language has something to do with one's
actual religiosity.

Philip Larkin, a contemporary British poet, makes a more subtle use
of diction in his poem "MCMXIV." He attempts to recapture in his
poem the spirit of that year, a time of innocence seldom seen before
and never seen since. The word "lark" in line 8 epitomizes Larkin's
feelings about life in 1914. Other words are important, especially as

they convey the distance, both cultural and chronological, that intrudes between then and now:" bleached," "tin advertisements," "all hazed over," "dust." His diction has a deliberately impressionistic, evocative quality that is perfectly suited to a contemporary poet looking back half a century to the eve of World War I.

MCMXIV

Those long uneven lines
Standing as patiently
As if they were stretched outside
The Oval or Villa Park,
The crowns of hats, the sun   5
On moustached archaic faces
Grinning as if it were all
An August Bank Holiday lark;

And the shut shops, the bleached
Established names on the sunblinds,   10
The farthings and sovereigns,
And dark-clothed children at play
Called after kings and queens,
The tin advertisements
For cocoa and twist, and the pubs   15
Wide open all day;

And the countryside not caring:
The place-names all hazed over
With flowering grasses, and fields
Shadowing Domesday lines   20
Under wheat's restless silence;
The differently-dressed servants
With tiny rooms in huge houses,
The dust behind limousines;

Never such innocence,   25
Never before or since,
As changed itself to past

Without a word—the men
Leaving the gardens tidy,
The thousands of marriages   30
Lasting a little while longer:
Never such innocence again.

—Philip Larkin

Title: the year in which World War I began. Many historians view that war as the beginning of the "modern" period, the age of technology. 11. *farthings and sovereigns*: coins of smallest and greatest worth in the British monetary system. 15. *twist*: a strong, twisted silk thread; also the kind of tobacco sold in the form of a rope cord. 20. *Domesday lines*: English boundary lines dating from the time of William the Conqueror's *Domesday Book*.

QUESTIONS

1. What specific scenes does Larkin describe? What appears to be the basis for his selection?

2. The "bleached/Established names on the sunblinds" are bleached because, being painted on the blinds of long-established businesses, they have endured much weather. But the names might be established and the signs bleached in another way: established in the sense of fixed, firm, stable; bleached in that from Larkin's perspective the stability that they represent is a thing of the past. What other phrases have a double meaning—one that describes the scene literally, and one that gives us a clue as to Larkin's attitude toward the era he is describing?

3. Larkin's word for the age is "innocence"; he uses it twice in the final section of his poem. Discuss the various meanings of innocence, and decide in what sense 1914 was an innocent year.

4. The poet's closing reference is to "thousands of marriages/Lasting a little while longer." Discuss the relationship between the marriages, innocence, and the rest of the poem. Is the poet using the rest of the poem as a preface to what he has to say about marriage, or is he using marriage as a summary of his picture of life before World War I?

5. Why is the title of the poem in roman numerals?

IMAGERY

Some words make a special appeal to one or more of the senses— usually to the sense of sight, but upon occasion to the senses of smell and taste and even touch. Poetry, which is more immediate than most writing, makes a greater use of these sensuously appealing words than does prose. The difference is the difference between "bright red" and "fire engine red." Through one phrase we are told that the red is bright; through the other an image is created in our mind's eye and we see that the red is bright. The former is abstract, the latter is concrete. The latter is imagistic, the former is not. In a similar fashion, "ghostly moan" and "mackerel-scented wharves" would appeal to our senses of hearing and smell, respectively. In one sense, then, imagery is concrete language that makes an appeal to one or more of our senses. Larkin's "MCMXIV," for example, contained many visual images.

In some cases, however, the term "imagery" is used in a looser sense to refer to an extended series of words all derived from the same source: "trade," "get," "spend," and "toil" (in Wordsworth's sonnet, "The World is Too Much With Us") are referred to as "commercial imagery," because all the words have something to do with commerce. "Holy," "saint," "prayer," "reverence," and "bless," although they are not concrete and do not appeal to any of our senses, might be called "religious imagery," because they are all words associated with religion. So there might be a pattern of sexual imagery or natural imagery or winter imagery in a poem. Read these two poems by Shakespeare carefully with an eye toward identifying the imagery used by the poet.

Spring

When daisies pied and violets blue
   And lady-smocks all silver-white
And cuckoo-buds of yellow hue
   Do paint the meadows with delight,
The cuckoo then, on every tree,   5
Mocks married men; for thus sings he,
          Cuckoo!
Cuckoo, cuckoo! O, word of fear,
Unpleasing to a married ear!

When shepherds pipe on oaten straws,   10
   And merry larks are ploughmen's clocks,
When turtles tread, and rooks, and daws,
   And maidens bleach their summer smocks,

The cuckoo then, on every tree,
Mocks married men; for thus sings he,   15
          Cuckoo!
Cuckoo, cuckoo! O, word of fear,
Unpleasing to a married ear!

                              —*William Shakespeare*

  9. *unpleasing*: the cuckoo (like the cowbird) lays its eggs in the nests of
other birds, and its call resembles the English word "cuckold." For these reasons its call would be unpleasing to a married ear.

Winter

When icicles hang by the wall,
    And Dick the shepherd blows his nail,
And Tom bears logs into the hall,
    And milk comes frozen home in pail,
When blood is nipped and ways be foul,   5
    Then nightly sings the staring owl:
        "Tu-whit, tu-who!"
        A merry note,
While greasy Joan doth keel the pot.

When all aloud the wind doth blow,   10
    And coughing drowns the parson's saw,
And birds sit brooding in the snow,
    And Marian's nose looks red and raw,
When roasted crabs hiss in the bowl,
    Then nightly sings the staring owl: 15
        "Tu-whit, tu-who!"
        A merry note,
While greasy Joan doth keel the pot.

                              —*William Shakespeare*

  9. *keel*: stir. 11. *saw*: proverb. 14. *crabs*: crab apples.

The imagery is complicated. On the simplest level the poems contain
natural imagery appropriate to the season: daisies, violets, cuckoo-buds,
straws, larks, turtledoves in spring; icicles, logs, owls, roasted crab
apples in winter. The appropriateness of the natural imagery and
the way it creates an immediate picture of the respective seasons have

been much admired by readers over the last three centuries. But look again at the imagery. The cuckoo of "Spring" has obvious sexual overtones. The daisies are pied (multi-colored) and have overtones of inconstancy. The other flowers also have sexual overtones: lady-smocks and cuckoo-buds. The oaten straws are phallic, and the treading turtles ("and rooks, and daws,/And maidens . . .") are overtly sexual, perhaps unpleasantly so. And the imagery of "Winter" is even more sexual and more unpleasant. It could be argued that the sexuality of Shakespeare's imagery is entirely unintentional—but anyone who knows the poet well knows both his fondness for double meanings and his tendency to drop the most frightening obscenities into the middle of his most beautiful and tender passages. It is quite probable that we are justified in reading double meanings into his imagery in these two songs, especially since that of "Spring" is suggested overtly in lines 8–9 and 17–18 of the poem itself. Is that duplicity necessarily self-contradictory? Does the poet have a point he's trying to make by using such two-sided imagery? Or is he merely being perverse? In your spare time read over *Love's Labours Lost,* from which these two songs are taken, and consider their meaning when put in the context of the whole play.

Suzanne

Suzanne takes you down
To her place near the river
You can hear the boats go by
You can spend the night beside her.
And you know that she's half crazy   5
But that's why you want to be there
And she feeds you tea and oranges
That come all the way from China.
And just when you mean to tell her
That you have no love to give her   10
Then she gets you on her wavelength
And she lets the river answer
That you've always been her lover
And you want to travel with her
And you want to travel blind   15
And you know that she will trust you
For you've touched her perfect body with your mind.

And Jesus was a sailor
When he walked upon the water
And he spent a long time watching 20
From his lonely wooden tower.
And when he knew for certain
Only drowning men could see him
He said, "All men will be sailors then
Until the sea shall free them." 25
But he himself was broken
Long before the sky would open
Forsaken, almost human,
He sank beneath your wisdom like a stone.
And you want to travel with him 30
And you want to travel blind
And you think maybe you'll trust him
For he's touched your perfect body with his mind.

Now Suzanne takes your hand
And she leads you to the river 35
She is wearing rags and feathers
From Salvation Army counters.
And the sun pours down like honey
On our lady of the harbour;
And she shows you where to look 40
Among the garbage and the flowers.
There are heroes in the seaweed,
There are children in the morning,
They are leaning out for love
And they will lean that way forever 45
While Suzanne holds the mirror.
And you want to travel with her
And you want to travel blind
And you know that you can trust her
For she's touched your perfect body with her mind. 50

                                        —*Leonard Cohen*

39. *our lady of the harbour*: many European harbor cities have large statues
of Christ or Mary on a hill adjacent to the harbor to bless ships as they pass.

In moving from "Spring'" and "Winter" to Leonard Cohen's "Suzanne"
we move from the profane to the sacred and from poetry that makes

at least some kind of literal sense to poetry that is almost entirely dependent on the connotations and associations of its imagery and the responses produced in a listener by the successive images. No matter what we want to say about the suggestions of "When icicles hang by the wall,/And Dick the shepherd blows his nail," the lines have a literal sense that is absent in lines like "Forsaken, almost human,/He sank beneath your wisdom/Like a stone." Perhaps because the literal meaning is absent, perhaps because the imagery is richer and more complex, "Suzanne" demands more attention than either of Shakespeare's songs. Central to the poem's meaning is an understanding of Suzanne, Jesus, the person addressed by the poet, and the interrelationships among the three. Although nothing definite is said by Cohen, we can make some reasonably precise statements about all three, based on the imagery with which the poet surrounds each. Suzanne loves: she loves you even before she meets you, she loves you enough to offer you tea and oranges (luxury items in most economies, carrying connotations of great value). Perhaps because of her totally selfless love, the world considers her half crazy. The effect of her love is so strong that it transforms even the garbage world of the waterfront: there are heroes in the seaweed. There is something vaguely religious about Suzanne, for religious imagery surrounds her: "our lady of the harbour," "Salvation Army counters," most of all, "love." On the other hand, she wears rags and feathers and lives down by the river: she may be not only half crazy, but a tramp as well. You can spend the night beside her. Her character is both religious and sexual, much like Cohen's Sisters of Mercy.

Jesus, like Suzanne, is associated with the water: she lives near the water; he was a sailor and walked upon it. Just as our wisdom cannot fathom Suzanne and we suspect she's crazy, Jesus sank beneath our wisdom "like a stone." Suzanne wastes a lot of love on the waterfront bums; Jesus spent his time hanging around with "drowning men."

The indefinite "you" of the poem provides the measure of both Suzanne and Jesus, because it is upon this character that they act. He is in need of love, but by instinct distrustful, perhaps because of previous experiences. He is probably one of the "drowning men" of line 23. He is desperately in need of direction and help, which he gains as the poem progresses: the imagery of the final stanza is richly affirmative. So we may say that the experience here is roughly similar to that of "Sisters of Mercy": the poet and an indefinite "you" meet with a semireligious woman who is able to transform their depression into affirmation.

The presence of Jesus in the poem and the wealth of water imagery bring a strong religious element into "Suzanne." Does water have its Christian significance of baptism here? Is that what is going on in the final stanza? Or is the baptismal significance subsumed into a broader connotation of water, that of regeneration and life? Is Suzanne given religious overtones in an attempt to suggest the effect she has on a man, or is her effect due to her position as a human agent of the divine Jesus? Might Suzanne be a Salvation Army lass? These are all possibilities supported to some extent by the imagery, although the poet is so vague that we cannot affirm or deny any of them for sure. Clearly the man experiences some sort of conversion, but the variety of the images for rebirth and the many images for death (drowning men) and life (the sun pouring down like honey) make it unclear whether the conversion is specifically Christian, broadly religious, or something else entirely.

Consider the imagery of the following two poems. To what senses does the imagery appeal? How does the imagery convey meaning?

To His Coy Mistress

Had we but world enough and time,
This coyness, lady, were no crime.
We would sit down and think which way
To walk, and pass our long love's day;
Thou by the Indian Ganges' side   5
Shouldst rubies find; I by the tide
Of Humber would complain. I would
Love you ten years before the Flood;
And you should, if you please, refuse
Till the conversion of the Jews.   10
My vegetable love should grow
Vaster than empires, and more slow.
An hundred years should go to praise
Thine eyes, and on thy forehead gaze;
Two hundred to adore each breast,   15
But thirty thousand to the rest;
An age at least to every part,

And the last age should show your heart.
For, lady, you deserve this state,
Nor would I love at lower rate.   20
　　But at my back I always hear
Time's wingèd chariot hurrying near;
And yonder all before us lie
Deserts of vast eternity.
Thy beauty shall no more be found,   25
Nor in thy marble vault shall sound
My echoing song; then worms shall try
That long preserved virginity,
And your quaint honor turn to dust,
And into ashes all my lust.   30
The grave's a fine and private place,
But none, I think, do there embrace.
　　Now therefore, while the youthful hue
Sits on thy skin like morning dew,
And while thy willing soul transpires   35
At every pore with instant fires,
Now let us sport us while we may;
And now, like am'rous birds of prey,
Rather at once our time devour,
Than languish in his slow-chapt power,   40
Let us roll all our strength, and all
Our sweetness, up into one ball;
And tear our pleasures with rough strife
Through the iron gates of life.
Thus, though we cannot make our sun   45
Stand still, yet we will make him run.

　　　　　　　　　　　　　　　　　　　—Andrew Marvell

　　1. *world*: space. 7. *Humber*: a river in England; *complain*: see the section on
genres, "complaints." 29. *quaint*: quite possibly a pun on quaint = old and ME
queynte = female private parts. 40. *chapt*: cracked, roughened.

QUESTIONS

　　1. This poem has a more definite literal meaning than "Suzanne." In
fact, it reduces to a syllogism once the wealth of imagery is removed.
What specifically is the argument? Is it valid?

2. How does the poet change the imagery of each section of the argument to accord with his various premises?

3. Is the poet entirely serious in his argument, apparently an attempt at seduction? Is there something mildly humorous about the incongruity of a cold, rational argument tricked out with lush, sensual imagery? Is the poet conscious of this?

4. Compare the thought of the last line with the thought expressed in the poems by Millay and Yeats in chapter 6. Do you find this idea of rushing through life with a kind of savage eagerness for death reckless and grotesque, or is it something you too have felt at one time or another?

Silver

Slowly, silently, now the moon
Walks the night in her silver shoon;
This way, and that, she peers, and sees
Silver fruit upon silver trees;
One by one the casements catch   5
Her beams beneath the silvery thatch;
Couched in his kneel, like a log,
With paws of silver sleeps the dog;
From their shadowy cote the white breasts peep
Of doves in a silver-feathered sleep;   10
A harvest mouse goes scampering by,
With silver claws and a silver eye;
And moveless fish in the water gleam,
By silver reeds in a silver stream.

—Walter de la Mare

2. *shoon*: archaic plural of shoe. 9. *cote*: shelter for sleep.

QUESTIONS

1. Examine the images closely. At first they all appear to enhance the silvery quality of the landscape, and some of them—the water images especially—would definitely give off a silver shine in the moonlight. A few others might be silvery if seen in the proper light: the doves' white

breasts, the eye of the mouse. Others, however, are not silver in any light: the fruit, the straw thatch of the house. Is this a failure on de la Mare's part, or has the poet made a significant point about perception and the eye of the beholder?

2. Note the focusing down as the images proceed: from trees to housetop to dog to doves to mouse to fish. What does this focusing down add to the poem's effect? To its message?

3. "Like a log" in line seven: is this trite and used merely for the sake of a rhyme for "dog," or is there something deeper to it?

Some poems are little more than collections of images; the meaning is simply the net impact of all the connotations of all the images plus the interrelationships among those images. Usually such imagistic poems, like Cohen's "Suzanne" or the writing of some of the nineteenth century French poets, lack any semblance of literal meaning. Sometimes they have a literal meaning that is itself meaningless and functions only as a framework in which to set images. Imagistic poetry is to be explained in terms of its images, which (like those of "I Am the Walrus" and "Kubla Khan") are inevitably rich and elusive.

I Am the Walrus

I am he as you are he as you are me and we are all together.
See how they run like pigs from a gun see how they fly,
I'm crying.
Sitting on a cornflake—waiting for the van to come.
Corporation teashirt, stupid bloody tuesday man you been a   5
    naughty boy you let your face grow long.
I am the eggman, they are the eggmen—I am the walrus
GOO GOO GOO JOOB.
City policeman sitting pretty little policeman in a row,
See how they fly like Lucy in the sky—see how they run
I'm crying—I'm crying.   10
Yellow matter custard dripping from a dead dog's eye.
Crabalocker fishwife pornographic priestess boy you been a naughty
    girl, you let your knickers down.
I am the eggman, they are the eggmen—I am the walrus.
GOO GOO GOO JOOB.
Sitting in an English garden waiting for the sun,   15

If the sun don't come, you get a tan from standing in the English
  rain,
I am the eggman, they are the eggmen—I am the walrus.
GOO GOO GOO JOOB.
Expert texpert choking smokers don't you think the joker laughs at
  you? Ha ha ha!
See how they smile, like pigs in a sty, see how they snied.   20
I'm crying.
Semolina pilchard climbing up the Eiffel Tower.
Elementary penguin singing Hare Krishna man you should have
  seen them kicking
Edgar Allen Poe.
I am the eggman, they are the eggmen—I am the walrus.   25
GOO GOO GOO JOOB
GOO GOO GOO JOOB GOO GOO GOOOOOOOOOOOOJOOOOB

                                   —*John Lennon–Paul McCartney*

Some people have argued that "I Am the Walrus" is a put-on, a meaningless collage of images designed to elicit absurd responses from over-
ingenious listeners. Others view it as a good imagistic poem, as well as a
good song. At the crux of the matter is just what the walrus represents,
since we are all equal to I and "I am the walrus," and therefore we are
all walruses. Popular mythology would have the walrus be slang for
corpse, and the song about death. Many of the other images, however,
apparently have little to do with death: pornographic priestess, pigs in
a sty, the eggman. The music, from its opening wrenching cacophony
to its cyclonic conclusion, is vaguely unpleasant, harsh, and perhaps
terrifying—all of which may or may not suggest death. Someone appears
to be chanting "Everybody's a hunchback" as the song swirls to its
finish, and it very definitely ends with a quotation from Shakespeare's
King Lear, act *IV*, scene 6.

EDGAR	I know thee well—a serviceable villain,
	As duteous to the vices of thy mistress
	As badness would desire.
GLOUCESTER	What, is he dead?
EDGAR	Sit you down, father, rest you.

Lines 15–16 are set off from the rest of the song by virtue of their own unique musical setting—are they perhaps the key to unlocking the poem? Discuss the many images of the song, the effect they have on the senses, the effect the music has on them, and see if you can relate them coherently. Can anything be said about the theme of this poem, anything more definite than, "This is an extremely unpleasant poem about extreme unpleasantness?" Is that theme enough?

Kubla Khan

In Xanadu did Kubla Khan
A stately pleasure-dome decree:
Where Alph, the sacred river, ran
Through caverns measureless to man
   Down to a sunless sea.   5
So twice five miles of fertile ground
With walls and towers were girdled round:
And here were gardens bright with sinuous rills,
Where blossomed many an incense-bearing tree,
And here were forests ancient as the hills,   10
Enfolding sunny spots of greenery.

But oh! that deep romantic chasm which slanted
Down the green hill athwart a cedarn cover!
A savage place! as holy and enchanted
As e'er beneath a waning moon was haunted   15
By woman wailing for her demon-lover!
And from this chasm, with ceaseless turmoil seething,
As if this earth in fast thick pants were breathing,
A mighty fountain momently was forced,
Amid whose swift half-intermitted burst   20
Huge fragments vaulted like rebounding hail,
Or chaffy grain beneath the thresher's flail:
And 'mid these dancing rocks at once and ever
It flung up momently the sacred river.
Five miles meandering with a mazy motion   25
Through wood and dale the sacred river ran,

Then reached the caverns measureless to man,
And sank in tumult to a lifeless ocean:
And 'mid this tumult Kubla heard from far
Ancestral voices prophesying war!   30

   The shadow of the dome of pleasure
   Floated midway on the waves;
   Where was heard the mingled measure
   From the fountain and the caves.
It was a miracle of rare device,   35
A sunny pleasure-dome with caves of ice!

   A damsel with a dulcimer
   In a vision once I saw:
   It was an Abyssinian maid,
   And on her dulcimer she played,   40
   Singing of Mount Abora.
Could I revive within me
Her symphony and song,
To such a deep delight 'twould win me,
That music loud and long,   45
I would build that dome in air,
That sunny dome! those caves of ice!
And all who heard should see them there,
And all should cry, Beware! Beware!
His flashing eyes, his floating hair!   50
Weave a circle round him thrice,
And close your eyes with holy dread,
For he on honey-dew hath fed,
And drunk the milk of Paradise.

                                —*Samuel Taylor Coleridge*

This poem is so well known that it really needs little comment here. The poet claimed that he literally dreamt the poem up on an opium trip, then forgot most of it when interrupted in the process of writing it down. We have little reason to doubt him, although certainly some subconscious processes had been at work before the dream that might have produced a poem somewhat like this in due time, dream or no dream. So complex are the images that it took John Livingston Lowes a full book to discuss them, their sources, and their relationships. The narrative has a dreamlike inconsistency which makes it difficult to follow. What does Coleridge describe? What would you say is the theme of the poem? How does the first part relate to the second? How does the imagery create patterns of meaning?

Long poems, like "To His Coy Mistress" or "The Quaker Graveyard in Nantucket" (chap. 5), allow poets to change imagery as their subject changes or play back and forth on several different imagistic themes. The longer the poem, the greater the possibilities, of course, and the imagery in a four-hundred line poem like Eliot's "The Wasteland" or a several thousand line poem like Whitman's "Leaves of Grass" is so complex that extensive study is required before patterns begin to emerge. Many playwrights write in verse, and frequently that verse involves complex patterns of imagery of several varieties. Shakespeare was both a good poet and a first rate playwright, and the imagery and poetry of a play like *Romeo and Juliet* or *King Lear* are as fine as those of any poem in the English language. Act II, scenes 1 and 2 of *Romeo and Juliet* present a case in point. Shakespeare's imagery changes with his characters: Mercutio, who is exceptionally cynical and unromantic, uses considerable sexual imagery and many images of darkness. Romeo, whose love is sexual but romantic as well, uses sexual imagery of a more chaste nature, astronomical imagery, and extensive light imagery. Juliet echoes Romeo, and toward the end of the scene introduces falconry imagery. What is most important, however, is the pattern of light and dark imagery that pervades the speech of all the characters in these scenes—indeed—the whole play. The play is a battleground on which images of light war against images of darkness, and the wealth of connotative significance carried by light and darkness is what makes the play more than just a love story. It is not insignificant that the Prince of Verona begins the final speech of the play with the lines, "A glooming peace this morning with it brings,/ The Sun for sorrow will not show his head." Imagistically, light loses in the play. Trace the development of light and dark imagery, as well as other patterns of imagery, through these two scenes. Do they foreshadow imagistically the play's end, or do they imply a hope that the tragic ending will fail to fulfil?

Romeo and Juliet, Act II.

*Scene I. A lane by the wall
of Capulet's orchard.*

[*Enter* ROMEO.]

ROMEO   Can I go forward when my heart is here?
Turn back, dull earth, and find thy centre out.

[*He climbs the wall, and leaps down within it.*]

[*Enter* BENVOLIO *and* MERCUTIO]

BENVOLIO   Romeo! my cousin Romeo!

MERCUTIO   He is wise;
And, on my life, hath stol'n him home to bed.

BENVOLIO   He ran this way, and leap'd this orchard wall: 5
Call, good Mercutio.

MERCUTIO   Nay, I'll conjure too?
Romeo! humours! madman! passion! lover!
Appear thou in the likeness of a sigh:
Speak but one rhyme, and I am satisfied;
Cry but "Ay me!" pronounce but "love" and "dove;"   10
Speak to my gossip Venus one fair word,
One nick-name for her purblind son and heir,
Young Adam Cupid, he that shot so trim,
When King Cophetua loved the beggar-maid!
He heareth not, he stirreth not, he moveth not;   15
The ape is dead, and I must conjure him.
I conjure thee by Rosaline's bright eyes,
By her high forehead and her scarlet lip,
By her fine foot, straight leg and quivering thigh
And the demesnes that there adjacent lie,   20
That in thy likeness thou appear to us!

BENVOLIO   An if he hear thee, thou wilt anger him.

MERCUTIO   This cannot anger him: 'twould anger him
To raise a spirit in his mistress' circle
Of some strange nature, letting it there stand   25
Till she had laid it and conjured it down;
That were some spite: my invocation
Is fair and honest, and in his mistress' name
I conjure only but to raise up him.

BENVOLIO   Come, he hath hid himself among these trees,   30

To be consorted with the humorous night:
Blind is his love and best befits the dark.

MERCUTIO   If love be blind, love cannot hit the mark.
Now will he sit under a medlar tree,
And wish his mistress were that kind of fruit   35
As maids call medlars, when they laugh alone.
O, Romeo, that she were, O, that she were
An open et cætera, thou a poperin pear!
Romeo, good night: I'll to my truckle-bed;
This field-bed is too cold for me to sleep: 40
Come, shall we go?

BENVOLIO   Go, then; for 'tis in vain
To seek him here that means not to be found.
[*Exeunt.*]

6. *conjure*: raise up by incantation, as if Romeo were a spirit. 7. *humours*: the
bodily fluids, which men of the Renaissance assumed filled the body. In a healthy
man the humours were in balance; in madmen, lovers, and sick people, the
humours were out of balance. Love, insanity, sickness—it's all the same, Mercutio
implies; he's "in a bad humour." 11. *gossip*: friend. 12. *purblind*: totally blind.
13. *Adam*: hypocritical. 14. *Cophetua*: a ballad character. 17. *Rosaline*: before he
met Juliet, Romeo was in love with Rosaline. Mercutio is as yet unaware that
the object of Romeo's affections has changed. 20. *demesnes*: estates, areas, regions.
22. *anger him*: because of the obscene puns Mercutio has been making about a
subject that to Romeo is sacred. 34. *medlar*: a small fruit resembling a brown
apple. 39. *truckle-bed*: a small rollaway bed tucked under a standing bed during
the day time. 40. *field-bed*: a bed on the bare ground.

Scene II. Capulet's orchard.

[*Enter* ROMEO.]

ROMEO   He jests at scars that never felt a wound.
[*JULIET appears above at a window.*]
But, soft! what light through yonder window breaks?
It is the east, and Juliet is the sun.
Arise, fair sun, and kill the envious moon,
Who is already sick and pale with grief,   5
That thou her maid art far more fair than she:
Be not her maid, since she is envious;
Her vestal livery is but sick and green
And none but fools do wear it; cast it off.
It is my lady, O, it is my love!   10

O, that she knew she were!
She speaks, yet she says nothing: what of that?
Her eye discourses; I will answer it.
I am too bold, 'tis not to me she speaks:
Two of the fairest stars in all the heaven,   15
Having some business, do entreat her eyes
To twinkle in their spheres till they return.
What if her eyes were there, they in her head?
The brightness of her cheek would shame those stars,
As daylight doth a lamp; her eyes in heaven   20
Would through the airy region stream so bright
That birds would sing and think it were not night.
See, how she leans her cheek upon her hand!
O, that I were a glove upon that hand,
That I might touch that cheek!

JULIET   Ay me!
ROMEO   She speaks: 25
O, speak again, bright angel! for thou art
As glorious to this night, being o'er my head,
As is a wingèd messenger of heaven
Unto the white-upturnèd wondering eyes
Of mortals that fall back to gaze on him   30
When he bestrides the lazy-pacing clouds
And sails upon the bosom of the air.

JULIET   O Romeo, Romeo! wherefore art thou Romeo?
Deny thy father and refuse thy name;
Or, if thou wilt not, be but sworn my love,   35
And I'll no longer be a Capulet.

ROMEO   [Aside] Shall I hear more, or shall I speak at this?

JULIET   'Tis but thy name that is my enemy;
Thou art thyself, though not a Montague.
What's Montague? it is nor hand, nor foot,   40
Nor arm, nor face, nor any other part
Belonging to a man. O, be some other name!
What's in a name? that which we call a rose
By any other name would smell as sweet;
So Romeo would, were he not Romeo call'd,   45
Retain that dear perfection which he owes
Without that title. Romeo, doff thy name,

And for that name which is no part of thee
Take all myself.

ROMEO   I take thee at thy word:
Call me but love, and I'll be new baptized;   50
Henceforth I never will be Romeo.

JULIET   What man art thou that thus bescreen'd in night
So stumblest on my counsel?

ROMEO   By a name
I know not how to tell thee who I am:
My name, dear saint, is hateful to myself,   55
Because it is an enemy to thee;
Had I it written I would tear the word.

JULIET   My ears have not yet drunk a hundred words
Of that tongue's utterance, yet I know the sound:
Art thou not Romeo and a Montague?   60

ROMEO   Neither, fair saint, if either thee dislike.

JULIET   How camest thou hither, tell me, and wherefore?
The orchard walls are high and hard to climb,
And the place death, considering who thou art,
If any of my kinsmen find thee here.   65

ROMEO   With love's light wings did I o'erperch these walls,
For stony limits cannot hold love out,
And what love can do that dares love attempt;
Therefore thy kinsmen are no let to me.

JULIET   If they do see thee, they will murder thee.   70

ROMEO   Alack, there lies more peril in thine eye
Than twenty of their swords: look thou but sweet,
And I am proof against their enmity.

JULIET   I would not for the world they saw thee here.

ROMEO   I have night's cloak to hide me from their sight;   75
And but thou love me, let them find me here:
My life were better ended by their hate,
Than death proroguèd, wanting of thy love.

JULIET   By whose direction found'st thou out this place?

ROMEO   By love, who first did prompt me to inquire;   80
He lent me counsel and I lent him eyes.
I am no pilot; yet, wert thou as far
As that vast shore wash'd with the farthest sea,
I would adventure for such merchandise.

JULIET   Thou know'st the mask of night is on my face,   85
Else would a maiden blush bepaint my cheek
For that which thou hast heard me speak tonight.
Fain would I dwell on form, fain, fain deny
What I have spoke: but farewell compliment!
Dost thou love me? I know thou wilt say "Ay."   90
And I will take thy word: yet, if thou swear'st,
Thou mayst prove false; at lovers' perjuries,
They say, Jove laughs. O gentle Romeo,
If thou dost love, pronounce it faithfully:
Or if thou think'st I am too quickly won,   95
I'll frown and be perverse and say thee nay,
So thou wilt woo; but else, not for the world.
In truth, fair Montague, I am too fond,
And therefore thou mayst think my 'haviour light:
But trust me, gentleman, I'll prove more true   100
Than those that have more cunning to be strange.
I should have been more strange, I must confess,
But that thou overheard'st, ere I was ware,
My true love's passion; therefore pardon me,
And not impute this yielding to light love,   105
Which the dark night hath so discovered.

ROMEO   Lady, by yonder blessed moon I swear
That tips with silver all these fruit-tree tops—

JULIET   O, swear not by the moon, the inconstant moon,
That monthly changes in her circled orb,   110
Lest that thy love prove likewise variable.

ROMEO   What shall I swear by?

JULIET   Do not swear at all;
Or, if thou wilt, swear by thy gracious self,
Which is the god of my idolatry,
And I'll believe thee.

ROMEO   If my heart's dear love—   115

JULIET   Well, do not swear: although I joy in thee,
I have no joy of this contract to-night:
It is too rash, too unadvised, too sudden;
Too like the lightning, which doth cease to be
Ere one can say "It lightens." Sweet, good night!   120
This bud of love, by summer's ripening breath,

May prove a beauteous flower when next we meet.
Good night, good night! as sweet repose and rest
Come to thy heart as that within my breast!

ROMEO   O, wilt thou leave me so unsatisfied?   125
JULIET   What satisfaction canst thou have tonight?
ROMEO   The exchange of thy love's faithful vow for mine.
JULIET   I gave thee mine before thou didst request it:
And yet I would it were to give again.

ROMEO   Wouldst thou withdraw it? for what purpose, love?   130
JULIET   But to be frank, and give it thee again.
And yet I wish but for the thing I have:
My bounty is as boundless as the sea,
My love as deep; the more I give to thee,
The more I have, for both are infinite.   135

                       [NURSE *calls within.*]

I hear some noise within; dear love, adieu!
Anon, good nurse! Sweet Montague, be true.
Stay but a little, I will come again.

                            [*Exit, above.*

ROMEO   O blessèd, blessèd night! I am afeard,
Being in night, all this is but a dream,   140
Too flattering-sweet to be substantial.

            [*Re-enter* JULIET, *above.*]

JULIET   Three words, dear Romeo, and good night indeed.
If that thy bent of love be honourable,
Thy purpose marriage, send me word tomorrow,
By one that I'll procure to come to thee,   145
Where and what time thou wilt perform the rite;
And all my fortunes at thy foot I'll lay
And follow thee my lord throughout the world.

NURSE   [*Within*] Madam!
JULIET   I come, anon.—But if thou mean'st not well,   150
I do beseech thee—

NURSE   [*Within*] Madam!
JULIET   By and by, I come:—
To cease thy suit, and leave me to my grief:
To-morrow will I send.

ROMEO   So thrive my soul—
JULIET   A thousand times good night!   155

[Exit, above.

ROMEO   A thousand times the worse, to want thy light.
              Love goes toward love, as schoolboys from their books,
              But love from love, toward school with heavy looks.

[Retiring.

[Re-enter JULIET, above.]

JULIET   Hist! Romeo, hist! O, for a falconer's voice,
              To lure this tassel-gentle back again!   160
              Bondage is hoarse, and may not speak aloud;
              Else would I tear the cave where Echo lies,
              And make her airy tongue more hoarse than mine,
              With repetition of my Romeo's name.

ROMEO   It is my soul that calls upon my name: 165
              How silver-sweet sound lovers' tongues by night,
              Like softest music to attending ears!

JULIET   Romeo!

ROMEO   My dear?

JULIET   At what o'clock to-morrow
              Shall I send to thee?

ROMEO   At the hour of nine.

JULIET   I will not fail: 'tis twenty years till then.   170
              I have forgot why I did call thee back.

ROMEO   Let me stand here till thou remember it.

JULIET   I shall forget, to have thee still stand there,
              Remembering how I love thy company.

ROMEO   And I'll still stay, to have thee still forget,   175
              Forgetting any other home but this.

JULIET   'Tis almost morning; I would have thee gone:
              And yet no further than a wanton's bird;
              Who lets it hop a little from her hand,
              Like a poor prisoner in his twisted gyves,   180
              And with a silk thread plucks it back again,
              So loving-jealous of his liberty.

ROMEO   I would I were thy bird.

JULIET   Sweet, so would I:
              Yet I should kill thee with much cherishing.
              Good night, good night! parting is such sweet sorrow,   185
              That I shall say good night till it be morrow.

[Exit, above.

ROMEO   Sleep dwell upon thine eyes, peace in thy breast!
             Would I were sleep and peace, so sweet to rest!
             Hence will I to my ghostly father's cell,
             His help to crave, and my dear hap to tell.   190
                                                                   [*Exit.*

4. *Moon*: the goddess of the sphere of the moon was Diana, also goddess of virginity. Romeo's imagery here is working on two levels. 8. *vestal*: virgin. 20. *eyes*: the sun was frequently called the heaven's eye or the heaven's mind in Neo-Platonic thought. Romeo is working on a contrast between ordinary stars, whose places in the heavens Juliet's eyes are taking temporarily, and her eyes, which seem more like the sun than a star. 66. *o'erperch*: fly over. 99. *light*: immodest. A pun is intended. 109. *the inconstant moon*: because the moon alone among heavenly bodies appeared to change size, its sphere was viewed as the dividing line between things mutable and things immutable. Cf. "sublunary love" in Donne's "A Valediction: Forbidding Mourning." 160. *tassel-gentle*: a male tercel falcon. 180. *gyves*: fetters. 190. *crave*: request; *hap*: fortune.

SIMILE AND METAPHOR

Wallace Stevens suggested in "The Idea of Order at Key West" that one of the functions of the artist—perhaps his primary function—is ordering experience. The idea is not original with Stevens; it has a long and respectable history, as his reference to Fernandez suggests. Perhaps as the poet takes public and private experience and filters it through his own vision to create a poem, he also orders disordered events. There are many ways in which he can accomplish this, of course: by the imposition of regular rhythm and patterns of rhyme, by drawing metaphysical statements from events of human history, and by making comparisons between aspects of existence we did not suspect were similar in any way. The devices of *simile* and *metaphor* are particularly relevant to this last way of ordering experience, because they imply relationship between two or more fundamentally different things. Rhetorically, there is little difference between a simile and a metaphor —"My love is like a red, red rose" is a simile; "My love is a red, red rose" would be a metaphor. But in practice there is considerable difference in that metaphors tend to be more open-ended than similes. Both, however, make significant comparisons between two different things (roses and love, for example); both relate two previously unrelated aspects of existence.

Simile and metaphor are basic ingredients of most poetry, although modern poetry tends to concentrate on single experiences and allow comparisons only implicitly. What makes a poetic comparison different from any rhetorical exercise in comparison and contrast is insight: "he acts like a real ass," "my faith is like an oak tree: strong, healthy, and deep-rooted," and "she was built like the proverbial brick outside appurtenance" are all comparisons, but they are bad poetic similes. They are not fresh, they offer us no genuine insight. The oak doesn't say anything really significant about faith, nor the ass about a man's behavior. These comparisons lack depth. A good simile or metaphor has layers of meaning, has depth, and rewards reading and rereading; a bad simile or metaphor is either banal to begin with or else disintegrates to nonsense after careful thought. Unfortunately, poetry (or pseudo-poetry, such as that of Rod McKuen or Joyce Kilmer) is full of trivial, superficial, casual comparisons, and most readers seem to lack the intelligence to distinguish between the banal and the beautiful.

Come All You Fair and Tender Ladies

Come all you fair and tender ladies,
Take warning how you court young men.
They're like the stars of a summer's morning,
First they'll appear and then they're gone.

If I had known before I courted   5
I never would have courted none.
I'd have locked my heart in a box of golden
And fastened it up with a silver pin.

I wish I were some little swallow,
And I had wings and I could fly.   10
I'd fly away to my false true-lover
And when he'd speak I would deny.

But I am not a little swallow;
I have no wings, neither can I fly.
So I'll sit down here to weep in sorrow   15
And try to pass my troubles by.

                                                       —*anonymous*

QUESTIONS

1. What specifically has happened to the singer of this song? What is her attitude toward her experience?

2. What connotations do golden and silver have? How effective is the image of lines 7–8?

3. In what ways is the comparison between the lady and the swallow appropriate? And that between men and stars? Which do you think has more depth?

The Arsenal at Springfield

This is the Arsenal. From floor to ceiling,
   Like a huge organ, rise the burnished arms;
But from their silent pipes no anthem pealing
   Startles the villages with strange alarms.

Ah, what a sound will rise, how wild and dreary,   5
   When the death-angel touches those swift keys!
What loud lament and dismal Miserere
   Will mingle with their awful symphonies!

I hear even now the infinite fierce chorus,
   The cries of agony, the endless groan,   10
Which, through the ages that have gone before us,
   In long reverberations reach our own.

On helm and harness rings the Saxon hammer,
   Through Cimbric forest roars the Norseman's song.
And loud, amid the universal clamor,   15
   O'er distant deserts sounds the Tartar gong.

I hear the Florentine, who from his palace
   Wheels out his battle-bell with dreadful din,
And Aztec priests upon their teocallis
   Beat the wild war-drums made of serpent's skin;   20

The tumult of each sacked and burning village;
  The shout that every prayer for mercy drowns;
The soldiers' revels in the midst of pillage;
  The wall of famine in beleaguered towns;

The bursting shell, the gateway wrenched asunder,   25
  The rattling musketry, the clashing blade;
And ever and anon, in tones of thunder,
  The diapason of the cannonade.

Is it, O man, with such discordant noises,
  With such accursed instruments as these,   30
Thou drownest Nature's sweet and kindly voices,
  And jarrest the celestial harmonies?

Were half the power that fills the world with terror,
  Were half the wealth bestowed on camps and courts,
Given to redeem the human mind from error,   35
  There were no need of arsenals or forts.

The warrior's name would be a name abhorr'ed!
  And every nation, that should lift again
Its hand against a brother, on its forehead
  Would wear forevermore the curse of Cain.   40

Down the dark future, through long generations,
  The echoing sounds grow fainter and then cease;
And like a bell, with solemn, sweet vibrations,
  I hear once more the voice of Christ say, "Peace!"

Peace! and no longer from its brazen portals   45
  The blast of War's great organ shakes the skies!
But beautiful as songs of the immortals,
  The holy melodies of love arise.
                              —Henry Wadsworth Longfellow

7. *Miserere*: a musical setting for Psalm 51; a hymn of penitence. 14. *Cimbric*:
a tribe of Danes who long contested Roman rule in northern Europe. 19. *teocallis*:
ceremonial pyramidic structures of the Aztecs. 28. *diapason*: an organ stop. 40.
curse of Cain: see Genesis 4:11 ff.

QUESTIONS

1. The simile on which the whole poem is constructed is stated in the first two lines, then developed through the rest of the poem. The stacked weapons look like an organ; their sound when fired sounds like the deep noise of an organ; the triggers are like keys. Is the comparison between arsenal and organ apt, especially given the religious connotations of organs? Is it fresh, startling in its insight and development, or merely a rhetorical device worked out in a rather mechanical fashion?

2. Ostensibly, this is an antiwar poem; lines 29–40 are especially preachy in their pacificism. Yet even as this poem was being written (in 1845), voices in the North were calling for a holy war against the South. Does the knowledge that a scant fifteen years after the poem's composition the United States would be engaged in the Civil War undercut its effectiveness? Is that necessarily the poet's fault?

A Valediction: Forbidding Mourning

As virtuous men pass mildly away,
    And whisper to their souls, to go,
Whilst some of their sad friends do say,
    The breath goes now, and some say, no:

So let us melt, and make no noise,   5
    No tear-floods, nor sigh-tempests move,
T'were profanation of our joys
    To tell the laity our love.

Moving of th' earth brings harms and fears,
    Men reckon what it did and meant,   10
But trepidation of the spheres,
    Though greater far, is innocent.

Dull sublunary lovers' love
    (Whose soul is sense) cannot admit
Absence, because it doth remove   15
    Those things which elemented it.

But we by a love, so much refined
   That our selves know not what it is,
Inter-assurèd of the mind,
   Care less, eyes, lips, and hands to miss.   20

Our two souls therefore, which are one,
   Though I must go, endure not yet
A breach, but an expansion,
   Like gold to airy thinness beat.

If they be two, they are two so   25
   As stiff twin compasses are two,
Thy soul, the fixt foot, makes no show
   To move, but doth, if th' other do.

And though it in the center sit,
   Yet when the other far doth roam,   30
It leans, and hearkens after it,
   And grows erect, as that comes home.

Such wilt thou be to me, who must
   Like th' other foot, obliquely run;
Thy firmness makes my circle just,   35
   And makes me end, where I begun.

                                 —John Donne

This poem contains some of the most complicated workings-out of similes in the English language. In the first two stanzas, the poet compares the parting of himself and his lover to the death of virtuous men: because they have nothing to fear in the afterlife, they make no noise or "sigh-tempests" when they die—in fact, their death is so calm that friends are unsure about the exact moment of death. Donne suggests that the parting of himself and his love be just as peaceful, because a telltale commotion would cheapen their love (7–8) and imply that they feared separation as virtueless men fear death. Next Donne compares the parting to the movement of the heavenly bodies of the Ptolemaic system: when earth, the lowest of the nine spheres, moves, it causes great commotion among men who fear the significance of such motion; but when the highest spheres move, they are unnoticed. Since Donne's love is of a higher nature, the departure should cause no commotion. Then the poet compares the stretching of their love to the stretching of gold as it is beaten to a foil, and finally to the movement of the two legs of a compass, an instrument used to draw circles in geometry and to mark distances by navigators. His love, he argues, remains fixed at home, while he moves away from her and around her (two motions are involved here). But even though the points move apart, the two legs remain attached at the top; so their spiritual love will bind them together, even though they move away from each other. Donne develops the argument further: when the one leg moves away from the other (as when the navigator uses the compass to mark distances), the other leg moves sympathetically with it, and the efficacy of the entire instrument is predicated on the fixedness (the constancy) of the two legs; so their love will remain constant even though they are separated. Moreover, the rigidity (constancy) of the compass (love) causes the outside leg to move in a perfect circle, so that it ends where it began (Donne returns to his love).

The similes are rhetorically complex, and Donne manages to suggest a great deal in a little space. But a rhetorical analysis does not exhaust the possibilities of the poem by any means. The circle is a particularly apt image for love, since it is continuous, perfect, and has no beginning or end. The simile involving the celestial bodies is similarly significant: men of the Middle Ages and Renaissance viewed change and mutability as the law of the world (a reasonable assumption, even today), observing that everything on earth changed from life to death, from joy to unhappiness, from wealth to poverty (and occasionally vice versa). So too the moon changed. But as far as they could see the other planets did not change, so quite obviously the realm of mutability was confined to the sphere of the moon and below. "Sublunary" in line 13 implies more than higher and lower love, then; it implies a changing, inconstant love as contrasted to a changeless love. Look carefully at some of the diction in the poem: "stiff," "foot," "grows erect," and "firmness." Some people find the obvious sexual connotations of these words incompatible with the celestial love that Donne has been talking about. What is your reaction? Does the vulgar destroy the celestial or do they compliment each other? Might it be that the generation of the 1960's and 1970's is in a better position to appreciate this poem of the 1600's than was the generation of the 1940's or the Victorian period in England?

Bird on the Wire

Like a bird on the wire
Like a drunk in a midnight choir
I have tried in my way to be free
Like a worm on a hook
Like a knight from some old-fashioned book   5
I have saved all my ribbons for thee

  If I have been unkind
  I hope that you can just let it go by
  If I have been untrue,
  I hope you know it was never to you.   10

Like a baby stillborn
Like a beast with his horn
I have torn everyone who reached out for me
But I swear by this song
And by all that I have done wrong   15
I will make it all up to thee.

  I saw a beggar leaning on his wooden crutch
  He said to me, "You must not ask for so much."
  And a pretty woman leaning in her darkened door,
  She cried to me, "Hey, why not ask for more?"   20
                                 —*Leonard Cohen*

The rhetoric of this song is not nearly so complicated as that of Donne's "Valediction," but the similes are more enigmatic: in what sense are a bird on a wire and a drunk in a choir free? How are a baby and a beast alike? How do worms and knights save ribbons? But questions like these are probably answerable only after we have reached some sort of agreement on the singer's character and his relationship to the woman to whom the song is obviously addressed. Discuss the singer carefully, being as definite about his personality as you possibly can, but ignoring the similes. Then, after you have reached an agreement on his character, turn back to the similes and attempt to explain them one by one.

Ars Poetica

A poem should be palpable and mute
As a globed fruit,

Dumb
As old medallions to the thumb,

Silent as the sleeve-worn stone   5
Of casement ledges where the moss has grown—

A poem should be wordless
As the flight of birds.

A poem should be motionless in time
As the moon climbs,   10

Leaving, as the moon releases
Twig by twig the night-entangled trees,

Leaving, as the moon behind the winter leaves,
Memory by memory the mind—

A poem should be motionless in time   15
As the moon climbs.

A poem should be equal to:
Not true.

For all the history of grief
An empty doorway and a maple leaf.   20

For love
The leaning grasses and two lights above the sea—

A poem should not mean
But be.

> —*Archibald MacLeish*

More statements on poetry—this time, almost riddles. Some of the similes of the poem are easily penetrated: old medallions are worn medallions, and they do not yield a definite image to fingers when touched although there is a picture stamped on them that we can see with our eyes. In this sense they are dumb to the thumbs, and in this sense, MacLeish argues, poems should also be dumb: both speak to us, but not overtly. Other similes are more enigmatic: "wordless/As the flight of birds," for example. Work out each of the statements separately; taken individually and subjected to much thought, the similes yield a consistent statement about poetry and what MacLeish thinks poetry ought to be. "Ars Poetica" means "the art of poetry"; what does this poet have to say about that art? Does his poem follow his directions for creating a poem? Do you agree with him on what a poem should be?

Although the rhetorical definitions would not indicate it, metaphors tend to be less definite than similes. They therefore present more problems to critics attempting to translate multiple meanings into the cold, clear, denotative language of prose criticism. "Like" and "as" imply similarity in several respects; their omission leaves a naked "is," which is more all-encompassing. The difference is the difference between things that are only approximately equal and things that are ostensibly entirely equal. In simple comparisons, the difference is virtually negligible: there is no practical difference between "I am cold as ice" and "I am an ice cube." We get the picture. But suppose the simile "A poem should be motionless in time/As the moon climbs" had been written, "a poem is a climbing moon." A climbing moon does many things, and it would be only after much trouble that we might realize that the moon moves without the appearance of motion, that it acts without appearing to act, and that this comparison was what the poet had in mind. For all their problems, the similes of Cohen's "Bird on the Wire" are easier for critics to handle than the metaphors of Frank Davis' "Four Glimpses of Night." The following poems contain several metaphors,

some of them simple, some of them complex, some meaningful, others
absurd or ill-considered. Read the poems carefully and work out the details of the comparisons made by the poets, the bases for those comparisons, the way in which the legs of the metaphor supplement and
complement each other. Then form some evaluation of the poets' use of
metaphoric language.

Four Glimpses of Night

1

Eagerly
Like a woman hurrying to her lover
Night comes to the room of the world
And lies, yielding and content
Against the cool round face   5
Of the moon.

2

Night is a curious child, wandering
Between earth and sky, creeping
In windows and doors, daubing
The entire neighborhood   10
With purple paint.
Day
Is an apologetic mother
Cloth in hand
Following after.   15

3

Peddling
From door to door
Night sells
Black bags of peppermint stars
Heaping cones of vanilla moon   20
Until
His wares are gone
Then shuffles homeward

Jingling the gray coins
Of daybreak.   25

    4
Night's brittle song, silver-thin,
Shatters into a billion fragments
Of quiet shadows
At the blaring jazz
Of a morning sun.   30

                   —Frank Marshall Davis

QUESTIONS

1. In section 1, Davis sets up some pretty clear equivalents: night–woman, moon–lover, world–room. Ostensibly the purpose of the comparison of night to a woman rushing to her lover is to demonstrate how "eagerly" the night comes and how "yielding" it is. In what sense does the night come eagerly? In what sense does it yield to the moon? Does Davis have some further qualities of night in mind that he suggests in this comparison?

2. In section 2, night is a child, day his mother. What is the connotative difference between the two? The child daubs, the mother cleans: whose works is more interesting? In what sense does night daub and day clean?

3. What connotations do "black bags of peppermint stars" and "heaping cones of vanilla moon" have? Are grey coins adequate payment? If night is a person, is Davis inconsistent in making daybreak coins rather than another human being?

4. A yielding woman, a child painting pictures, peppermint candy and vanilla ice cream, a silver-thin song: all these are Davis' metaphors for night. In each case night is contrasted to light: a cool face, an erasing mother, some grey coins, blaring jazz. Which does Davis make you prefer?

Discovery

The petals of the vagina unfold
like Christopher Columbus
taking off his shoes.

Is there anything more beautiful
than the bow of a ship   5
touching a new world?

                              —*Richard Brautigan*

QUESTIONS

   1. What is the subject of the poem? Of course it's about sexual intercourse, but what specifically about sexual intercourse?
   2. The poem's basis is two metaphors and a simile: petals, a ship,
and Christopher Columbus' shoes. In what senses are these good or bad
metaphors? How are they related?

she being Brand

she being Brand

-new;and you
know consequently a
little stiff i was
careful of her and(having   5

thoroughly oiled the universal
joint tested my gas felt of
her radiator made sure her springs were O.

K.)i went right to it flooded-the-carburetor cranked her

up,slipped the   10
clutch(and then somehow got into reverse she
kicked what
the hell)next
minute i was back in neutral tried and

again slo-wly;bare,ly nudg.   ing(my   15

lev-er Right-
oh and her gears being in

A 1 shape passed
from low through
second-in-to-high like   20
greasedlightning)just as we turned the corner of Divinity

avenue i touched the accelerator and give

her the juice,good

                    (it
was the first ride and believe i we was   25
happy to see how nice she acted right up to
the last minute coming back down by the Public
Gardens i slammed on
the
internalexpanding   30
&
externalcontracting
brakes Bothatonce and

brought allofher tremB
-ling   35
to a:dead.

stand-
;Still)

                                             —*e. e. cummings*

QUESTIONS

1. More sex, although a reexamination of the poem will show that
the subject is never mentioned overtly. Is this poem merely clever and
dirty, or does the poet make a pretty significant statement about trying
out women as one tries on a pair of shoes or a new car? Do you prefer
this poem or that of Brautigan as a work of art? Or neither? Why?

2. Discuss cummings' use of typographical disarrangement to further
poetic effect.

The Chambered Nautilus

This is the ship of pearl, which, poets feign,
   Sails the unshadowed main,—
   The venturous bark that flings
On the sweet summer wind its purpled wings
In gulfs enchanted, where the Siren sings,   5
   And coral reefs lie bare,
Where the cold sea-maids rise to sun their streaming hair.

Its webs of living gauze no more unfurl;
   Wrecked is the ship of pearl!
   And every chambered cell,   10
Where its dim dreaming life was wont to dwell,
As the frail tenant shaped his growing shell,
   Before thee lies revealed,—
Its irised ceiling rent, its sunless crypt unsealed!

Year after year beheld the silent toil   15
   That spread his lustrous coil;
   Still, as the spiral grew,
He left the past year's dwelling for the new,
Stole with soft step its shining archway through,
   Built up its idle door,   20
Stretched in his last-found home, and knew the old no more.

Thanks for the heavenly message brought by thee,
   Child of the wandering sea,
   Cast from her lap, forlorn!
From thy dead lips a clearer note is born   25
Than ever Triton blew from wreathed horn!
   While on mine ear it rings,
Through the deep caves of thought I hear a voice that sings:—

Build thee more stately mansions, O my soul,
   As the swift seasons roll!   30
   Leave thy low-vaulted past!
Let each new temple, nobler than the last,

Shut thee from heaven with a dome more vast,
  Till thou at length art free,
Leaving thine outgrown shell by life's unresting sea!   35
                                —*Oliver Wendell Holmes*

3. *bark*: ship. 5. *Sirens*: mythological creatures, half woman and half bird, reputed to lure sailors to their deaths by the sweet sound of their singing. 26. *Triton*: son of Poseidon, the God of the sea, who carried a horn made out of a conch shell.

QUESTIONS

1. Words like "feign," "main," "venturous bark," and "purpled wings" (and many, many others) are conscious attempts by Holmes to use a high level of diction, a "poetic diction." Does such self-consciously high diction help or hurt the poem?

2. Point out the various metaphors used by the poet, beginning with the ship of pearl and ending with "life's unresting sea." Are they as a rule superficial or insightful, fresh or stale? Are they consistent?

3. This poem is a staple of American literature. Is its reputation justified?

"Hope" is the thing with feathers

"Hope" is the thing with feathers—
That perches in the soul—
And sings the tune without the words—
And never stops—at all—

And sweetest—in the Gale—is heard—   5
And sore must be the storm—
That could abash the little Bird
That kept so many warm—

I've heard it in the chillest land—
And on the strangest Sea—   10
Yet, never, in Extremity,
It asked a crumb—of Me.
                                —*Emily Dickinson*

QUESTIONS

1. How does Dickinson's use of the "storm of life" metaphor compare with Housman's in "On Wenlock Edge" (chap. 7)? What does she mean by the "crumb" of line 12?

2. How does Dickinson's comparison of hope and a bird relate to the swallow in "Come All You Fair and Tender Ladies" we discussed earlier? Is the bird a natural representative of freedom and aspiration? Why?

No Expectations

Take me to the station
And put me on a train.
I've got no expectations
To pass through here again.

Once I was a rich man   5
And now I am so poor,
But never in my sweet, short life
Have I felt like this before.

Your heart is like a diamond,
You throw your pearls at swine,   10
And as I watched you leaving me
You packed my peace of mind.

Our love was like the water
That splashes on a stone,
Our love is like our music,   15
It's here and then it's gone.

So take me to the airport
And put me on a plane.
I've got no expectations
To pass through here again.   20

—Mick Jagger–Keith Richards

Discuss the situation that prompts the words of this Rolling Stones lyric, the singer's attitude toward those experiences to which he alludes, and Jagger's use of imagery, simile, and metaphor. Listen to the song as it is recorded by both the Stones and by Joan Baez, and discuss which rendition better captures the spirit of the words.

SYMBOL

Rhetorically, the difference between a simile and a metaphor is the presence of "like" or "as" in the simile. Rhetorically, the difference between a metaphor and a *symbol* is that the metaphor names both legs of the comparison, but the symbol leaves one implicit: "My love is like a rose" is a simile; "My love is a rose" is a metaphor; "a rose" could be a symbol of love. All this is purely rhetorical, of course, because some things happen to metaphors when we turn them into symbols—if, indeed, that is the way symbols are made. Symbols are far more open-ended than similes or metaphors can ever be. Confronted with the word "rose" out of any context, we have no real way of knowing whether it symbolizes love, the Virgin Mary, beauty, the house of Lancaster or of York, or nothing at all. Even contexts sometimes fail to make the exact meaning of a symbol clear. And even when rose is used to symbolize love, it carries muted overtones of all its other symbolic meanings as well.

Symbols are nothing strange or unusual; they surround us constantly in our everyday life. The flag is a symbol, the cross is a symbol, a swimming pool in the back yard and a Cadillac car can be symbols. The familiar "V" sign made with the middle and index fingers is a symbol, although it means different things to different people: to the young it symbolizes peace, to older folk, victory. And here is an important point about symbols: they change meaning. Even symbols whose meaning has already been generally agreed upon can change. The flag of the United States, for instance: at one time, and not very long ago either, it was a nearly universal symbol of freedom; now it has come to be widely regarded as a symbol of repression, colonialism, and militarism. Or the swastika, once a cosmic or religious symbol, now a symbol of fascistic totalitarianism and despotism. Each age fashions its own symbols, sometimes adopting those of a previous generation, sometimes turning old symbols around 180 degrees in their connotations. The meaning of a symbol, even of a public symbol, depends on context and on the time and place in which it is used.

Poets use symbols too and, like public symbols, their symbols depend upon context for meaning. Some poetic symbols are also public symbols and give us little trouble when we read them. Others are poetic, but are used often enough to have a universal meaning: water for faith, life, and potentiality; winter for death and old age; dove for peace. But some poetic symbols represent the poet's own creation or his own special usage. They may be conjured up just for the moment (*nonce symbols*, the meaning of which depends entirely on context) or they may be used again and again in the poet's work (in which case a knowledge of the poet's other usages is helpful in determining meaning). Peter Yarrow's "Great Mandella" is a public symbol: his song is but one poem in a great body of mandella literature stretching back to the middle ages; for Judy Collins, Paris and Ohio become personal nonce symbols in "My Father"; for William Butler Yeats, the gyre was a personal symbol that appeared and reappeared in his later poems. Determining whether a word really is a symbol, and whether it is used in its public sense or in a special private sense, requires a bit of practice and experience.

The Great Mandella

The Wheel of Life

So I told him that he'd better
Shut his mouth and do his job like a man
And he answered, "Listen Father,
I will never kill another."
He thinks he's better than his brother that died.   5
What the hell does he think he is doing
To his father who brought him up right?

Take your place on
The Great Mandella
As it moves through your brief moment of time.   10
Win or lose now,
You must choose now;
And if you lose you're only losing your life.

Tell the jailer not to bother
With his meal of bread and water today—   15
He is fasting 'til the killing's over.
He's a martyr, he thinks he's a prophet,
But he's a coward, he's just playing a game.
He can't do it, he can't change things;
It's been going on for ten thousand years.   20

Tell the people they are safe now;
Hunger stopped him, he lies still in his cell.
Death has gagged his accusations.
We are free now, we can kill now,
We can hate now, now we can end the world.   25
We're not guilty, he was crazy;
And it's been going on for ten thousand years.

Take your place on
The Great Mandella
As it moves through your brief moment of time.   30
Win or lose now,
You must choose now;
And if you lose you've only wasted your life.

                                                                    —*Peter Yarrow*

It is certainly not difficult to untangle the events with which this song
deals, or the conflicting attitudes embodied in the son on the one hand
and the father and the rest of us ("We" of lines 24 ff.) on the other.
What makes the poem especially memorable, however, is the wheel
symbol and all the connotations it conjures up. Certainly it suggests a
cyclical process in nature, as do Yeats' gyres in "The Second Coming"
or Ochs' "circle-studded skies" in "The Crucifixion." The wheel also
suggests a carnival wheel or a roulette wheel, because an element of
choice and loss is involved with the wheel in the poem. During the
middle ages and Renaissance, the wheel was associated with the goddess
Fortune or the goddess Mutability (frequently the same character), a
fickle creature whose governance accounted for the rising and falling of
men's fortunes here on earth. It may be that some of these connotations
of the wheel as Fortune's symbol are operative here, meant to suggest

that just as men's fortunes change, so too will the dominant mentalities. Things do not go on eternally; they can be and will be changed. Ten thousand years or no, the son's pacificism will ultimately prevail even though the boy has died. In the light of the various possible associations of the wheel in this poem, is it possible to determine just who has wasted—not lost, *wasted*—his life in the final line?

Here is Phil Ochs' commentary on the state of modern America. His main symbol, a flower, is frequently used—it is a public symbol. But the meaning it carries as a public symbol is vague and ill-defined, and Ochs' usage adds a private meaning to the public symbolic connotations. The flower is juxtaposed against rich and poor strangers, quarreling lovers, sterile artists, arguing students and soldiers, lost drunk souls, and disillusioned old folk. They all complain, they all argue angrily with each other or within themselves, and none feel or communicate. In this context, the flower becomes a symbol for the healing communication based on a genuine sensitivity to others that would, to borrow a phrase, "bring us together again." None of these people in the poem realize what the flower symbolizes, however; ironically, even the flower lady no longer knows.

The Flower Lady

Millionaires and paupers walk the hungry street,
Rich and poor companions of the restless feet.
Strangers in a foreign land strike a match with a tremblin' hand
Learned too much to ever understand.
But nobody's buying flowers from the flower lady.   5

Lovers quarrel, snarl away their happiness,
Kisses crumble in a web of loneliness.
It's written by the poison pen; voices break before they bend
The door is slammed, it's over once again,
But nobody's buying flowers from the flower lady.   10

Poets agonize, they cannot find the words.
The stone stares at the sculptor, asks are you absurd,
The painter paints his brushes black; through the canvas runs a
    crack.

The portrait of the pain never answers back.
But nobody's buying flowers from the flower lady.   15

Soldiers, disillusioned, come home from the war.
Sarcastic students tell them not to fight no more;
And they argue through the night, black is black and white is white,
Walk away both knowing they are right.
Still nobody's buying flowers from the flower lady.   20

Smoke dreams of escaping soul are drifting by.
Dull the pain of living as they slowly die.
Smiles change into a sneer, washed away by whiskey tears.
In the quicksand of their minds they disappear.
But nobody's buying flowers from the flower lady.   25

Feeble aged people almost to their knees
Complain about the present using memories.
Never found their pot of gold, wrinkled hands pound weary holes.
Each line screams out you're old, you're old, you're old—
But nobody's buying flowers from the flower lady.   30

And the flower lady hobbles home without a sale;
Tattered shreds of petals leave a fading trail.
Not a pause to hold a rose, even she no longer knows.
The lamp goes out, the evening now is closed.
And nobody's buying flowers from the flower lady.   35

                                        —*Phil Ochs*

Symbols come from all areas of human experience, but nature and geography provide more than their proportional share. What symbolic significances do Africa, Ohio, and Paris take on in the following poems? To what extent are these meanings public? How does the delicacy of the music of Judy Collins' performance add to or detract from the effect of the words?

My Father

My father always promised us
    that we would live in France,
We'd go boating on the Seine
    and I would learn to dance.
We lived in Ohio then;   5
    he worked in the mines.
On his streams like boats
    we knew we'd sail in time.

All my sisters soon were gone
    to Denver and Cheyenne,   10
Marrying their grownup dreams,
    the lilacs and the man.
I stayed behind the youngest still,
    only danced alone,
The colors of my father's dreams   15
    faded without a sigh.

And I live in Paris now,
    my children dance and dream
Hearing the ways of a miner's life
    in words they've never seen.   20
I sail my memories afar
    like boats across the Seine,
And watch the Paris sun
    set in my father's eyes again.

My father always promised us   25
    that we would live in France,
We'd go boating on the Seine
    and I would learn to dance.
We lived in Ohio then;
    he worked in the mines.   30
On his streams like boats
    we knew we'd sail in time.

                                     —*Judy Collins*

24. *my father's eyes*: Collins' father was blind.

Afro–American Fragment

So long,
So far away
Is Africa.
Not even memories alive
Save those that history books create,   5
Save those that songs
Beat back into the blood—
Beat out of blood with words sad-sung
In strange un-Negro tongue—
So long,   10
So far away
Is Africa.

Subdued and time-lost
Are the drums—and yet
Through some vast mist of race   15
There comes this song
I do not understand,
This song of atavistic land,
Of bitter yearnings lost
Without a place—   20
So long,
So far away
Is Africa's
Dark face.

—*Langston Hughes*

18. *atavistic*: marked by the reappearance in later generations of a characteristic of remote ancestors that has not shown up in the intervening generations.

The following two poems are a matched set by the English Romantic poet William Blake. One comes from a collection called *Songs of Innocence,* the other from *Songs of Experience.* Both are very much admired as poetic statements of attitudes symbolized perfectly by the animals of the titles.

The Lamb

Little Lamb, who made thee?
Dost thou know who made thee?
Gave thee life, and bid thee feed
By the stream and o'er the mead;
Gave thee clothing of delight,   5
Softest clothing, wooly, bright;
Gave thee such a tender voice,
Making all the vales rejoice?
Little Lamb, who made thee?
Dost thou know who made thee?   10

Little Lamb, I'll tell thee,
Little Lamb, I'll tell thee:
He is callèd by thy name,
For he calls himself a Lamb.
He is meek, and he is mild;   15
He became a little child.
I a child, and thou a lamb,
We are callèd by his name.
Little Lamb, God bless thee!
Little Lamb, God bless thee!   20

—William Blake

QUESTIONS

1. Make a list of all the possible symbolic significations for "lamb." Which of them are operative in this poem? How can you be sure?

2. Could it be said that the poem tells us more about the speaker than about the animal itself? Do you suppose this is the poet's intention?

3. Do some of the lines, especially "He is meek and he is mild/He became a little child" remind you of a Sunday School hymn (for instance, "Jesus loves me, this I know/For the Bible tells me so")? Is the similarity accidental?

4. Discuss the relationships among the child who speaks the poem, the lamb to whom it is addressed, and God.

The Tyger

Tyger! Tyger! burning bright
In the forests of the night,
What immortal hand or eye
Could frame thy fearful symmetry?

In what distant deeps or skies   5
Burnt the fire of thine eyes?
On what wings dare he aspire?
What the hand dare seize the fire?

And what shoulder, and what art
Could twist the sinews of thy heart?   10
And when thy heart began to beat,
What dread hand? and what dread feet?

What the hammer? what the chain?
In what furnace was thy brain?
What the anvil? what dread grasp   15
Dare its deadly terrors clasp?

When the stars threw down their spears,
And water'd heaven with their tears,
Did he smile his work to see?
Did he who made the Lamb make thee?   20

Tyger! Tyger! burning bright
In the forests of the night,
What immortal hand or eye,
Dare frame thy fearful symmetry?

—William Blake

QUESTIONS

1. What does the tiger symbolize? Is it a vaguer symbol than the lamb?
2. What is the nature of the relationship between the lamb and the

tiger? What questions about the nature of creation does the pair pose?

3. Much of the imagery of the poem suggests a forge, with its fires and anvil and furnace. What makes the forge an appropriate image in this poem?

4. Lines 17–18 may be a reference to the Fall of Adam and Eve, at which time, we have it on the best authority, all creation groaned aloud. Why would such a reference suit the poem's theme and subject?

5. The poem is a series of rhetorical questions, as is the first stanza of "The Lamb." But unlike the questions in that poem, those here are unanswered. There is only a significant shift from "Could frame thy fearful symmetry?" to "Dare frame thy fearful symmetry?" Why?

6. Consider for a moment the implications of "fearful symmetry." To what exactly does the phrase refer? What does it suggest? Is there anything inherently fearful about symmetry, or is it merely the tiger's symmetry that inspires terror?

The Windhover

To Christ Our Lord

I caught this morning morning's minion, king-
    dom of daylight's dauphin, dapple-dawn-drawn Falcon, in his
    riding
    Of the rolling level underneath him steady air, and striding
High there, how he rung upon the rein of a wimpling wing
In his ecstasy! then off, off forth on swing,   5
    As a skate's heel sweeps smooth on a bow-bend: the hurl and
    gliding
    Rebuffed the big wind. My heart in hiding
Stirred for a bird,—the achieve of, the mastery of the thing!

Brute beauty and valour and act, oh, air, pride, plume, here
    Buckle! AND the fire that breaks from thee then, a billion   10
Times told lovelier, more dangerous, O my chevalier!

    No wonder of it: sheer plod makes plough down sillion
Shine, and blue-bleak embers, ah my dear,
    Fall, gall themselves, and gash gold-vermilion.
                          —*Gerard Manley Hopkins*

The first step in discussing the symbolism of Hopkin's windhover is to straighten out the poem—no simple matter. The first three lines might be roughly paraphrased to read, "This morning I saw the morning's lord, the dauphin of the kingdom of daylight, the falcon who is dappled like the dawn, as he rode the air that was actually windy but seemed steady underneath him." Nothing particularly mysterious here, especially to those who know the windhover, a kind of falcon with an uncanny ability to hover in the air with its head to the wind, then glide quickly in a long arc ("swing/As a skate's heel sweeps smooth on a bow-bend") across the sky. The focus is on the apparent stasis, then the sudden motion, and on the swiftness with which the transition is made. This and other aspects of the bird are contrasted to the poet's own station: the freedom, grace, beauty, and swiftness provide a contrast to the poet's earthbound situation. The word "buckle" in line 10 is a problem: it might mean either "join together" or "collapse"—or both at once. The "thee" of that line is also a problem; does it address the windhover or "my chevalier?" Clearly there is a contrast between the falcon and "my chevalier," just as there is a contrast between the poet and the bird, although the nature of this contrast is different and serves to mitigate the feelings of inferiority the poet felt in the bird's presence. The poet draws on the strength of Christ, presumably his chevalier, who is a billion times lovelier than the windhover. In fact, in Christ even the menial labor of the earth-bound poet becomes beautiful, in much the same way that ashes when they fall break open to reveal a gold-vermilion inside.

The falcon is an old symbol for Christ (to whom the poem is dedicated), a symbol used widely during the Middle Ages with overtones of chivalry and feudalism. Is this traditional meaning the symbolic meaning of the windhover in this poem? How has Hopkins moved beyond traditional significations with his own personal signification? Is it possible for a symbol to function on a literal level as a contrast to the very thing it signifies on the symbolic level, as the windhover seems to in this poem? Is such complexity self-contradictory or enriching?

ALLEGORY

Symbols or extended metaphors set moving in a narrative framework produce *allegory,* a term so loosely defined as to be almost (but not entirely) meaningless. The symbols may make sense on a literal level, in which case they can be read as a simple narrative with allegorical significance—but this is not always the case. In many allegories, the narrative is so surrealistic as to preclude any possibility of a plausible literal level. Usually allegories have symbolic meaning on several different levels, although some function on only one. Usually we demand that an allegory be consistent. If a character designates one abstraction (perhaps avarice) in one part of the allegory, he must designate that abstraction in all other parts of the narrative. There are, however, well-known allegories in which the symbolic significance of characters changes. (In *Piers Plowman,* for example, Piers represents at various times Christ, St. Peter, a priest, and any Christian.) Usually, allegorical figures are personifications of abstractions, although they may symbolize historical people or concrete things. Armed with a working knowledge of four or five of the more famous allegories—*Piers Plowman, The Phoenix, Dante's Comedy, Everyman, The Faerie Queene, Pilgrim's Progress*—almost any student of literature could with little difficulty refute any generalization made about allegory—including, perhaps, the definition of allegory as "symbols in a narrative framework."

Allegory was an extremely popular form during the Middle Ages and Renaissance, but it fell into a long period of disrepute thereafter, from which it has only recently recovered. "Puff" is reputed to be a multilevel allegory (although its composer vigorously denies the third level): a literal fairy story, an allegory of a youngster growing up, and an allegory of a drug-user giving up marijuana ("puff, the magic drag on") and moving on to other dope. Much of what Bob Dylan wrote in the mid-to-late 1960's seems vaguely allegorical, although a song like "All Along the Watchtower" is extremely elusive in its meaning. And Pete Seeger uses allegory in his poem about the Vietnamese War, a piece which was quickly suppressed by most of the major broadcasting companies almost as soon as it was released.

Puff

Puff, the magic dragon, lived by the sea
And frolicked in the autumn mist in a land called Honahlee,
Little Jackie Paper loved that rascal, Puff,
And brought him strings and sealing wax and other fancy stuff.

Puff, the magic dragon lived by the sea,   5
And frolicked in the autumn mist in a land called Honahlee.

Together they would travel on a boat with billowed sail,
Jackie kept a lookout perched on Puff's gigantic tail,
Noble kings and princes would bow whene'er they came,
Pirate ships would low'r their flag when Puff roared out his name.   10

A dragon lives forever but not so little boys,
Painted wings and giant rings make way for other toys.
One grey night it happened, Jackie Paper came no more
And Puff that mighty dragon, he ceased his fearless roar.

His head was bent in sorrow, green scales fell like rain,   15
Puff no longer went to play along the cherry lane.
Without his life-long friend, Puff could not be brave
So Puff that mighty dragon, sadly slipped into his cave.

Puff, the magic dragon lived by the sea,
And frolicked in the autumn mist in a land called Honahlee.   20
                                                —Peter Yarrow

Examine carefully the lyrics to the song. To what extent are the three
allegorical interpretations we mentioned before justified? Paul McCartney, in an interview with the *Washington Post,* denied an LSD interpretation to "Lucy in the Sky with Diamonds," although he admitted
in retrospect that the song could be read that way. Is Peter Yarrow
denying the obvious when he denies that the song has anything to do
with marijuana? Or are his denials mere "public relations," not to be
taken at face value? The music of the song is in no way suggestive; in
fact, "Puff" sounds like any high-spirited children's song. Do you think
that fact is significant or merely deceptive?

Waist Deep in the Big Muddy

It was back in nineteen forty-two,
I was part of a good platoon;
We were on maneuvers in a-Loozianna,
One night by the light of the moon;
The captain told us to ford a river,   5
And that's how it all begun.
We were knee deep in the Big Muddy
But the big fool said to move on.

The sergeant said, "Sir, are you sure,
This is the best way back to the base?"   10
"Sergeant, go on; I once forded this river
Just a mile above this place;
It'll be a little soggy but just keep slogging,
We'll soon be on dry ground."
We were waist deep in the Big Muddy   15
And the big fool said to push on.

The seargeant said, "With all this equipment
No man'll be able to swim";
"Sergeant, don't be a nervous nellie,"
The Captain said to him;   20
"All we need is a little determination;
Men, follow me, I'll lead on."
We were neck deep in the Big Muddy
And the big fool said to push on.

All of a sudden, the moon clouded over,   25
We heard a gurgling cry;
A few seconds later, the captain's helmet
Was all that floated by;
The sergeant said, "Turn around men,
I'm in charge from now on."   30

And we just made it out of the Big Muddy
With the captain dead and gone.

We stripped and dived and found his body
Stuck in the old quicksand;
I guess he didn't know that the water was deeper   35
Than the place he'd once before been;
Another stream had joined the Big Muddy
Just a half mile from where we'd gone.
We'd been lucky to escape from the Big Muddy
When the damn fool said to push on.   40

Well, maybe you'd rather not draw any moral,
I'll leave that to yourself;
Maybe you're still walking and you're still talking
And you'd like to keep your health;
But every time I read the papers   45
That old feeling comes on:
Waist deep in the Big Muddy
And the big fool says to push on.

Waist deep in the Big Muddy
And the Big Fool says to push on;   50
Waist deep in the Big Muddy
And the Big Fool says to push on;
Waist deep! Neck deep! Soon even a tall
Man'll be over his head!
Waist deep in the Big Muddy   55
And the Big Fool says to push on!

—Pete Seeger

There is little doubt about what the poet is suggesting in his allegory, and probably the reference to President Johnson as the "big fool" captain was behind the song's dismissal from the airwaves. Phil Ochs is less overt in a song like "The Scorpion Departs and Never Returns," or in the following haunting narrative, sung by Ochs to a melody as beautiful and evocative as any in modern music.

Pleasures of the Harbor

And the ship sets the sail.
They've lived the tales to carry to the shore,
Straining at the oars or staring from the rails.
And the sea bids farewell.
She waves and swells and sends them on their way.   5
Time has been her pay, and time will have to tell.

Oh! Soon your sailing will be over.
Come and take your pleasures of the harbor.

And the anchor hits the sand,
The hungry hands have tied them to the port,   10
The hour will be short for the leisure on the land.
And the girls scent the air,
They seem so fair, with paint upon their face,
Soft is their embrace to lead them up the stairs.

In the room dark and dim,   15
The touch of skin, he asks her of her name.
She answers with no shame and not a sense of sin.
The fingers draw the blind,
The sip of wine, the cigarette of doubt
Till the candle is blown out, the darkness is so kind.   20

And the shadows frame the light,
The same old sight, the thrill has flown away.
All alone they lay, two strangers in the night.
Then his heart skips a beat,
He's on his feet, to shipmates he must join.   25
She's counting up the coins, he's swallowed by the street.

In the bar hangs a cloud,
The whiskey's loud, there's laughter in their eyes.
The lonely in disguise are clinging to the crowd
And the bottle fills the glass,   30
The haze is fast, he's trembling for the taste
Of passions gone to waste, in memories of the past.

In the alley wet with rain,
A cry of pain, for love was but a smile
Teasing all the while, now dancing down the drain.   35
Till the boys reach the dock,
They gently mock, and lift him on their backs
To lay him on his rack, to sleep beneath the clock.

And the ship sets the sail.
They've lived the tales to carry to the shore,   40
Straining at the oars or staring from the rails.
And the sea bids farewell.
She waves and swells and sends them on their way.
Time has been her pay, and time will have to tell.

Oh! Soon your sailing will be over.   45
Come and take your pleasures of the harbor.

                                                    —*Phil Ochs*

The song makes perfect sense on the literal level: it tells about a brief port call and the various ways sailors spend their hour or so. But the "you" has a generalizing effect on the song—we are all not sailors except in the symbolic sense. The song then becomes an allegory of man sailing through life, tasting the pleasures of relaxation between long periods of labor and work. As an allegory it has both a literal and a symbolic meaning, and both are equally important.

In English literature, some of the finest allegories are the earliest poems. Here is a translation of two segments of *The Phoenix*, a long Anglo-Saxon poem on the life and significance of that bird, written probably around 800 A.D. perhaps by the poet Cynewulf. The first section comes from the story of the phoenix' death and resurrection, the second section from the poet's detailed explanation of the allegory, an explanation that is as long as the story itself.

The Phoenix

   When the gem of the sky   in the summer season,
The burning sun,   shines over the shades
Scanning the world,   the Phoenix sits

Fain of departure,   fulfilling his fate.
His house is kindled   by heat of the sun;   5
The herbs grow hot,   the pleasant hall steams
With sweetest odours;   in the surging flame,
In the fire-grip, burns   the bird with his nest.
The pyre is kindled,   the fire enfolds
The home of the heart-sick.   The yellow flame   10
Fiercely rages;   the Phoenix burns,
Full of years,   as the fire consumes
The fleeting body.   The spirit fades,
The soul of the fated.   The bale-fire seizes
Both bone and flesh.
                        But his life is reborn   15
After a season,   when the ashes begin
After the fire-surge   fusing together
Compressed to a ball.   The brightest of nests,
The house of the stout-heart,   by force of the flame
Is clean consumed;   the corpse grows chill;   20
The bone-frame is broken;   the burning subsides.
From the flame of the fire   is found thereafter
In the ash of the pyre   an apple's likeness,
Of which grows a worm   most wondorous fair,
As it were a creature   come from an egg,   25
Shining from the shell.   In the shadow it grows
Fashioned first   as an eagle's young,
A comely fledgeling;   then flourishing fair
Is like in form   to a full-grown eagle
Adorned with feathers   as he was at first,   30
Brightly gleaming. . . .

            Brightly the King,
Fair Gem of light,   from His lofty seat
Shall beam on the holy.   Blessed is he
In that fearful hour   who finds favour with God!
    Then go glad-hearted   the pure of sin;   5
Souls pass back again   into their bodies
While high to the heavens   the bale-fires burn.
Bitter for many   that fearful blaze
When blessed or sinful,   body and soul,

Each from the grave   goes to God's Judgment   10
Shaking with fear.   The fire rages
Consuming the sinful;   but blessed souls
After their exile   are garbed in good works,
The deeds they have done.   These are sweet spices,
The winsome herbs   wherewith the wild bird   15
Besets his nest   till it burns with fire,
And the Phoenix with it   flames in the sun;
Then after the burning   the bird is reborn!
So every soul   shall be swathed in flesh,
Shall be young and fair,   who fervently strives   20
By his deeds on earth   that on Judgment Day
The King of glory,   Almighty God,
Gracious and mild   may show him mercy.

—Cynewulf (?)
(translated by *Charles Kennedy*)

Allegorically, the phoenix represents the good Christian, the fire his death, the rebirth of the bird his resurrection, and the spices in the bird's nest his good works. The allegory is ingenious, perhaps too ingenious—such an explanation would probably not be tolerated in a freshman English composition!

Not all allegories are as simply explained as those of "Big Muddy" and *The Phoenix,* or even "Puff" or "Pleasures of the Harbor." "A Poison Tree" is clear enough in its general outline, but the nature of the apple is a bit obscure. Certainly the poem's allegorical meaning cannot be reduced to something like "it is better to tell people that you're mad at them than it is to nurse your anger along," as some people would like to paraphrase it. What do you make of the allegory?

A Poison Tree

I was angry with my friend:
I told my wrath, my wrath did end.
I was angry with my foe:
I told it not, my wrath did grow.

And I water'd it in fears,   5
Night and morning with my tears;
And I sunned it with smiles,
And with soft deceitful wiles.

And it grew both day and night,
Till it bore an apple bright;   10
And my foe beheld it shine,
And he knew that it was mine,

And into my garden stole
When the night had veil'd the pole:
In the morning glad I see   15
My foe outstretch'd beneath the tree.

                                        —*William Blake*

Equally vague is this poem by Wallace Stevens.

Anecdote of the Jar

I placed a jar in Tennessee,
And round it was, upon a hill.
It made the slovenly wilderness
Surround that hill.

The wilderness rose up to it,   5
And sprawled around, no longer wild.
The jar was round upon the ground
And tall and of a port in air.

It took dominion everywhere.
The jar was gray and bare.   10
It did not give of bird or bush,
Like nothing else in Tennessee.

                                        —*Wallace Stevens*

The jar is an art object in the midst of the Tennessee wilderness. Like all art it is sterile: it does not foster animal or vegetable life. It does, however, have an effect on the surrounding wilderness in which life thrives. What is that effect? How close is the theme of this poem to that of "The Idea of Order at Key West" (chap. 1)? Which poem develops the theme better?

The Corpus Christi Carol

Lully, lullay, lully, lullay,
The faucon hath borne my make away.

He bare him up, he bare him down,
He bare him into an orchard brown.

In that orchard ther was an hall   5
That was hanged with purple and pall.

And in that hall ther was a bed:
It was hanged with gold so red.

And in that bed ther lith a knight,
His woundes bleeding by day and night.   10

By that beddes side ther kneeleth a may,
And she weepeth both night and day.

And by that beddes side ther standeth a stoon:
Corpus Christi written theron.

—anonymous

2. *faucon*: falcon; *make*: mate. 6. *pall*: black velvet. 9. *lith*: lies. 11. *may*: maid. 13. *stoon*: stone. 14. *Corpus Christi*: "the body of Christ," the communion host.

"The Corpus Christi Carol" has puzzled readers for centuries, and the key to its allegory is probably now lost in antiquity, buried with the medieval poet who wrote it. It does, however, illustrate how a little research can enlighten puzzling poems. We know from Hopkins' "The Windhover" that the falcon is a traditional symbol for Christ, so the identification of the two here should come as no surprise. The action, though, remains unclear until we know that in some medieval churches it was customary to move the host (the *Corpus Christi*) from the main altar to a side altar hung with purple during the period between Good Friday and Easter Sunday, and to keep a watch constantly over the host at that altar. Although such information does not explain every detail of the story, it does go a long way toward clearing up some of the mystery of the allegory.

Paysage Moralisé

Hearing of harvests rotting in the valleys,
Seeing at end of street the barren mountains,
Round corners coming suddenly on water,
Knowing them shipwrecked who were launched for islands,
We honour founders of these starving cities   5
Whose honour is the image of our sorrow,

Which cannot see its likeness in their sorrow
That brought them desperate to the brink of valleys;
Dreaming of evening walks through learned cities
They reined their violent horses on the mountains,   10
Those fields like ships to castaways on islands,
Visions of green to them who craved for water.

They built by rivers and at night the water
Running past windows comforted their sorrows;
Each in his little bed conceived of islands   15
Where every day was dancing in the valleys
And all the green trees blossomed on the mountains
Where love was innocent, being far from cities.

But dawn came back and they were still in cities;
No marvellous creatures rose up from the water;   20
There was still gold and silver in the mountains
But hunger was a more immediate sorrow,

Although to moping villagers in valleys
Some waving pilgrims were describing islands . . .

"The gods," they promise, "visit us from islands,   25
Are stalking, head-up, lovely, through our cities;
Now is the time to leave your wretched valleys
And sail with them across the lime-green water,
Sitting at their white sides, forget your sorrow,
The shadow cast across your lives by mountains."   30

So many, doubtful, perished in the mountains,
Climbing up crags to get a view of islands,
So many, fearful, took with them their sorrow
Which stayed them when they reached unhappy cities,
So many, careless, dived and drowned in water,   35
So many, wretched, would not leave their valleys.

It is our sorrow. Shall it melt? Ah, water
Would gush, flush, green these mountains and these valleys,
And we rebuild our cities, not dream of islands.
                                                —*W. H. Auden*

Here is a long, complex allegory involving sorrow and five other symbols: water, cities, mountains, islands, and valleys. The verse form is a
sestina: a series of six six-line stanzas, the lines of which all end with
the same six words in six different orders, followed by a three-line coda
that repeats them all again. By its very nature the verse form puts
considerable emphasis on the six repeated words, and it is in terms of
their symbolic meaning that this allegory is to be explained.

QUESTIONS

1. List the symbolic meanings of the elements of this "moralised
landscape." Are they traditional symbolic values, or nonce usages?
What other symbols are used in the poem?

2. Auden makes a distinction between "our sorrow" (lines 6, 27)
and "their sorrow" (lines 7, 14). Who are "they" and "we"? Are the
respective sorrows different? In what ways?

3. What transformation takes place in the fourth stanza? Are the men of this stanza the same men who "reigned their violent horses on the mountains" and "built by rivers?" What has happened allegorically?

4. What kind of misdirected effort is suggested in the sixth stanza? If these responses to sorrow are ill-conceived and inadequate, what would be the appropriate response? Does Auden give us a suggestion in the final three lines?

5. Would you call the poem entirely optimistic, guardedly hopeful, or totally pessimistic in its final conclusions? Have the situation described by the poet and the possibilities for regeneration changed much since the poem was written?

Some of the most haunting and evocative allegorical landscapes in all modern literature and music were created by Bob Dylan on his *John Wesley Harding* album. One of them is "All Along the Watchtower." Like "The Sick Rose," this song suggests many possibilities, none of which is totally satisfactory. What allegorical equations explain the symbolic meanings contained within the joker, the thief, the watchtower, the wildcat, and their story? Is it possible that Dylan is simply trying to write a haunting pseudo-allegory and is using highly charged language to create an impression rather than to tell an allegorical narrative? If that is the case, what is the theme of the song?

All Along the Watchtower

"There must be some way out of here,"
Said the joker to the thief,
"There's too much confusion,
I can't get no relief.
Businessmen, they drink my wine,   5
Plowmen dig my earth,
None of them along the line
Know what any of it is worth."

"No reason to get excited,"
The thief he kindly spoke,   10

"There are many here among us
Who feel that life is but a joke.
But, you and I, we've been through that,
And this is not our fate,
So, let us not talk falsely now,   15
The hour is getting late."

All along the Watchtower
Princes kept the view,
While all the women came and went,
Barefoot servants too.   20
Outside in the distance
A wildcat did growl,
Two riders were approaching,
The wind began to howl.

—*Bob Dylan*

PERSONIFICATION,
SYNECDOCHE, METONYMY

Some kinds of metaphor have special names because they are used so frequently in rhetoric and poetry. *Personification* compares an abstraction, an animal, or some inanimate object with a human being by endowing the nonhuman with human characteristics; *metonymy* substitutes a closely related word for the word the author really means; *synecdoche* uses a part to represent a whole. All three figures offer many possibilities for metaphoric comparisons, and they can be used to imbue a poem with considerable interest and significance. They are not peculiar only to poetry, either. Death is regularly personified as "the grim reaper"; we have all heard variations of the synecdoche "get your ass over here"; "to give someone a buzz" usually means to give him a telephone call. All of these are by now trite usages, but some songs and many poems use the figures very effectively. Consider the personification in this song, recorded by Joan Baez.

One Day at a Time

I live one day at a time,
I dream one dream at a time;
Yesterday's dead and tomorrow is blind,
I live one day at a time.

Bet you're surprised to see me back at home;   5
You don't know how I miss you when you're gone.
Don't ask how long I plan to stay,
It never crossed my mind.
I live one day at a time.

There's a swallow flyin' across a cloudy sky   10
Lookin' for a patch of sky; so am I.
Don't ask how long I have to follow him,
Perhaps I won't sometime,
But I live one day at a time.

I live one day at a time,   15
I dream one dream at a time;
Yesterday's dead and tomorrow is blind;
I live one day at a time.

—Willie Nelson

"One Day at a Time"—words and music by Willie Nelson. Copyright © 1965, reprinted by permission of the publisher, Tree Publishing Co., Inc.

QUESTIONS

1. Discuss the character of the speaker. Is his statement "I live one day at a time" entirely truthful in light of the third stanza? Is he a hardheaded realist about things, or does he suffer from some neo-romantic illusions? If so, what are they?

2. What does the speaker mean when he says "Yesterday's dead and tomorrow is blind?" The personification of the day is not a particularly unique thing; is this line merely trite convention, or is it something fresh?

3. How does Nelson's usage of the swallow-as-symbol measure up to

Dickinson's bird and the swallow of "Come All You Fair and Tender Ladies?"

Eight O'clock

He stood, and heard the steeple
   Sprinkle the quarters on the morning town.
One, two, three, four, to market-place and people
   It tossed them down.

Strapped, noosed, nighing his hour,   5
   He stood and counted them and cursed his luck;
And then the clock collected in the tower
   Its strength, and struck.

                        —*A. E. Housman*

The subject of this poem is a prisoner about to be hanged, and the hour being tolled is the man's last. Some interesting things happen over the eight lines, making the poem more complex and subtle than it at first appears. The clock and the steeple are personified throughout the poem, suggesting a similarity between them and men, perhaps between them and the condemned man listening. But the animation of the clock all seems directed toward striking the hour, and one gets the impression that after the hour is struck the clock's energies will be gone—as will its most human characteristic, its strength. Of course the man about to be hanged will lose his strength too with the striking of the hour; he will become a corpse, a thing, rather than a living person. For eight lines, then, the clock is made like the man; after that eighth line, the man will be like the clock. Interestingly, the poem ends for us just as it does for the dead man: with the striking of the hour, with this sudden shift from the land of the animate to the land of the inanimate. It is almost as if we too were involved in the episode. The use of personification to animate the entire scene, the sharp distinction between living and dead, and the forced identification of the reader with the subject of the poem all combine to create a highly effective eight-line poem.

Sparrow

Who will love a little sparrow
Who's traveled far and cries for rest?
"Not I," said the oak tree.
"I won't share my branches with no sparrow's nest;
My blanket of leaves won't warm a cold breast."   5

Who will love a little sparrow,
And who will speak a kindly word?
"Not I," said the swan.
"The entire idea is utterly absurd;
I'd be laughed at and scorned if the other swans heard."   10

Who will take pity in his heart,
And who will feed a starving sparrow?
"Not I," said the golden wheat.
"I would if I could, but I cannot I know;
I need all my grain to prosper and grow."   15

Who will love a little sparrow?
Will no one write her eulogy?
"I will," said the earth.
"For all I've created returns unto me:
From dust are ye made, and dust ye shall be."   20

                                        —*Paul Simon*

QUESTIONS

    1. Four symbols and a personified mother earth are presented in
this song. The sparrow symbolizes the downtrodden, the swan symbolizes the proud, the oak symbolizes the self-centered, and the wheat
symbolizes those who hoard. Is it necessary for the poet to personify
these symbols when their symbolic meaning already makes it clear that
they represent types of people? Is anything gained by personification?
Is anything lost?
    2. "Cold breast" is a synecdoche for the whole sparrow; why does

Simon choose the breast to represent the whole, rather than a leg or the head? Only for the sake of rhyme? How fresh is the breast synecdoche or the metonymy "dust" in the last line?

3. Upon what biblical elements does Simon draw to create this song?

I like to see it lap the Miles

I like to see it lap the Miles—
And lick the Valleys up—
And stop to feed itself at Tanks—
And then—prodigious step

Around a Pile of Mountains—   5
And supercilious peer
In Shanties—by the sides of Roads—
And then a Quarry pare

To fit its sides
And crawl between   10
Complaining all the while
In horrid—hooting stanza—
Then chase itself down Hill—

And neigh like Boanerges—
Then—prompter than a Star   15
Stop—docile and omnipotent
At its own stable door—

                                            —*Emily Dickinson*

The "it" of this poem is usually the subject of much discussion. Some people simply refuse to believe that the poem's subject is a railroad train "personified" into a horse. If anything, they argue, line 14 involves the personification of the horse into a human being. What is there about the poem that strongly suggests that Dickinson is talking about an iron horse rather than an animate horse? How apt is her comparison? How fresh?

APOSTROPHE

Another rhetorical device frequently used by poets is *apostrophe*: the direct address of persons not actually present, of abstract ideas, or of nonexistent personages. The thing addressed may be a personification or it may be a real person; what is important is that the poet shifts from first or third person to second. The effect of apostrophe is to make the situation more immediate, more vivid, more impressive. Insofar as immediacy and vividness are desirable in poetry—and other forms of writing as well—apostrophe is an effective rhetorical device. Perhaps because of its overuse by rhetoricians, perhaps because the Romantic poets used it so frequently, perhaps because of other considerations, many people think of apostrophe as the epitome of pretension in poetry —something foreign to the language of sane men. Such is not the case; one of the most popular songs in the repertoire of Judy Collins makes effective use of apostrophe as she addresses a personified sea shore.

Who Knows Where the Time Goes?

Across the morning sky
All the birds are leaving.
Ah, how can they know
It's time for them to go?
Before the winter fire,   5
We'll still be dreaming,
I do not count the time,
Who knows where the time goes,
Who knows where the time goes?

Sad deserted shore   10
Your fickle friends are leaving,
Ah, but then you know
It's time for them to go,
But I will still be here,
I have no thought of leaving,   15
I do not count the time,

Who knows where the time goes,
Who knows where the time goes?

And I'm not going
While my love is near me,   20
And I know it will be so,
Till it's time to go,
So come the storms of winter
And the birds of spring again,
I do not fear the time,   25
Who knows how my love grows?
Who knows where the time goes?

                                        —*Sandy Denny*

QUESTIONS

1. Is winter used symbolically in the first and third stanzas? Who
are the "we" of line 6? Can you characterize "we"? Does the refrain
suggest anything?

2. Is the shore addressed in line 14 as well as in lines 10–13? Who
is? What is the relationship between the shore and the lover, the birds
and the singer? Is the shore a symbol for the singer's lover, or is it a
contrast?

3. To what does "Till it's time to go" refer? Why might the poet
"fear the time?"

To Daffodils

Fair daffodils, we weep to see
    You haste away so soon;
As yet the early-rising Sun
    Has not attain'd his noon.
        Stay, stay,   5
        Until the hasting day
            Has run
        But to the evensong;
And, having pray'd together, we
        Will go with you along.   10

We have short time to stay, as you,
    We have as short a Spring;
As quick a growth to meet decay,
    As you, or anything.
        We die,   15
    As your hours do, and dry
        Away,
    Like to the Summer's rain;
Or as the pearls of Morning's dew,
    Ne'er to be found again.   20

                                 —Robert Herrick

   8. *evensong*: a service of worship for evening, vespers.

In this seventeenth century poem Herrick uses an extended apostrophe
to the flowers, then draws a comparison between them and human
beings similar to that drawn by Denny between shore and lover in
"Who Knows Where the Time Goes."

QUESTIONS

   1. Are the similes of the last few lines appropriate to the central
metaphor of the poem. How?

   2. Is the sun a symbol of anything or anyone in particular, or is it
merely the star?

   3. What devices and phrases does the poet use to strengthen the
identification between the reader and the daffodils?

Death, Be Not Proud

Death, be not proud, though some have called thee
Mighty and dreadful, for thou art not so,
For those whom thou think'st thou dost overthrow
Die not, poor Death, nor yet canst thou kill me.
From rest and sleep, which but thy pictures be,   5
Much pleasure, then from thee much more must flow;
And soonest our best men with thee do go—

Rest of their bones and souls' delivery!
Thou'rt slave to fate, chance, kings and desperate men,
And dost with poison, war, and sickness dwell,   10
And poppy or charms can make us sleep as well,
And better than thy stroke; why swell'st thou then?
One short sleep past, we wake eternally,
And death shall be no more: Death, thou shalt die!

—*John Donne*

11. *poppy*: the source of opium. 12. *swell'st*: swell (with pride).

This is one of the "Holy Sonnets," written by Donne after his conversion from a rogue and a rake to a Christian clergyman. Like "Valediction," which we considered earlier, the poem is ruggedly intellectual.

QUESTIONS

1. What specific reasons does the poet give why Death should not
be proud? Death is usually called a grim reaper; here Death is "poor
Death." This is certainly startling; is it convincing?

2. The Middle Ages and Renaissance, ages of literalistic Christianity,
had a vivid sense of the fact that although the devil may have been
real and at times frightening, he was also fighting a losing battle,
wrong in all his assumptions and logic, and—as Ben Jonson succinctly
put it—an ass. The devils of medieval mystery plays are comic buffoons.
Does all of this help explain Donne's attitude toward death, the metaphorical son of the devil?

These are the days when Birds come back

These are the days when Birds come back—
A very few—a Bird or two—
To take a backward look.

These are the days when skies resume
The old—old sophistries of June—   5
A blue and gold mistake.

Oh fraud that cannot cheat the Bee—
Almost thy plausibility
Induces my belief.

Till ranks of seeds their witness bear—   10
And softly thro' the altered air
Hurries a timid leaf.

Oh Sacrament of summer days,
Oh Last Communion in the Haze—
Permit a child to join.   15

Thy sacred emblems to partake—
Thy consecrated bread to take
And thine immortal wine!

                                        —*Emily Dickinson*

QUESTIONS

1. What season of the year is Dickinson portraying? How can you be sure?

2. In lines 6ff., is the poet talking about the June or Indian summer? When she addresses the season as a fraud, is she addressing (and therefore calling fraudulent) the pretensions of Indian summer or the promise of June? How important is this distinction to the theme of the poem?

3. Toward the end of the poem, the poet uses considerable religious imagery. What comment is made by June and Indian summer on religion? And vice versa? Is the exact identity of the fraud of line 7 important in determining what the poem suggests about religion?

4. What personifications are used in the poem? How do they increase its effectiveness?

Ode to the West Wind

I

O wild West Wind, thou breath of Autumn's being,
Thou, from whose unseen presence the leaves dead
Are driven, like ghosts from an enchanter fleeing,

Yellow, and black, and pale, and hectic red,
Pestilence-stricken multitudes: O thou, 5
Who chariotest to their dark wintry bed

The wingèd seeds, where they lie cold and low,
Each like a corpse within its grave, until
Thine azure sister of the Spring shall blow

Her clarion o'er the dreaming earth, and fill 10
(Driving sweet buds like flocks to feed in air)
With living hues and odours plain and hill:

Wild Spirit, which art moving everywhere;
Destroyer and preserver; hear, oh, hear!

2

Thou on whose stream, 'mid the steep sky's commotion, 15
Loose clouds like earth's decaying leaves are shed,
Shook from the tangled boughs of Heaven and Ocean,

Angels of rain and lightning: there are spread
On the blue surface of thine airy surge,
Like the bright hair uplifted from the head 20

Of some fierce Mænad, even from the dim verge
Of the horizon to the zenith's height
The locks of the approaching storm. Thou dirge

Of the dying Year, to which this closing night
Will be the dome of a vast sepulchre, 25
Vaulted with all thy congregated might

Of vapours, from whose solid atmosphere
Black rain, and fire, and hail will burst: oh, hear!

3

Thou who didst waken from his summer dreams
The blue Mediterranean, where he lay, 30
Lulled by the coil of his crystalline streams,

Beside a pumice isle in Baia's bay,
And saw in sleep old palaces and towers
Quivering within the wave's intenser day,

All overgrown with azure moss and flowers   35
So sweet, the sense faints picturing them! Thou
For whose path the Atlantic's level powers

Cleave themselves into chasms, while far below
The sea-blooms and the oozy woods which wear
The sapless foliage of the ocean, know   40

Thy voice, and suddenly grow gray with fear,
And tremble and despoil themselves: oh, hear!

4

If I were a dead leaf thou mightest bear;
If I were a swift cloud to fly with thee;
A wave to pant beneath thy power, and share   45

The impulse of thy strength, only less free
Than thou, O uncontrollable! If even
I were as in my boyhood, and could be

The comrade of thy wanderings over Heaven,
As then, when to outstrip thy skiey speed   50
Scarce seemed a vision; I would ne'er have striven

As thus with thee in prayer in my sore need.
Oh, lift me as a wave, a leaf, a cloud!
I fall upon the thorns of life! I bleed!

A heavy weight of hours has chained and bowed   55
One too like thee: tameless, and swift, and proud.

5

Make me thy lyre, even as the forest is:
What if my leaves are falling like its own!
The tumult of thy mighty harmonies

Will take from both a deep, autumnal tone,   60
Sweet though in sadness. Be thou, Spirit fierce,
My spirit! Be thou me, impetuous one!

Drive my dead thoughts over the universe
Like withered leaves to quicken a new birth!
And, by the incantation of this verse,   65

Scatter, as from an unextinguished hearth
Ashes and sparks, my words among mankind!
Be through my lips to unawakened Earth

The trumpet of a prophecy! O Wind,
If winter comes, can Spring be far behind?   70
                    —*Percy Bysshe Shelley*

21. *Maenad*: a female attendant of Bacchus, hence, any wild or frenzied woman. 32. *Baia*: an ancient resort city in southwest Italy. 57. *lyre*: an aeolian harp, played by the wind passing over its strings.

QUESTIONS

1. In this complicated collage of symbols, personifications, and metaphors, the poet expresses his discontent with winter and his hope that spring will soon come. Are winter and spring themselves metaphors? For what? If biographical criticism tell us that the poem was indeed written toward the end of winter, and that the poet did indeed become very depressed during that season, can we—should we—still read winter and spring as metaphors or symbols? Why?

2. Sections 1, 2, and 3 each involve an examination of the relationship between the symbolic wind and an equally symbolic piece of nature: a leaf, a cloud, a wave. Why does Shelley choose these three particular things? They are compared to other things in complex webs of similes and metaphors. Consider each section individually, and explain why the poet chooses the metaphors he does.

3. Section 4 brings the three major images of the previous sections together and identifies them with the poet. Why? Does the symbolic meaning of the West Wind begin to emerge in this section?

4. In lines 43–45, the poet is—hypothetically at least—the leaf, the cloud, the wave upon which the wind acts; in line 56 he identifies

himself with the wind. Why? Does the symbolic meaning of the West Wind begin to emerge in this section?

5. What complex symbolic thoughts develop in the final section? Why is the harp image especially appropriate here? And the ashes and sparks?

6. Discuss Shelley's diction (to which many people object). Do you find it pretentiously poetic? Do you find lines like "I fall upon the thorns of life! I bleed!" a bit much? Is this personal taste, is it a preference of the twentieth century, or are these lines simply bad poetry?

7. It might be argued that in couching the whole poem in an extended apostrophe to the wind the poet puts himself in the somewhat awkward position of telling it what it is and what it does, which it would presumably already have known. What advantages of apostrophe outweigh the possible disadvantages in this case?

PARADOX, OXYMORON, AMBIGUITY

In several of the poems that we have discussed already the poets appeared at times to be deliberately ambiguous or enigmatic. The Dickinson poem "These are the days when Birds come back" was not at all clear about whether June or late summer was a fraud; Donne's "Death, Be Not Proud" contained the apparently self-contradictory line "Death, thou shalt die." Contradiction and ambiguity may, of course, be the result of sloppy thinking, but the fact is that life is full of apparent contradictions and ambiguities, and philosophical speculation on life is invariably full of speculation on such paradox and ambiguity. Whether poetry mirrors life or transforms it, inevitably some of the paradox of life must be reflected in poetry. Used carefully, such contradictions that are not contradictions and ambiguities that are really multiple meanings can enrich a poem considerably, as in the Dickinson and Donne poems. Paul Simon reduced paradox to a three-word phrase in his song "Sound of Silence," and the oxymoron (a condensed paradox) produced one of the most effective songs he ever wrote. But paradox need not be condensed to a phrase like "Death, thou shalt die" or "Sound of Silence", it may be spread across an entire poem, as in this poem by Ransom. The poet takes considerable time piling up images of action and motion, which he contrasts sharply to a "brown study/Lying so primly propped" to give us the sense of surprise and vexation he feels at the viewing of John Whiteside's daughter. Work out the details of the poem and the paradox that underlies its theme.

Bells for John Whiteside's Daughter

There was such speed in her little body,
And such lightness in her footfall,
It is no wonder her brown study
Astonishes us all.

Her wars were bruited in our high window.   5
We looked among orchard trees and beyond,
Where she took arms against her shadow,
Or harried unto the pond

The lazy geese, like a snow cloud
Dripping their snow on the green grass,   10
Tricking and stopping, sleepy and proud,
Who cried in goose, Alas,

For the tireless heart within the little
Lady with rod that made them rise
From their noon apple-dreams and scuttle   15
Goose-fashion under the skies!

But now go the bells, and we are ready,
In one house we are sternly stopped
To say we are vexed at her brown study,
Lying so primly propped.   20

                                        —*John Crowe Ransom*

    3. *brown study*: state of reverie or abstraction. 5. *bruited*: rumored.

Here is a poem by Yeats that, like many of his poems, is built on the paradox of the sacred in the profane, the celestial within the mundane. What specific images develop this theme?

The Magi

Now as at all times I can see in the mind's eye,
In their stiff, painted clothes, the pale unsatisfied ones
Appear and disappear in the blue depth of the sky
With all their ancient faces like rain-beaten stones,
And all their helms of silver hovering side by side,   5
And all their eyes still fixed, hoping to find once more,
Being by Calvary's turbulence unsatisfied,
The uncontrollable mystery on the bestial floor.
                                        —*William Butler Yeats*

Ambiguity is a less perceptible and striking form of paradox, in that we find it paradoxical that the same words can mean two different, and apparently mutually exclusive, things. Just as paradox brings us up short because of an apparent contradiction, ambiguity surprises us with multiple meanings. And just as both sides of a paradox prove upon examination to be valid, so all possible meanings of a deliberate ambiguity prove significant. A phrase like "I'd like to make it with you," used in a song popular only a few years ago, contains obvious deliberate ambiguity; so too does the Lennon–McCartney song "All You Need is Love." "What kind of love?" we ask ourselves, and scraps of music playing in the back of the song give us all sorts of answers: the modern, unromanticized love of "She Loves You, Yeh, Yeh, Yeh, Yeh," the romantic love of "Greensleeves," the Christian *agape* of Christmas and the old carol "What Child Is This?" But it is possible, we discover when we think about it, that "love" encompasses all of these meanings, that they encompass each other, and that the love we need is multi-dimensional. The song exploits the possibilities of an ambiguous love to make an important—if not particularly original—point.

Consider the ambiguities in the following lyric, also by Lennon–McCartney.

Let It Be

When I find myself in times of trouble
Mother Mary comes to me

Speaking words of wisdom,
Let it be.

And in my hour of darkness   5
She is standing right in front of me
Speaking words of wisdom,
Let it be.

Let it be,
Let it be,   10
Let it be,
Let it be,
Whisper words of wisdom,
Let it be.

And when the broken hearted people   15
Living in the world agree
There will be an answer,
Let it be.

For though they may be parted
There is still a chance that they will see   20
There will be an answer,
Let it be.

Let it be,
Let it be,
Let it be,   25
Let it be,
There will be an answer,
Let it be.

And when the night is cloudy
There is still a light that shines on me   30
Shine until tomorrow,
Let it be.

I wake up to the sound of music.
Mother Mary comes to me
Speaking words of wisdom,   35
Let it be.

Let it be,
Let it be,
Let it be,
Let it be,   40
Whisper words of wisdom,
Let it be.

—John Lennon–Paul McCartney

The most clearly ambiguous phrase (to use an oxymoron) is the title, "Let It Be." To what does "it" refer? To an answer? An answer to what question? And just how do we "let it be?" But another and perhaps more important ambiguity may lie in "Mother Mary," who speaks the words of wisdom. In rock lyrics Mary is frequently a personification of marijuana ("Along Comes Mary," "Just Like a Woman," "Proud Mary"), and she may be just that here. But Mother Mary suggests Mary, Christ's mother, and some religious implications are added to the poem. If the figure is deliberately ambiguous, what would be the point of combining the associations of the Virgin Mary and marijuana? Does the rest of the poem assume added meaning in light of this ambiguous Mary? Does it explain what the answer might be, how "it" might be, what "it" might resolve?

One obvious form of ambiguity is the *pun,* a word that has two different meanings, both unrelated, both appropriate to the context in which the word is used. Usually puns make bad poetry and occasionally bad drama: Shakespeare had a fondness for puns, a fondness that many readers consider a grave fault. Consider the following poem by the rake-turned-clergyman John Donne. In view of his history and his name, what ambiguities do lines 2, 5, 11, 17 take on? And line 15? Is this poem just clever, or is it witty (that is, both clever and insightful), or is it a brilliantly contrived philosophical ambiguity?

A Hymn to God the Father

Wilt thou forgive that sin where I begun,
    Which is my sin, though it were done before?
Wilt thou forgive that sin through which I run,
    And do run still, though still I do deplore?

When thou hast done, thou hast not done; 5
        For I have more.

Wilt thou forgive that sin which I have won
  Others to sin, and made my sins their door?
Wilt thou forgive that sin which I did shun
  A year or two, but wallowed in a score? 10
When thou hast done, thou hast not done;
        For I have more.

I have a sin of fear, that when I've spun
  My last thread, I shall perish on the shore;
But swear by thyself that at my death thy Son 15
  Shall shine as he shines now and heretofore;
And having done that, thou hast done;
        I fear no more.

                            —*John Donne*

BALANCE, REPETITION, REFRAINS

A favorite device of the classical rhetoricians was to pattern language into parallel syntactical units; or better still, to produce a series of parallel constructions beginning or ending—or in exceptional cases both beginning and ending—with the same words. There is no doubt that such series can be highly effective rhetorically: "I have never been a member of the communist party, I am not now a member of the communist party, and I never shall be a member of the communist party!" Whether such devices used in poetry remain mere rhetorical ornamentation or become effective methods of increasing the poem's communication depends largely on the skill of the individual poet. The fact is that balance, repetition, and refrains (a form of repetition) are a useful part of the poet's bag of tricks, and he uses them often. Usually we demand that repetition or balanced series of constructions widen the perspective of the poem as we progress through them; if there is no increment in meaning, no development of idea, the devices remain insignificant ornament, mere rhetoric. Used carefully, however, they can be enormously effective, as in the case of the initial line of each stanza of the following poem.

A Man Come into Egypt

There is a man come into Egypt,
And Moses is his name,
When he saw the grief upon us
In his heart there burned a flame.

There is a man come into Egypt,   5
His eyes are full of light,
Like the sun come up in Egypt,
Come to drive away the night.

There is a man come into Egypt;
He is come for you and me,   10
On his lips a word is singing,
And the word is liberty.

There is a man come into Egypt,
To stir the soul of man;
We will follow him to freedom,   15
Never wear those chains again.

                                        —*anonymous*

The significance of Moses, the man come into Egypt, emerges gradually over the course of the poem, over the course of the repeated initial
lines. In the first stanza he is simply the historical Moses who sees the
grief upon the captive Israelites and conceives in his heart a hope for
them. The flame suggests his talk with God in the burning bush, but
probably its primary function is to symbolize hope. The second stanza
tells us more about this man: the light in his eyes is like the light of the
sun, and both drive away night (the one a physical the other a metaphysical darkness). So Moses is taking on some symbolic significance:
he is a savior. In the third stanza the poem's scope widens considerably:
"He is come for you and me," the poet tells us. Moses-savior is now removed from his limiting historical context; "the word is liberty" makes
him even more contemporary. By the fourth repetition of the line, both
man and Egypt have become symbols: no longer merely an Israelite

and a country, they are savior and land of bondage in general. Obviously the "we" of line 15 is not a reference to Israelites, and the "him" of that line is not an historical Moses. The song proves to be something of a protest song; Moses could be Martin Luther King or Malcolm X, Egypt could be Little Rock or Chicago. It really doesn't matter, because the historicity of the song has been lost in its symbolic meaning. The poem has developed: at its end it is something much more than it was at the beginning. The repetition of the initial line of each stanza is incremental; it adds to the poem. Listen to Peter, Paul, and Mary perform this song on their *Moving* album. They repeat the last line of each stanza several times. Does this repetition have the same incremental effect over the short run that the repetition of the title line has over the poem's whole length?

Lord Randall

"O where hae ye been, Lord Randall, my son?
O where hae ye been, my handsome young man?"
"I hae been to the wildwood; mother, make my bed soon,
For I'm weary wi' hunting, and fain wald lie down."

"What gat ye to your dinner, Lord Randall, my son?   5
What gat ye to your dinner, my handsome young man?"
"I gat eels boiled in broo; mother, make my bed soon,
For I'm weary wi' hunting, and fain wald lie down."

"What became of your bloodhounds, Lord Randall, my son?
What became of your bloodhounds, my handsome young man?" 10
"O they swell'd and they died; mother, make my bed soon,
For I'm weary wi' hunting, and fain wald lie down."

"O I fear ye are poisoned, Lord Randall, my son!
O I fear ye are poisoned, my handsome young man!"
"O yes! I am poisoned; mother make my bed soon,   15
For I'm sick at the heart, and I fain wald lie down."

              —*anonymous*

1. *hae*: have. 4. *fain wald*: would like to.

Here is a popular ballad, also once a song, that makes considerable use of incremental repetition—this time in a refrain line as well as in the initial line of each stanza. There are any number of versions of this ballad in Scottish and English and American and even Italian traditions; this one is late medieval Scottish. Point out the various repetitions and how they change in their significance as the situation unfolds and as the stanzas progress. Does the gradual unravelling of the plot partially explain the ballad's popularity? Is the true-love a witch—or merely a bitch?

Refrains may be whole choruses as well as individual lines, whole stanzas as well as phrases. Look back at "Let it Be." How useful is all the repetition in that song? How about the chorus of "One Day at a Time?" Or some of the repeated lines in "The Lamb?"

Stopping by Woods on a Snowy Evening

Whose woods these are I think I know.
His house is in the village though;
He will not see me stopping here
To watch his woods fill up with snow.

My little horse must think it queer   5
To stop without a farmhouse near
Between the woods and frozen lake
The darkest evening of the year.

He gives his harness bells a shake
To ask if there is some mistake.   10
The only other sound's the sweep
Of easy wind and downy flake.

The woods are lovely, dark and deep.
But I have promises to keep,
And miles to go before I sleep,   15
And miles to go before I sleep.

—*Robert Frost*

"Stopping by Woods" is one of Frost's best-known pieces, and you are probably already familiar with both the poem and various interpretations of it. The poet claimed in a letter to have intended a five-stanza poem, the last stanza of which was never written. "With great presence of mind," the poet recalls, "I instantly struck the line out [what had been line 16] and made my exit with a repeat end." What is the effect of this repetition on the poem? How heavily do the interpretations you know lean on the hypnotic or incremental effects of this repetition?

More complicated than any of the poems we have yet considered, Whitman's "Noiseless Patient Spider" makes use of parallelisms balanced one against the other and repeated individual words.

A Noiseless Patient Spider

A noiseless patient spider,
I mark'd where on a little promontory it stood isolated,
Mark'd how to explore the vacant vast surrounding,
It launch'd forth filament, filament, filament, out of itself,
Ever unreeling them, ever tirelessly speeding them.   5

And you O my soul where you stand,
Surrounded, detached, in measureless oceans of space,
Ceaselessly musing, venturing, throwing, seeking the spheres to
    connect them,
Till the bridge you will need be form'd, till the ductile anchor hold,
Till the gossamer thread you fling catch somewhere, O my soul.   10
                                                —Walt Whitman

QUESTIONS

1. Some of the words are repeated two and even three times. Why? Is there a genuine expansion of the poem's meaning—if not in its denotative meaning, then in its emotional impact on the reader?

2. Consider the effect of line 5, with its two parallel phrases; or the tripartite balance of the three "till" clauses in lines 9–10. Is there any development in the poem as a result of these parallelisms, or is Whitman merely wasting time? Consider the series of appositive verbs in line 8; is this padding, or is the poem's meaning expanded?

3. Consider Whitman's metaphor in all its ramifications. How appropriate is it?

Of all poets in English, Whitman probably makes most frequent and effective use of long passages of extended parallelisms, balanced phrases, and repeated expressions. Another major repository of poetry of this sort is the Bible, particularly the Psalms and the books of the prophets. Work out the balances and the parallelisms in the following two Psalms from the Revised Standard Version of the Bible. In what ways do the second and third rephrasings enlarge the scope of statements they repeat? Do the last lines of Psalm 150 suggest a particular reason for the poet's use of "praise him" to begin nine different clauses?

Psalm 95

O come, let us sing to the Lord;
   let us make a joyful noise to the rock of our salvation!
Let us come into his presence with thanksgiving;
   let us make a joyful noise to him with songs of praise!
For the Lord is a great God,
   and a great King above all gods.
In his hand are the depths of the earth;
   the heights of the mountains are his also.
The sea is his, for he made it;   5
   for his hands formed the dry land.

O come, let us worship and bow down,
   let us kneel before the Lord, our Maker!
For he is our God,
   and we are the people of his pasture,
   and the sheep of his hand.

O that today you would hearken to his voice!
Harden not your hearts, as at Meribah,
   as on the day at Massah in the wilderness,
when your fathers tested me,
   and put me to the proof, though they had seen my work.
For forty years I loathed that generation   10

and said, "They are a people who err in heart,
and they do not regard my ways."
Therefore I swore in my anger
that they should not enter my rest.

Psalm 150

Praise the Lord!
Praise God in his sanctuary;
praise him in his mighty firmament!
Praise him for his mighty deeds;
praise him according to his exceeding greatness!

Praise him with trumpet sound;
praise him with lute and harp!
Praise him with timbrel and dance;
praise him with strings and pipe!
Praise him with sounding cymbals;
praise him with loud clashing cymbals!   5
Let everything that breathes praise the Lord!
Praise the Lord!

ALLUSION

Frequently, a poet finds it useful to make reference to or to allude to
a poem or a person or a place or an historical event other than the one
that he is treating in his own particular poem. Such *allusions* allow a
poet to expand significantly the scope of his own subject by implying a
comparison between his subject and the one to which he alludes. The
casual allusions to the Cimbri and the Aztecs in "The Arsenal at Springfield," for example, widen the perspective of that poem so that it em-
braces not only the arsenal at Springfield, Mass., but all warfare at all
periods of human history. The allusions allow the poet to imply a similarity between Springfield's militarism and the militarism of societies that
Americans of 1845 would have thought barbaric and uncivilized. But
despite the widened scope the allusions give Longfellow's poem, its sub-

ject remains what it was: the arsenal at Springfield. A poem describing the Fall of Adam is not an allusion; the fall is the subject of the poem. But a reference to the Fall in a poem on, say, the loss of childish innocence (see Thomas' "Fern Hill") in order to draw an analogy between the two events is an allusion. Usually allusions are only a matter of a few words or a brief quotation; they are so subtle that an unperceptive reader may miss them entirely. Occasionally, however, allusions are so important that they constitute the major part of a poem's significance, as is the case in MacLeish's "You, Andrew Marvell" or Phil Ochs' "William Butler Yeats Visits Lincoln Park and Escapes Unscathed." The poems are not *about* Andrew Marvell or William Butler Yeats— they are about the rise and fall of civilization and the Chicago Lincoln Park massacre respectively—but the poets named in their titles are important to the whole meaning of the poems. Although specific references are confined to titles, allusions in the poems are of great importance to any understanding of the poems.

Terence, This Is Stupid Stuff

'Terence, this is stupid stuff:
You eat your victuals fast enough;
There can't be much amiss, 'tis clear,
To see the rate you drink your beer.
But, oh, good Lord, the verse you make,   5
It gives a chap the belly-ache.
The cow, the old cow, she is dead;
It sleeps well, the horned head:
We poor lads, 'tis our turn now
To hear such tunes as killed the cow.   10
Pretty friendship 'tis to rhyme
Your friends to death before their time
Moping melancholy mad.
Come, pipe a tune to dance to, lad.'

    Why, if 'tis dancing you would be,   15
There's brisker pipes than poetry.
Say, for what were hop-yards meant,
Or why was Burton built on Trent?

Oh many a peer of England brews,
Livelier liquor than the Muse,   20
And malt does more than Milton can
To justify God's ways to man.
Ale, man, ale's the stuff to drink
For fellows whom it hurts to think:
Look into the pewter pot   25
To see the world as the world's not.
And faith, 'tis pleasant till 'tis past:
The mischief is that 'twill not last.
Oh I have been to Ludlow fair
And left my necktie God knows where,   30
And carried half-way home, or near,
Pints and quarts of Ludlow beer:
Then the world seemed none so bad,
And I myself a sterling lad;
And down in lovely muck I've lain,   35
Happy till I woke again.
Then I saw the morning sky:
Heigho, the tale was all a lie;
The world, it was the old world yet,
I was I, my things were wet,   40
And nothing now remained to do
But begin the game anew.

    Therefore, since the world has still
Much good, but much less good than ill,
And while the sun and moon endure   45
Luck's a chance, but trouble's sure,
I'd face it as a wise man would,
And train for ill and not for good.
'Tis true, the stuff I bring for sale
Is not so brisk a brew as ale: 50
Out of a stem that scored the hand
I wrung it in a weary land.
But take it: if the smack is sour,
The better for the embittered hour;
It should do good to heart and head   55
When your soul is in my soul's stead;

And I will friend you, if I may,
In the dark and cloudy day.

   There was a king reigned in the East:
There, when kings will sit to feast,   60
They get their fill before they think
With poisoned meat and poisoned drink.
He gathered all that springs to birth
From the many-venomed earth;
First a little, thence to more,   65
He sampled all her killing store;
And easy, smiling, seasoned sound,
Sate the king when healths went round.
They put arsenic in his meat
And stared aghast to watch him eat;   70
They poured strychnine in his cup
And shook to see him drink it up:
They shook, they stared as white's their shirt:
Them it was their poison hurt.
—I tell the tale that I heard told.   75
Mithridates, he died old.

                        —A. E. Housman

   59ff. The story comes from Pliny's *Natural History.*

This poem is largely uncomplicated by the freight of symbols, meta-phors, and personifications that serve to confuse much of the poetry we have been reading; it comes close to being pure poetry of statement, es-pecially in the example that fills the final lines. The identity of Terence may at first be confusing, but when we discover that A. E. Housman at first intended to call *A Shropshire Lad* by a different title—*Poems by Terence Hearsay*—the mystery is cleared up instantly. The poet's friends complain to him that his verse is depressing because of its content, that it killed the cow and now it's killing them, and would he please quit writing poetry or change his subject. Terence answers that if they want enjoyment and dancing, they might better go out and get drunk as he himself does on occasion; but since the world offers more trouble than good fortune, more ill than good, it would be wise to prepare, like Mithridates, for trouble. And to prepare for trouble, he implies, means listening to his gloomy poems, familiarizing oneself with the dark side of existence rather than the bright aspects of human experience. To prove the point, Terence recounts the Mithridates story. All that calls for real critical comment are a few allusions, literary and geographical, in the second section. "Ludlow fair" should be self-explanatory, although it is worth noting that Housman himself was from Worcestershire and would have been familiar with the place (it is doubtful, however, that the University of London classics professor ever lay drunk in a ditch overnight). And it should be equally self-evident that Burton-on-Trent is a center of the brewing industry in England. Lines 21–22 present the only real problem in the poem, the only lines that require much comment. The explanation is to be found in the opening lines of Milton's *Paradise Lost,* in which the poet asks an unidentified spirit for help in composing his poem, the object of which is made clear in the final line.

> And chiefly Thou O Spirit, that dost prefer
> Before all Temples th'upright heart and pure,
> Instruct me, for Thou kno'st; Thou from the first
> Wast present, and with mighty wings outspread
> Dove-like satst brooding on the vast Abyss
> And mad'st it pregnant: What in me is dark
> Illumine, what is low raise and support:
> That to the highth of this great Argument
> I may assert Eternal Providence,
> And justify the ways of God to men.

In light of these lines Housman's allusion is perfectly clear. Housman, as we have mentioned, taught classics at the University of London, and would have had *Paradise Lost* virtually memorized; is it possible that the allusion is too obscure in the 1970's to be effective without a footnote?

The allusion to *Paradise Lost* is a matter of a few lines in Housman's poem. It is glancing, casual, off-the-cuff; we would be puzzled but not totally mystified if it were never explained. Certainly the poem could function if we never understood it. The extensive references to *Alice in Wonderland* and *Through the Looking Glass* in "The White Rabbit" are much less peripheral; and yet the poem is not properly *about* characters from *Alice in Wonderland,* it is about a twentieth-century individual confronted with a variety of pills (some of which make him

larger, some smaller, and others that do nothing at all) and his reaction
to those pills.

White Rabbit

One pill makes you larger
And one pill makes you small.
And the ones that mother gives you
Don't do anything at all.
Go ask Alice   5
When she's ten feet tall.

And if you go chasing rabbits
And you know you're going to fall,
Tell 'em a hookah smoking caterpillar
Has given you the call.   10
Call Alice
When she was just small.

When men on the chessboard
Get up and tell you where to go.
And you've just had some kind of mushroom,   15
And your mind is moving low.
Go ask Alice
I think she'll know.

When logic and proportion
Have fallen sloppy dead,   20
And the White Knight is talking backwards
And the Red Queen's lost her head.

Remember what the dormouse said:
"Feed your head.
Feed your head.   25
Feed your head."

—Grace Slick

9. *hookah*: a large water pipe.

QUESTIONS

1. What is the real subject of the song? What sort of pills confront the person to whom it is addressed?

2. How do you explain the wealth of allusions to Lewis Carroll's fiction? To what specific incidents does Slick allude? What about the subject of the song and the nature of the books makes the allusions appropriate?

3. What did the dormouse have to say in *Alice in Wonderland*? Of what relevance is that here? The song builds, somewhat like Ravel's "Bolero," to a spectacular conclusion in which Slick fairly shrieks at us on the record. This performance, coupled with the fact that the advice is repeated three times, places considerable emphasis on this line. Why?

The Unicorn Tapestries

You stay in the grove
To ambush the unicorn.
I don't know what the hunters gave,
But all the money of the sun
Falling between the shadows of your face   5
In yellow coin,
Could not bribe away the scorn
Which fastens up your mouth.

For whom are those hard lips?
The hunters creeping through the green   10
Beside their iron-collared hounds,
Or that towered head who soon
Will close his eyes
Between your aproned knees?

And when the animal is leashed   15
To the pomegranate tree,
Don't come by my prison room,
Singing your victory,
Or charm the guards to untie the chains
With which I was bound before the hunt,   20
When I cried I was a man.

You stay in the grove
To ambush the unicorn.
And after wander to the poisoned stream
Which the unicorn will never clean,   25
And greet the good beasts thirsting there,
Then follow through the holes and caves
The animals who poisoned it,
And cohabit in each lair.

I don't know what the hunters gave,   30
But all the money of the sun
Falling between the shadows of your face
In yellow coin,
Could not bribe away the scorn
Which fastens up your mouth.   35

—Leonard Cohen

This poem is specifically about a series of tapestries in The Cloisters (part of New York's Metropolitan Museum of Art) depicting the hunt and capture of the unicorn. It is addressed to the lady who appears in one of them. She is the poem's subject. The content of the poem derives from the tapestries, including the two legends to which Cohen refers: a unicorn is so fierce and wild that he can be taken only by a virgin, in whose lap he trustingly falls asleep and is thereby rendered powerless to resist the hunters; the unicorn purifies poisoned water by touching it with his horn, thereby providing animals and men with fresh, potable water to insure their survival. These legends, then, are not properly allusions, since they are depicted in the tapestries that are the subject of the poem itself. It may be, however, that the phrase "coin" in conjunction with "bribe" (lines 33, 34) refers to something outside the tapestries proper: the sale of Christ by Judas (Matt. 26:14–16). Such an allusion, if Cohen actually intends it, would be quite appropriate, because in medieval typology the unicorn was frequently a type or a symbol for Christ. It would, however, be very oblique.

In the tapestry, as you can tell from Cohen's poem, the virgin's face shows obvious scorn, although it is not at all clear at whom the scorn is directed. Discuss Cohen's interpretation of the tapestry, the way he relates himself to the lady and the unicorn, and the way he expects his readers to relate to the scene.

You, Andrew Marvell

And here face down beneath the sun
And here upon earth's noonward height
To feel the always coming on
The always rising of the night:

To feel creep up the curving east   5
The earthly chill of dusk and slow
Upon those under lands the vast
And ever-climbing shadow grow

And strange at Ecbatan the trees
Take leaf by leaf the evening strange   10
The flooding dark about their knees
The mountains over Persia change

And now at Kermanshah the gate
Dark empty and the withered grass
And through the twilight now the late   15
Few travelers in the westward pass

And Baghdad darken and the bridge
Across the silent river gone
And through Arabia the edge
Of evening widen and steal on   20

And deepen on Palmyra's street
The wheel rut in the ruined stone
And Lebanon fade out and Crete
High through the clouds and overblown

And over Sicily the air   25
Still flashing with the landward gulls

And loom and slowly disappear
The sails above the shadowy hulls

And Spain go under and the shore
Of Africa the gilded sand   30
And evening vanish and no more
The low pale light across that land

Nor now the long light on the sea:
And here face downward in the sun
To feel how swift how secretly   35
The shadow of the night comes on . . .

                              —*Archibald MacLeish*

    9. *Ecbatan*: once the capital of Media. 13. *Kermanshah*: ancient city in Iran.
21. *Palmyra*: ancient city in Syria.

Reread and digest Andrew Marvell's "To His Coy Mistress" if you do
not remember it well. Then read "You, Andrew Marvell" again carefully. Obviously the two poems are not on the same subject: one is a
seduction poem, the other has something to do with the decline of civili-
zations of the past and the probable decline of our own contemporary
civilization. But some definite links exist. Both poems are concerned
with the process of time and its ravages, and the position of MacLeish
as he lies "face down beneath the sun" makes it obvious that it is "at
his back" that he hears time's winged chariot hurrying near. The poem
may also draw on a book by Oswald Spengler, *The Decline of the West,*
in which the author argued that civilization, like the sun, moved from
east to west, and that European and even American civilization were
doomed to decline in the very near future. Why might MacLeish find
it useful to recall Andrew Marvell's poem in his own?

Babiy Yar

Over Babiy Yar
there are no memorials.
The steep hillside like a rough inscription.

I am frightened.
Today I am as old as the Jewish race.   5
I seem to myself a Jew at this moment.
I, wandering in Egypt.
I, crucified. I perishing.
Even today the mark of the nails.
I think also of Dreyfus. I am he.   10
The Philistine my judge and my accuser.
Cut off by bars and cornered,
ringed round, spat at, lied about;
the screaming ladies with the Brussels lace
poke me in the face with parasols.   15
I am also a boy in Belostok,
the dropping blood spreads across the floor,
the public-bar heroes are rioting
in an equal stench of garlic and of drink.
I have no strength, go spinning from a boot,   20
shriek useless prayers that they don't listen to;
with a cackle of 'Thrash the kikes and save Russia!'
the corn-chandler is beating up my mother.
I seem to myself like Anna Frank
to be transparent as an April twig   25
and am in love, I have no need for words,
I need for us to look at one another.
How little we have to see or to smell
separated from foliage and the sky,
how much, how much in the dark room   30
gently embracing each other.
They're coming. Don't be afraid.
The booming and banging of the spring.
It's coming this way. Come to me.
Quickly, give me your lips.   35
They're battering in the door. Roar of the ice.

Over Babiy Yar
rustle of the wild grass.
The trees look threatening, look like judges.
And everything is one silent cry.   40
Taking my hat off

I feel myself slowly going grey.
And I am one silent cry
over the many thousands of the buried;
am every old man killed here,   45
every child killed here.
O my Russian people, I know you.
Your nature is international.
Foul hands rattle your clean name.
I know the goodness of my country.   50
How horrible it is that pompous title
the anti-semites calmly call themselves,
Society of the Russian People.
No part of me can ever forget it.
When the last anti-semite on the earth   55
is buried for ever
let the International ring out.
No Jewish blood runs among my blood,
but I am as bitterly and hardly hated
by every anti-semite   60
as if I were a Jew. By this
I am a Russian.

—*Yevgeny Yevtushenko*
(translated by *Robin Milner–Gulland and Peter Levi*)

57. *International*: the communist "national" anthem.

Like Cohen's poem, this one is about the place that provides the title, the site in Russia of a major Jewish massacre during World War II; unlike Cohen's poem, "Babiy Yar" contains numerous definite allusions to historical events and persons other than Babiy Yar: "wandering in Egypt," "crucified," "Dreyfus." How many of the allusions can you identify and explain? How does the poet relate himself to Babiy Yar, the massacre, the Jewish people? Yevtushenko is a well-known contemporary Russian poet, popular not only in Russia but abroad as well. So popular is this poem that if the poet has not read it by the end of a poetry reading, so the story goes, Russian audiences break into a chant, "Babiy Yar, Babiy Yar" and will not let him leave until he has recited it. Do you think the popularity of the poem is to be explained more in terms of technique or in terms of content?

William Butler Yeats Visits Lincoln Park and Escapes Unscathed

As I went out one evening
To take the evening air,
I was blessed by a blood-red moon,
In Lincoln Park, the dark was turning;

I spied a fair young maiden   5
And a flame was in her eye,
And on her face lay the steel-blue sky
Of Lincoln Park, the dark was turning, turning.

They spread their sheets upon the ground
Just like a wandering tribe,   10
And the wise men walked in their robes, yeh robes,
Through Lincoln Park, the dark was turning.

The towers trapped an' tremblin'
And the boats were tossed about
When the fog rolled in and the gas rolled out   15
From Lincoln Park, the dark was turning.

Like wild horses freed at last
We took the streets of wine;
But I searched in vain, for she stayed behind,
In Lincoln Park the dark was turning, turning.   20

I'll go back to the city
Where I can be alone,
And tell my friend that she lies in stone,
In Lincoln Park the dark was turning.

—*Phil Ochs*

QUESTIONS

1. Is the speaker of this poem actually the Irish poet Yeats, or is the American Ochs merely comparing himself to Yeats? Yeats was active in

the cause of Irish nationalism (he has several poems on the subject), and fell passionately in love with Maude Gonne, a very beautiful woman also involved in the movement. Examine the other poems by Yeats and Ochs in this book, consider the above remarks, and explain why Ochs would find it useful to allude to Yeats and Irish nationalism in his song.

2. Apart from the title, what else about Ochs' song suggests Yeats and his work?

3. What does this close connection of Phil Ochs (American) and the Lincoln Park disturbances with Yeats (Irishman) and the cause of Irish nationalism tell us about the way Ochs views what happened at the Democratic Convention of 1968? What are the implications of the line repeated at the end of each stanza, "the dark was turning, turning?"

4. Examine the song carefully for examples of the poetic devices we have been discussing (simile, metaphor, balance, and repetition) and evaluate Ochs' use of these techniques.

The Second Coming

Turning and turning in the widening gyre
The falcon cannot hear the falconer;
Things fall apart; the center cannot hold;
Mere anarchy is loosed upon the world,
The blood-dimmed tide is loosed, and everywhere   5
The ceremony of innocence is drowned;
The best lack all conviction, while the worst
Are full of passionate intensity.
Surely some revelation is at hand;
Surely the Second Coming is at hand.   10
The Second Coming! Hardly are those words out
When a vast image out of *Spiritus Mundi*
Troubles my sight: somewhere in sands of the desert
A shape with lion body and the head of a man,
A gaze blank and pitiless as the sun,   15
Is moving its slow thighs, while all about it
Reel shadows of the indignant desert birds.
The darkness drops again; but now I know
That twenty centuries of stony sleep

Were vexed to nightmare by a rocking cradle,   20
And what rough beast, its hour come round at last,
Slouches towards Bethlehem to be born?

—*William Butler Yeats*

QUESTIONS

1. How does the imagery of this poem help explain Ochs' reference to Yeats in the song we just discussed?

2. This poem is rich and complicated in its allusions. The title suggests the Christian apocalypse, and images like "ceremony of innocence" and "some new Bethlehem" develop that suggestion. "*Spiritus Mundi*" suggests Jung and the collective subconscious, in which are stored various prototypes of human and superhuman figures, figures that appear to all of us in our dreams and figure in the myths all cultures create. This particular image is the sphinx, who seems to symbolize the qualities of the new civilization. The gyres suggest Yeats' own quasi-religious prose tract, *The Vision,* in which the poet developed his own personal religion and theory of time and history. To what extent is a knowledge of Christianity, Jung, and *The Vision* necessary for an understanding of this poem? Does Yeats make inordinate demands on our time, patience, and understanding?

3. In what ways is the new civilization that Yeats foresees like or unlike our present civilization? What connotations of which images suggest its nature?

A Whiter Shade of Pale

We skipped the light fandango
And turned cartwheels cross the floor.
I was feeling kind of seasick
But the crowd called out for more.
The room was humming harder   5
As the ceiling flew away

When we called out for another drink
The waiter brought a tray
And so it was that later
As the miller told his tale   10
That her face at first just ghostly
Turned a whiter shade of pale.

She said, "There is no reason,
And the truth is plain to see,"
But I wandered through my playing cards   15
And would not let her be
One of sixteen vestal virgins
Who were leaving for the coast
And although my eyes were open
They might just have well been closed.   20
And so it was that later
As the miller told his tale
That her face at first just ghostly
Turned a whiter shade of pale.

—Keith Reid–Gary Brooker

In "A Whiter Shade of Pale," we are presented with an interesting collection of images set to a very un-rockish piece of music adapted from
Bach. As a song, "A Whiter Shade of Pale" is certainly successful
enough, although the disparity between the measured, orderly progres-
sion of its music and the wild disorder of its lyrics suggests that Reid
and Brooker are being either highly ironic or incoherent. The issue that
concerns us here, however, is the matter of the allusions to Chaucer's
"Miller's Tale" and the Roman vestal virgins: are these allusions functional? Is it important that the allusion is made to the "Miller's Tale"
and not to the "Knight's Tale," or to Milton's *Paradise Lost*? Why the
vestal virgins and not some Maenad? Are the Miller and the virgins in
the song to allude to the past in the same way that the music alludes to
Bach in the musical past? To what point? Or are Reid and Brooker
merely looking for any images, past or present, to work into a collage
disarrayed enough to function as an ironic contrast to the music? If this
is the case, the Miller and the virgins are virtually meaningless as al-

lusions; it may even be that the song mongers allusions the way that Donovan Leitch mongers images. Involved in the answers to these questions, of course, is one's interpretation of the song and what it attempts to do. If it is a juxtaposition of musical order and verbal disorder, then the allusions have no real function. If it juxtaposes past and present (or, perhaps, past within the present?), then the Miller functions as a remembrance of things past and nothing more. If, however, the lyrics themselves have a thematic coherence (like the lines of Dan Smyth's poem "Letter from Maine" in chapter 7), the allusions should be functional. Discuss your interpretation of the song and your evaluation of the function of the allusions.

TONE

One function of the imagery, diction, balance, and repetition, even of rhythm and rhyme in a poem, is to create a mood in a poem, a tone. Sometimes individual words give a key to a poem's tone, like "plastic" in "Twentieth Century Fox"; in other instances metaphors are important, as in Paul Simon's popular "I Am a Rock." Careful poets can use even the rhythm of a poem to create tone, as we shall note when we discuss rhythm and rhyme. Usually, however, tone is a function of the meaning of words, a result of the collective connotations of all the words in a poem. Tone amounts to the poet's attitude toward his subject as it colors his selection of vocabulary. And because the vocabulary of a poem colors our own attitudes, tone may also be said to be our own attitudes toward the poem's subject. Occasionally there are confusions, as we shall see: poems in which the tone intended by the author is not quite the tone received by his reader—but such occasions are few and far between, and usually the result of changes in public taste and temperament beyond the control of the poet. Poems can be lightly or bombastically funny; they can be somber, sarcastic, serious, reminiscent, sentimental, bitter, ironic, solemn, or as in the case of Hardy's "Neutral Tones," simply neutral. What is important is that the tone be appropriate to the subject of the poem and that the poet be careful in his use of language not to use words or phrases that destroy the tone he is trying to create—or worse yet, create a mood inappropriate to his subject. Consider the song "Honey," popular not too long ago.

Honey

See the tree, how big it's grown,
But friend it hasn't been too long,
It wasn't big.
I laughed at her and she got mad,
The first day that she planted it   5
Was just a twig.
Then the first snow came and she
Ran out to brush the snow away
So it wouldn't die,
Came runnin' in all excited,   10
Slipped and almost hurt herself,
I laughed 'til I cried.

She was always young at heart,
Kind-a dumb and kind-a smart
And I loved her so.   15
I surprised her with a puppy,
Kept me up all Christmas eve,
Two years ago.
And it would sure embarrass her
When I came home from working late   20
'cause I would know
That she's been sittin' there and cryin'
Over some sad and silly
Late, late show.

And Honey, I miss you   25
And I'm being good
And I'd love to be with you;
If only I could.

She wrecked the car and she was sad,
And so afraid that I'd be mad,   30
But what the heck.
Though I pretended hard to be,
Guess you could say she saw through me

And hugged my neck.
I came home unexpectedly   35
And found her crying needlessly
In the middle of the day,
And it was in the early Spring,
When flowers bloom and Robins sing,
She went away.   40

And Honey, I miss you
And I'm being good
And I'd love to be with you;
If only I could.

Yes, one day, while I wasn't home,   45
While she was there and all alone,
The Angels came.
Now all I have is memories
Of Honey, and I wake up nights
And call her name.   50
Now my life's an empty stage,
Where Honey lived, and Honey played,
And love grew up.
A small cloud passes over head
And cries down in the flower bed   55
That Honey loved.

And Honey, I miss you
And I'm being good
And I'd love to be with you;
If only I could.   60

—*Bobby Russell*

Not long after the song was first played, the Smothers Brothers did a
short sketch on their now defunct television show on "Honey House,"
a tourist clip joint through which visitors were guided by one of the
brothers singing this song and showing at appropriate places a growing
tree, a puppy, a wrecked car protruding through the wall, and a pile of
tissues where "Honey" had obviously been crying needlessly. Each re-

peat of "And I'm being good" brought a suggestive glance at one of the women on the tour. The sketch was probably one of the funniest things the two comedians ever did, but questions were immediately raised about its appropriateness. Did the song really deserve that kind of treatment? Some people saw the sketch as a crude and unwarranted attempt to deface a beautiful song; others felt that the song had it coming.

For the song has obvious defects, and they are defects of tone. We must feel sorry for the singer, for he has lost someone who meant much to him; but it is unfortunate that he wallows in his grief the way he does, for his expression of remorse becomes an exercise in self-indulgence. In short, the song is sentimental in the literary rather than the popular sense: it indulges in emotion for emotion's sake. What exact phrases give rise to the sentimental tone of the lyric? Certainly the business about the angels, accompanied on the record by heart-rending angelic "ooh" and "aah." The tree, the puppy, and the speaker's absurd reaction to the destruction of his automobile do their fair share. Perhaps the character of the narrator as projected in the song is important, since he is obviously an emotional simpleton who savors every miserable memory of his dead wife. Perhaps it is the unrealistic characterization of Honey, the "kind-a dumb and kind-a smart" (?) child bride, whose superhuman strength helped her conceal the secret of her disease from her husband, the tender heart crying over the late show. Perhaps the poet's own attitude is important: clearly he enjoys the song's story for the sake of emotions it contains. But the sentimentality defies precise analysis; it is, like most tones, a product of the poem as a whole, and the whole is always more than the sum of parts. Sentimentalism had its day (the latter part of the nineteenth century) and the modern age is perhaps too hard on anything that smacks of Victorian sentimentalism—but certainly this song oversteps the bounds of even the most generous readers and listeners.

Here is a song by Curly Putnam that might or might not be sentimental. The potential *does* exist in the composer's subject. Read it, listen to it—Johnny Cash's recording is probably the best, Joan Baez's one of the worst—and decide whether Putnam manages to avoid the stickiness of "Honey" or whether he too is sucked into the quagmire. Think about some other songs—"Teen Angel" or "Don't It Make You Want to Go Home"—and poems—"The Soldier" by Rupert Brooke or Vachel Lindsay's "General William Booth Enters into Heaven"—and movies or novels—*Love Story*, for example—and decide the extent to which sentimentality still permeates popular literature and poetry. Do some composers and poets seem more prone to this tone than others? What is your own reaction to "decently sentimental" literature?

Green, Green Grass of Home

The old home town looks the same as I step
  down from the train
And there to meet me is my Mama and Papa
And down the road I look and there runs Mary
  hair of gold and lips like cherries   5
It's good to touch the green, green grass of home
Yes they'll all come to meet me arms a-reaching
  smiling sweetly
It's good to touch the green, green grass of home

The old house is still standing tho' the paint   10
  is cracked and dry
And there's that old oak tree that I used to play on
Down the lane I walk with my sweet Mary
  hair of gold and lips like cherries
It's good to touch the green, green grass of home   15

Then I awake and look around me at the gray walls
  that surround me
And I realize that I was only dreaming
For there's a guard and there's a sad old Padre
  arm and arm we'll walk at daybreak   20
Again I'll touch the green, green grass of home

Yes they'll all come to see me in the shade of that
  old oak tree
As they lay me 'neath the green, green grass of home.
                          —Curly Putnam

The opposite of too much emotion is no emotion at all. At its worst, this means a stiff-upper-lip attitude, such as the one adopted by A. E. Housman in his poem "1887." Used effectively, this lack of emotion can produce a poem like "Neutral Tones."

1887

From Clee to heaven the beacon burns,
    The shires have seen it plain,
From north and south the sign returns
    And beacons burn again.

Look left, look right, the hills are bright,   5
    The dales are light between,
Because 'tis fifty years to-night
    That God has saved the Queen.

Now, when the flame they watch not towers
    About the soil they trod,   10
Lads, we'll remember friends of ours
    Who shared the work with God.

To skies that knit their heartstrings right,
    To fields that bred them brave,
The saviours come not home to-night: 15
    Themselves they could not save.

It dawns in Asia, tombstones show
    And Shropshire names are read;
And the Nile spills his overflow
    Beside the Severn's dead.   20

We pledge in peace by farm and town
    The Queen they served in war,
And fire the beacons up and down
    The land they perished for.

'God save the Queen' we living sing,   25
    From height to height 'tis heard;
And with the rest your voices ring,
    Lads of the Fifty-third.

Oh, God will save her, fear you not:
    Be you the men you've been,   30
Get you the sons your fathers got,
    And God will save the Queen.

                                                —*A. E. Housman*

    20. *Severn*: a river in western England.

One of Housman's readers took this poem to be a tremendously effective satire of the typical British "thing" about war and the Queen
and patriotism, and told the poet so; Housman was much upset, and
replied that he had meant exactly what he said. The story raises some
questions about the intentional fallacy—what the artist actually produces and what he intended to produce—as well as some questions
about the tone of the poem. Was the student's reaction valid, or was
he perhaps imposing his own attitudes toward the subject on Housman's poem? Is there something absurd in the poem itself that undercuts its seriousness and suggests such an interpretation? Certainly, if
the poem failed to create the tone Housman desired he failed as an
artist, and Housman's poetry does contain such failures. On the other
hand, a poet is not to be condemned because another reader of
another generation imposes his values on that poet's creation. What
do you think?

Neutral Tones

We stood by a pond that winter day,
And the sun was white, as though chidden of God
And a few leaves lay on the starving sod;
    —They had fallen from an ash, and were gray.

Your eyes on me were as eyes that rove   5
Over tedious riddles of years ago;
And some words played between us to and fro
  On which lost the more by our love.

The smile on your mouth was the deadest thing
Alive enough to have strength to die;   10
And a grin of bitterness swept thereby
  Like an ominous bird a-wing. . . .

Since then, keen lessons that love deceives,
And wrings with wrong, have shaped to me
Your face, and the God-curst sun, and a tree,   15
  And a pond edged with grayish leaves.

                                               —*Thomas Hardy*

    2. *chidden*: scolded, faulted. 12. *ominous bird a-wing*: the Greeks and Romans believed that certain birds seen in certain positions indicated impending good fortune or disaster.

QUESTIONS

    1. Read the poem carefully and describe the situation in which it is written. What people are involved? What is happening as the speaker says the poem? What has happened in the past to which he refers? How many different points in time does the poem involve?

    2. Examine carefully the similes and metaphors: "white, as though chidden of God," "as eyes that rove/Over tedious riddles of years ago," "the deadest thing/Alive enough to have strength to die," "Like an ominous bird a-wing." How do they reflect back on the speaker or his former love, and to what times in their relationship do these similes and metaphors refer?

    3. The title itself identifies the tone of this poem; why should it be "neutral?" What imagery contributes to the tone?

    4. Given your own experience, do you identify with this poem? Do you think love affairs of any consequence ever really burn out so entirely that they leave neither love nor hate, only nothing?

  Read the following poem by Countee Cullen, a black poet. It raises questions concerning a number of seemingly inexplicable injustices and contradictions: what did the mole do to deserve his blindness; how is it that men, who are created in God's image, are mortal while God is not; are Tantalus and Sisyphus assigned their punishments in Dante's *Inferno* out of justice or caprice? All these questions God might resolve if he deigned to explain them to man; all are paradoxes only because man sees through the glass darkly. And then Cullen concludes, "Yet do I marvel at this curious thing: To make a poet black, and bid him sing!" The implication is that the poet is not at all surprised at the other apparent injustices and contradictions, but this contradiction outrages him. Would you say the tone of the poem is bitter, cynical, skeptical, dubious, puzzled, or what? How does its tone compare with that of Dickinson in "These are the days when Birds come back?"

Yet Do I Marvel

I doubt not God is good, well-meaning, kind,
And did He stoop to quibble could tell why
The little buried mole continues blind,
Why flesh that mirrors Him must someday die,
Make plain the reason tortured Tantalus   5
Is baited by the fickle fruit, declare
If merely brute caprice dooms Sisyphus
To struggle up a never-ending stair.
Inscrutable His ways are, and immune
To catechism by a mind too strewn   10
With petty cares to slightly understand
What awful brain compels His awful hand.
Yet do I marvel at this curious thing:
To make a poet black, and bid him sing!

                                              —*Countee Cullen*

2. *quibble*: argue, discuss. 5. *Tantalus*: son of Zeus, condemned to stand up to his neck in water that he could not drink, below a tree laden with fruit that he could not eat for all eternity as punishment for revealing secrets of the gods. 7. *Sisyphus*: a king of Corinth condemned in Hell to roll a heavy stone up a hill, only to have it fall down again just when he neared the top.

Robert Frost is a master of tone, although he is usually deceitfully ambiguous in all aspects of his art. Is the following poem an exception to the rule of ambiguity, or do successive readings produce layers of meaning and tone?

Provide, Provide

The witch that came (the withered hag)
To wash the steps with pail and rag,
Was once the beauty Abishag,

The picture pride of Hollywood.
Too many fall from great and good   5
For you to doubt the likelihood.

Die early and avoid the fate.
Or if predestined to die late,
Make up your mind to die in state.

Make the whole stock exchange your own!   10
If need be occupy a throne,
Where nobody can call *you* crone.

Some have relied on what they knew;
Others on being simply true.
What worked for them might work for you.   15

No memory of having starred
Atones for later disregard,
Or keeps the end from being hard.

Better to go down dignified
With boughten friendship at your side   20
Than none at all. Provide, provide!

                                        —*Robert Frost*

One form of irony involves saying one thing while actually meaning another, or making a statement that is obviously false in light of information you yourself have provided. Is Frost being ironic when he admonishes us to "Provide, provide!" Or is he quite serious?

One of the favorite modes of poets and readers alike is *satire*. In its classical sense, a satire is any criticism of any aspect of human existence cast into a formal poem; in its more modern usage, satire usually means a combination of criticism, humor, and derision in the tone of the poem. Satire implies criticism, but the criticism is usually indirect because satrical poems criticise by pretending to support, or condemn by imitating the deficiencies of style in another work. In the one case, the conventions or style being satirized is implicitly criticised by the stupidity with which it is used; in the other, conventions and style are debased by the inanity of the subject of the imitation. Both usages of satire involve a tone that is ironic and usually funny; the disparity between diction and content usually elicits laughter.

Satire may be light hearted and gently critical or bitter and scathing in the abuse it heaps upon the object of its scorn. *Parody* is usually gentler than what we call satire, although the former is really a subclass of the latter. Either can be a dangerous weapon in the hands of an unscrupulous satirist: people too busy laughing at the satire or parody all too frequently fail to question whether or not the object of the satire really deserves the treatment it is given.

There has been much satire and parody in music of late, most of it bad, some of it good. The Beatles' white album, which surveyed music in virtually all of its mutations and varieties, often appeared to parody the styles of other musicians and groups in a light-hearted manner. In his *Rhymes and Reasons* album, John Denver sings a version of a parody of country and western music.

You Done Stompt on My Heart

I told you that I loved you
And you said "That is good."
I called you my darlin'
And I thought I always would.
But now you've gone and left me   5
And don't know where you're at.
You done stompt on my heart
And mashed that sucker flat!

You done stompt on my heart,
You broke it all apart.   10
Sweetheart you just sorta
Stompt on my aorta.
You started stepping out with guys,
I felt us drift apart
And every step you took   15
Was a stomp upon my heart.

I only hope that someday,
When you have got the blues
In some lonely room
You look down at your shoes.   20
And think about the tender heart
You crushed beneath the soles
When your young body craved
Good times and fancy clothes.

—Mason Williams

QUESTIONS

1. What specific lines and phrases contribute to the light tone of this song? What makes them humorous?

2. What expressions, situations, conventions of country and western songs are parodied here?

3. Listen to John Denver's recording. Obviously his version is significantly different from this. Which do you prefer? Why? What elements of Denver's pronunciation contribute to the tone of the song? Would you call it gentle or bitter?

Williams' song satirizes the conventions of a whole style of writing; it is also possible to parody an individual poem, to satirize a single song. Here is a poem by the English Romantic poet Robert Southey, followed by Lewis Carroll's parody of the poem. Note how the parody borrows from the original poem in its phrasing, how it apparently flatters by imitation but really criticises by making the imitation absurd.

The Old Man's Comforts

And How He Gained Them

"You are old, Father William," the young man cried,
  "The few locks which are left you are gray;
You are hale, Father William, a hearty old man,
  Now tell me the reason, I pray."

"In the days of my youth," Father William replied,   5
  "I remembered that youth would fly fast,
And abused not my health, and my vigor at first,
  That I never might need them at last."

"You are old, Father William," the young man cried,
  "And pleasures with youth pass away;   10
And yet you lament not the days that are gone,
  Now tell me the reason, I pray."

"In the days of my youth," Father William replied,
  "I remembered that youth could not last;
I thought of the future, whatever I did,   15
  That I never might grieve for the past."

"You are old, Father William, the young man cried,
  "And life must be hastening away;
You are cheerful, and love to converse upon death,
  Now tell me the reason, I pray."   20

"I am cheerful, young man," Father William replied,
  "Let the cause thy attention engage;
In the days of my youth I remember'd my God!
  And He hath not forgotten my age."

                      —*Robert Southey*

You Are Old, Father William

"You are old, Father William," the young man said
  "And your hair has become very white;

And yet you incessantly stand on your head—
  Do you think, at your age, it is right?"

"In my youth," Father William replied to his son,   5
  "I feared it might injure the brain;
But, now that I'm perfectly sure I have none,
  Why, I do it again and again."

"You are old," said the youth, "as I mentioned before.
  And have grown most uncommonly fat;   10
Yet you turned a back-somersault in at the door—
  Pray, what is the reason of that?"

"In my youth," said the sage, as he shook his grey locks,
  "I kept all my limbs very supple
By the use of this ointment—one shilling the box—   15
  Allow me to sell you a couple?"

"You are old," said the youth, "and your jaws are too weak
  For anything tougher than suet;
Yet you finished the goose, with the bones and the beak—
  Pray, how did you manage to do it?"   20

"In my youth," said his father, "I took to the law,
  And argued each case with my wife;
And the muscular strength, which it gave to my jaw
  Has lasted the rest of my life."

"You are old," said the youth, "one would hardly suppose   25
  That your eye was as steady as ever;
Yet you balanced an eel on the end of your nose—
  What made you so awfully clever?"

"I have answered three questions, and that is enough,"
  Said his father. "Don't give yourself airs!   30
Do you think I can listen all day to such stuff?
  Be off, or I'll kick you down-stairs!"

                                        —*Lewis Carroll*

What deficiencies in Southey's poem does the parody point up? How would you describe the tone of each poem? How effective is parody as literary criticism?

Here finally is William Shakespeare's satire of the Petrarchan conventions popular in love poems of his day. Coral lips and eyes like the sun have since disappeared from serious love poetry, but the fact that we still recognize the objects of his satire suggests that Petrarchan conventions are still quite alive in bad contemporary verse.

Sonnet 130

My mistress' eyes are nothing like the sun;
Coral is far more red than her lips' red;
If snow be white, why then her breasts are dun;
If hairs be wires, black wires grow on her head.
I have seen roses damask'd, red and white,   5
But no such roses see I in her cheeks,
And in some perfumes there is more delight
Than in the breath that from my mistress reeks.
I love to hear her speak, yet well I know
That music hath a far more pleasing sound.   10
I grant I never saw a goddess go;
My mistress, when she walks, treads on the ground:
And yet, by heaven, I think my love as rare
As any she belied with false compare.
                                        —*William Shakespeare*

3. *dun*: greyish-brown. 5. *damask'd*: multi-colored, like damask silk.

3
Critical Terminology: Words as Sound

Thus far we have been talking about words as symbols for ideas, about words as meaning—about paradox, symbolism, metaphor, personification, irony. The meaning of poetry has received much attention in the twentieth century, so much as to give the impression that we ought to disregard everything about a poem except the meaning of the words. Hence, so much concentration on symbol, simile, and metaphor as the basic ingredients of poetry, the *sine qua non* without which a verse is not a poem. This is a mistaken impression of poetry, however, that may arise from any number of causes: from overreaction against late nineteenth-century poetry, which, at least in English, was basically sound-oriented; from the notion among modern readers that poetry has to be about heavy subjects and therefore must concern itself with ideas, which can be heavy, rather than with sounds, which cannot; or from the obvious fact that when one lives in an age in which poetry has become more a matter of the printed than spoken word, it is much easier to talk about words as symbols for meaning than words as sounds. In any event, the idea that the essence of poetry is related exclusively to meaning is erroneous and should be retired along with the myth of the international communist conspiracy and the invincible Green Bay Packers.

Words are sounds, and the sound of a word has a great deal to do with its total impression on a listener. There are people, for example, who object more strenuously to relatively innocuous four letter words than to really hard core profanity because the former "sound so ugly." "Farkle," a product of the Laugh-In television show, has virtually no denotative meaning at all—it just sounds obscene because of the hard "f" and "k" and the way we move the muscles of our mouth when we pronounce it. The sound gives it connotative meaning, and connotative meaning is all the meaning it has. In like manner, other combinations of letters and words can be made to sound unpleasant, soothing, rough, smooth, somber, light, heavy, or almost anything else the poet wishes. And the poet does indeed make use of the sound aspects of words regularly, sometimes in a way that makes the sound of the poem carry most of its meaning. There are even people who argue that poetry is sound, that we should ignore entirely the meaning of words and use them only as sound values. Such an idea is quite as nonsensical as maintaining that poetry is only meaning; the logical end of such an argument is that poetry in a foreign language that we cannot understand is more capable of being appreciated than poetry in our native tongue, where the meaning of the words keeps getting in the way of our concentration on sound. A good poet is aware of both sound and sense, and he makes the one parallel the other to create a coherent, well-integrated unity. Hence poetry must be verbalized to be appreciated fully, even when read in the privacy of one's own room for one's own enjoyment. It is for this reason that poets give readings, that they record their poetry, that there is no real substitute for actually hearing Vachel Lindsay performing "General William Booth" or Bob Dylan singing "Sad-Eyed Lady of the Lowlands."

ALLITERATION

The use of sound with which virtually everyone is familiar, the use people invariably associate with poetry, is *rhyme:* the repetition of the same vowel and consonant sounds in words in close proximity. But the fact is that rhyme is a relatively recent innovation in English poetry. Neither classical Greek nor Latin poetry rhymed, and until the Norman invasion of 1066 English poetry was not rhymed either. What ties early English poetry together is not rhyme but *alliteration:* the repetition of the same consonant sound on accented syllables of words in close proximity ("*f*ine *f*eathered *f*riend," "The *e*pitome of *p*omposity"). Alliteration surrounds us because politicians and the Madison Avenue crowd both know that phrases that alliterate are both cohesive and catchy ("*P*epsi *p*ours it on," "*k*ooks and *c*ommies," "*p*eace, *p*rogress, and *p*rosperity"). Early English poets found alliterative patterns effective for

unifying their poems, and they wrote in a verse form that tried to alliterate at least two and preferably three syllables of every line. Here,
roughly transcribed, are some lines from Beowulf, followed by a translation of those same lines by Charles Kennedy.

from Beowulf

Gewat that neosian, sythan niht becom,
hean huses, hu hit Hring-Dene
aefter beorthege gebun haefdon.
Fand tha thaer inne aethelinga gedriht
swefan aefter symble; sorge ne cuthon,
wonsceaft wera. Wiht unhaelo,
grim ond graedig, gaero sona waes,
reoc ond rethe, ond on raeste genam
thritig thegna; thanon eft gewat
huthe hremig to ham faran,
mid thaere waelfylle wica neosan.

(lines 115–25)

Then, under cover of night, Grendel came
to Hrothgar's lofty hall to see how the Ring-Danes
were disposed after drinking ale all evening;
and he found there a band of brave warriors,
well-feasted, fast asleep, dead to worldly sorrow,
man's sad destiny. At once that hellish monster,
grim and greedy, brutally cruel,
started forward and seized thirty thanes
even as they slept; and then, gloating
over his plunder, he hurried from the hall,
made for his lair with all those slain warriors.
                              —*anonymous* (translated by Charles Kennedy)

The cohesive effect on each line of the repeated consonant sounds is
obvious.
    Alliteration can serve several functions. It can exist as an ornament

to attract a reader's attention or to make an impression on his mind; it can act as a unifying element in a poem, especially when spread over several lines; it can promote the poem's meaning, both denotative and connotative, by repetition of appropriate sounds. Poe, for all his monotonous rhythm and other weaknesses, has a strong sense of the sound of words, and both "The Raven" and "The Bells," poems known to virtually every high school student, allow him to show off his ability. Examine carefully the uses of alliteration in this stanza of "The Raven," and observe how they act not merely to ornament the verse but as devices for conveying meaning as well.

> And the silken, sad, uncertain rustling of each purple
>   curtain
> Thrilled me—filled me with fantastic terrors never felt before;
> So that now, to still the beating of my heart, I stood repeating,
> " 'Tis some visitor entreating entrance at my chamber door—
> Some late visitor entreating entrance at my chamber door—
>   This it is and nothing more."

Then read—or better still, listen to—the following song by Phil Ochs.

I Kill Therefore I Am

Meet the king of cowboys; he rides a pale pony
He fights the bad boys; brings them to their knees.
He patrols the highways from the air;
He keeps the country safe from long hair;
I am the masculine American man; I kill therefore I am.   5

I don't like the blackman, for he does not know his place.
Take the back of my hand or I'll spray you with my mace.
I'm as brave as any man could be;
I find my courage through chemistry.
I am the masculine American man; I kill therefore I am.   10

I don't like the students now; they don't have no respect.
They don't like to work now; I think I'll wring their necks.
They call me pig although I'm underpaid,

I'll show those faggots that I'm not afraid.
I am the masculine American man; I kill therefore I am.   15

Farewell to the gangster; we don't need him anymore.
We've got the police force; they're the ones who break the laws.
He's got a gun and he's a hater;
He shoots first, he shoots later.
I am the masculine American man; I kill therefore I am.   20

                          —*Phil Ochs*

For pure unadultered rancor, this song is unrivaled in even Phil Ochs'
repertoire. The title is a most uncomplimentary play on Descartes'
famous dictum, *Cogito, ergo sum* (*I think, therefore I am*), the one
virtually unchallengable generalization upon which the philosopher
built his entire philosophical system. The implication is that the policeman builds his whole rationale not on thinking but on killing, that
killing serves as the one unchallengeable "truth" in his existence. Such
an insinuation is echoed and developed in line 19, a play on the old
aphorism "shoot first and ask questions later": the policeman shoots
first—and instead of asking questions, shoots again. Just as he is incapable of thought, he is incapable of asking questions, of engaging
in civilized discourse. Killing is tied in not only with the rationale of
the policeman, but with his masculinity as well. The gun as surrogate
for the emasculated American male's penis is a persistent motif in
contemporary literature and art, and Ochs clearly implies as much in
the refrain line of each stanza. To these characteristics of violence,
compulsive brutality, and sexual perversion is added simple childish-
ness: "Meet the king of cowboys," we are told. In one sense the cowboy is the representative symbol of the great American tradition of guns
and violence, of which the policeman is only a late descendant. In
another sense the cowboy represents a childish black–white, good guy–
bad guy morality—a game children play, an infantile but religious belief in fictions now all suddenly and tragically taken seriously by this
big kid with the gun in his hand, this king of cowboys, the cop. The
song is entirely uncomplimentary and without a drop of sympathy in
its explicit statements, in its use of allusions, in its imagery and
implications.

    The song is also very alliterative. Phrases like "king of cowboys," "pale pony," and "masculine American man" stick in the mind and will not go away. Is Ochs' use of alliteration confined to ornamentation, or does it have other functions? Explain.

The Eagle

He clasps the crag with crooked hands;
Close to the sun in lonely lands,
Ringed with the azure world, he stands.

The wrinkled sea beneath him crawls;
He watches from his mountain walls,
And like a thunderball he falls.

—Alfred, Lord Tennyson

Here is Tennyson's description of an eagle. The poem is simple enough; it plays on two contrasting states—stasis and motion—and the swiftness with which the eagle moves from one to the other. The images of height and depth—the sun, the wrinkled sea, the mountain walls—all emphasize contrasts of high and low, stasis and motion. But what is especially memorable about this brief poem is the first line: "He clasps the crag with crooked hands." Certainly the personification implicit in "hands" accounts for some of the line's effect, but most of it derives from the alliteration Tennyson uses. Is there something especially appropriate about the hard "c" sound, especially when used in conjunction with the "l" and the "r?" What qualities do the sound and the eagle share? Does the bird give the impression of being hard and powerful and perhaps a bit ugly in his proud power? And the consonant sounds—are they also hard and a bit ugly in their harshness? Or is this reading too much into the poem?

Pied Beauty

Glory be to God for dappled things—
For skies of couple-colour as a brinded cow;
For rose-moles all in stipple upon trout that swim;

Fresh-firecoal chestnut-falls; finches' wings;
  Landscape plotted and pieced—fold, fallow, and plough;   5
    And áll trádes, their gear and tackle and trim.

All things counter, original, spare, strange;
  Whatever is fickle, freckled (who knows how?)
    With swift, slow; sweet, sour; adazzle, dim;
He fathers-forth whose beauty is past change: 10
        Praise him.
          —*Gerard Manley Hopkins*

"Pied Beauty" is another poem constructed on paradoxes: all things changing and various are the creations of a God who himself never changes, for which reason the poet bids us praise him. The command to praise is given twice; the majority of the poem is taken up with lists of the various dappled things created by God, a list that upon close examination appears much less varied than first impression makes it seem. The skies of line 2, the stream in which the trout of line 3 presumably swim, and the landscape of line 5 cover the three realms of life: air, sea, and land. The cow, the trout, and the finch survey the inhabitants of these realms. The plotted and pieced land suggests farming, and "all trades" suggests commerce; the two categories include most of the occupations known to man. Lines 7–9 enumerate several opposites, some obvious (swift and slow, sweet and sour), others more oblique (counter and original). And after this catalogue of all the variety of God's creation comes an affirmation of its togetherness and the sameness of the Creator. The paradox is startling here, especially in what it implies about apparently fickle and freckled human experience.

Hopkins is a very musical poet, and it is not surprising to find a considerable amount of alliteration in one of his poems. But could it be argued that in this poem the alliteration has a special function? The subject of the poem is the sameness in opposites, similarities in things that are dissimilar. Does the sameness of the sounds "adazzle, dim" reflect similarity in dissimilar words? Might the insistence on the "f" sound throughout the whole poem be a verbal insistence on unity among a list of disparate elements? Reexamine carefully all the patterns of consonants in the poem, note how pervasive the alliteration is, and evaluate the sophistication of Hopkins' use of sound.

ASSONANCE

Like consonants, vowels can be used to create patterns of sound in spoken language, although repeated vowel sounds are not nearly so perceptible as repeated consonants. The fact that in the history of language vowel patterns and qualities in words change with far greater frequency than consonant patterns and values suggests that the vowel sounds are less definite, looser, more prone to variation than consonant sounds. For this reason the study of *assonance* requires a more careful ear and frequently some kind of regional or historical reconstruction that is not usually necessary in the study of alliteration. In some areas of the country the "i" of "condition" and the "e" of "see" sound alike; it may well be that the names of Keats and Yeats rhymed —or would have to John Keats. It is also possible for vowels that do not have exactly the same qualities to give a generally assonant effect, as Bob Dylan demonstrates in many of his lyrics: the sounds of the long "a" and "o" and of the short "i" and "e" are actually quite similar.

Consider the vowel qualities of the words of this haunting portrait of a rock madonna.

Sad-Eyed Lady of the Lowlands

With your merc'ry mouth in the missionary times,
And your eyes like smoke and your prayers like rhymes,
And your silver cross, and your voice like chimes,
Oh, who do they think could bury you?
With your pockets well-protected at last,   5
And your streetcar visions which you place on the grass
And your flesh like silk, and your face like glass,
Who among them do they think could carry you?

Sad-eyed lady of the lowlands,
Where the sad-eyed prophet says that no man comes,   10
My warehouse eyes my Arabian drums
Should I put them by your gate,
Or sad-eyed lady, should I wait?

With your sheets like metal and your belt like lace
And your deck of cards missing the jack and the ace   15
And your basement clothes and your hollow face
Who among them can think he could outguess you?
With your silhouette when the sunlight dims
Into your eyes where the moonlight swims
And your matchbook songs and your gypsy hymns   20
Who among them could try to impress you?

The kings of Tyrus with their convict list
Are waiting in line for the geranium kiss
And you wouldn't know it would happen like this,
But who among them really wants just to kiss you?   25
With your childhood flames on your midnight rug
And your Spanish manners and your mother's drugs
And your cowboy mouth and your curfew plugs,
Who among them do you think could resist you?

Oh, the farmers and the businessmen, they all did decide   30
To show you the dead angels that they used to hide,
But why did they pick you to sympathize with their side
Oh how could they ever stake you?
They wish you'd accepted the blame for the farm
But with the sea at your feet and the phony false alarm   35
And the child of the hoodlum wrapped up in your arms
How could they ever have persuaded you?

With your sheet metal memory of cannery row
And your magazine husband who one day just had to go
And your gentleness now which you just can't help but show   40
Who among them do you think would employ you?
Now you stand with your thief, you're on his parole
With your holy medallion which fingertips fold
And your saint-like face and your ghost-like soul
Oh who among them do you think could destroy you?   45

Sad-eyed lady of the lowlands,
Where the sad-eyed prophet said that no man comes,
My warehouse eyes my Arabian drums

Should I put them by your gate,
Or sad-eyed lady, should I wait?   50

—*Bob Dylan*

"Sad-Eyed Lady" is one of Dylan's most admired songs, although all
attempts to explain the nature of its attraction have proven embarass-
ingly inadequate. Perhaps, as everyone assumes, the key to the poem
is the profusion of images, similes, and metaphors (at times paradoxical
and self-contradictory in their connotations) that fill the song almost,
but not quite, to excess. But these images are a very mixed bag,
sometimes banal ("With your silhouette when the sunlight dims"),
sometimes startling in their freshness and insight ("mercury mouth,"
"magazine husband"), sometimes totally enigmatic ("missionary times,"
"matchbook songs"). Although they convey a generally smooth, saintly
impression of the lady, they will not take us very far for all their
wealth of connotative information. Perhaps the song is incapable of
being grasped between the thumb and forefinger of rational, purely
denotative discourse; perhaps it can only be "experienced," never explained. Or perhaps the right place to begin is not with the imagery
but with the sound values of the words.

   There is much alliteration in the song, mostly of the liquid "l" and
the nasal "m" and "n" consonants. And there is much assonance: the
long "a" of "Arabian," "Lady," and "gate" in the refrain; the long "i"
of lines 22, 23, 24: the long "e" of line 35. But even vowel qualities
that are not identical (those of the phrase "sad-eyed lady," for example) have an assonant effect because of the proximity of the sound
of the "a" of "sad" to that of the "a" of "lady." Both are liquid, soft and
smooth. They are not sharp and do not hurt like the short "i" of "wit"
or "sit." They do not whine like the "a" of "asp." The poem is filled
with long, languid vowel sounds that reproduce in the ear the effect
that images like silk and glass and sheet metal produce in the mind;
to this extent sound follows sense. But it may well be that in this
song sound precedes sense; that the most important aspect of "Sad-
Eyed Lady of the Lowlands" is not the imagery but the sound; that
the soft rich music of the words tells us more about Dylan's lady than
all the images combined.

   Listen carefully to the poet's own performance of the song, trying
to determine exactly the poem's effect on a listener, and from what

elements of the lyrics the effect derives. The song has also been recorded by Dylan's friend Joan Baez, whose voice is, according to many
critics, tonally richer and "better" than Dylan's. Whose recording better
captures the spirit of the poem?

Elusive Butterfly

You might wake up some morning
To the sound of something moving
Past your window in the wind.
And if you're quick enough to rise,
You'll catch the fleeting glimpse   5
Of someone's fading shadow

Don't be concerned, it will not harm you.
It's only me pursuing something I'm not sure of.
Across my dream, with nets of wonder,
I chase the bright elusive butterfly of love.   10

Out on the new horizon,
You may see the floating motion
Of a distant pair of wings.
And if the sleep has left your ears,
You might hear footsteps   15
Running through an open meadow.
You might have heard my footsteps
Echo softly in the distance
Through the canyons of your mind.
I might have even called your name   20
As I ran searching after
Something to believe in.

Don't be concerned, it will not harm you.
It's only me pursuing something I'm not sure of.
Across my dream, with nets of wonder.   25
I chase the bright elusive butterfly of love.

You might have seen me running
Through the long abandoned ruins
Of the dreams you left behind.
If you remember something there   30
That glided past you followed
Close by heavy breathing,

Don't be concerned, it will not harm you.
It's only me pursuing something I'm not sure of,
Across my dream, with nets of wonder,   35
I chase the bright elusive butterfly of love.

—Bob Lind

QUESTIONS

1. What is the relationship between the speaker and the person to whom the song is spoken? Have they once been lovers (lines 27–31), or is the song an invitation to love for the first time (lines 8, 21–22)?

2. Can you visualize the literal situation described in the poem, however surrealistic it may seem? Who does what where? Are "open meadows" and "ruined canyons" contradictory images?

3. What is the metaphoric situation? Can the meadows and canyons and ruins be explained in terms of their metaphoric or symbolic significance?

4. In the refrain, the composer speaks about his dreams; in line 29 he tells the listener that her dreams have been left behind. Is he mixed up, has he confused the situation, or does this tell us something about the speaker and the listener?

5. How appropriate is the butterfly as a symbol of love?

6. How effective is the assonance in lines 12, 13? In line 14? In line 28? What other instances of assonance and alliteration do you find in this song. How would you evaluate the composer's use of sound in general?

The Lotos-Eaters

"Courage!" he said, and pointed toward the land,
"This mounting wave will roll us shoreward soon."
In the afternoon they came unto a land

In which it seemèd always afternoon.
All round the coast the languid air did swoon,   5
Breathing like one that hath a weary dream.
Full-faced above the valley stood the moon;
And like a downward smoke, the slender stream
Along the cliff to fall and pause and fall did seem.

A land of streams! some, like a downward smoke,   10
Slow-dropping veils of thinnest lawn, did go;
And some through wavering lights and shadows broke,
Rolling a slumbrous sheet of foam below.
They saw the gleaming river seaward flow
From the inner land; far off, three mountain-tops,   15
Three silent pinnacles of aged snow,
Stood sunset-flushed; and, dewed with showery drops,
Up-clomb the shadowy pine above the woven copse.

The charmèd sunset lingered low adown
In the red West; through mountain clefts the dale   20
Was seen far inland, and the yellow down
Bordered with palm, and many a winding vale
And meadow, set with slender galingale;
A land where all things always seemed the same!
And round about the keel with faces pale,   25
Dark faces pale against that rosy flame,
The mild-eyed melancholy Lotos-eaters came.

Branches they bore of that enchanted stem,
Laden with flower and fruit, whereof they gave
To each, but whoso did receive of them,   30
And taste, to him the gushing of the wave
Far far away did seem to mourn and rave
On alien shores; and if his fellow spake,
His voice was thin, as voices from the grave;
And deep-asleep he seemed, yet all awake,   35
And music in his ears his beating heart did make.

They sat them down upon the yellow sand
Between the sun and moon upon the shore;

And sweet it was to dream of Fatherland,
Of child, and wife, and slave; but evermore 40
Most weary seemed the sea, weary the oar,
Weary the wandering fields of barren foam.
Then someone said, "We will return no more";
And all at once they sang, "Our island home
Is far beyond the wave; we will no longer roam." 45
　　　　　　　　　　　　—Alfred, Lord Tennyson

27. *Lotos-eaters*: The lotos-berry is about the size of an olive and tastes like a fig or date, Herodotus tells us. Tennyson's lotos (and Homer's) may well be the Arabic Sidr, used in the preparation of a rich amber liquor drunk today on the island of Djerba. Cf. Louis Golding. *Goodbye to Ithaca* (London, 1955) pp. 89–93.

The situation described by Tennyson in the poem is that in which Ulysses and his men found themselves in Book 10 of *The Odyssey*: plagued by a nine-day storm and driven far off course, the Greeks came to the island of the lotos-eaters, a people who ate a fruit of forgetfulness that produced in them a state of enervation, lethargy, and listlessness similar to the state produced by marijuana. These folk innocently gave the fruit to a few of Ulysses' men, and it was only with great difficulty that Ulysses dragged them back to his ship and embarked for what proved to be the island of the cyclops.

QUESTIONS

1. What specific lines in the poem tell the story?
2. What images convey the dream-like effect of the lotos fruit?
3. What sounds does Tennyson use to develop verbally the dream-like quality of the world as seen through the eyes of the lotos-eaters, and the slow pace at which they react?
4. Closely analyze lines 27 and 45. Would you agree that, given Tennyson's meaning, the sounds of these lines work very well to echo their sense?
5. If "White Rabbit" is a head song, are "The Lotos-Eaters" and "Kubla Khan" head poems?

EUPHONY AND CACOPHONY

Sometimes lines that are not properly alliterative or assonant just sound pleasant (*euphonic*) or unpleasant (*cacophonic*), as in the case of Bob Dylan's "Mister Tambourine Man," one of the finest things he ever composed.

Mister Tambourine Man

Hey! Mister Tambourine Man play a song for me,
I'm not sleepy and there is no place I'm goin' to.
Hey! Mister Tambourine Man play a song for me
In the jingle jangle mornin' I'll come followin' you.

Though I know that evenin's empire has returned into sand,   5
Vanished from my hand,
Left me blindly here to stand but still not sleepin'!
My weariness amazes me, I'm branded on my feet.
I have no one to meet
And the ancient empty street's too dead for dreamin'.   10

Take me on a trip upon your magic swirlin' ship
My senses have been stripped,
My hands can't feel to grip
My toes too numb to step
Wait only for my boot heels to be wanderin'.   15
I'm ready to go anywhere, I'm ready for to fade
Into my own parade, cast your dancin' spell my way
I promise to go under it.

Though you might hear laughin' spinnin' swingin' madly across
     the sun
It's not aimed at anyone,   20
It's just escapin' on the run

And but for the sky there are no fences facin'
And if you hear vague traces of skippin' reels of rhyme
To your tambourine in time,
It's just a ragged clown behind   25
I wouldn't pay it any mind,
It's just a shadow you're seein' that he's chasin'.

Then take me disappearin' through the smoke rings of my mind
Down the foggy ruins of time
Far past the frozen leaves   30
The haunted, frightened trees
Out to the windy beach
Far from the twisted reach of crazy sorrow
Yes, to dance beneath the diamond sky with one hand wavin' free
Silhouetted by the sea,   35
Circled by the circus sands
With all memory and fate
Driven deep beneath the waves
Let me forget about today until tomorrow.

Hey! Mister Tambourine Man play a song for me,   40
I'm not sleepy and there is no place I'm going to.
Hey! Mister Tambourine Man play a song for me
In the jingle jangle mornin' I'll come followin' you.

                                        —*Bob Dylan*

The poem certainly makes extensive use of both alliteration and assonance, and "jingle-jangle" is *onomatopoetic:* the word has no meaning
other than the sound it makes. The title phrase represents a subtle combination of assonance and alliteration that goes far to account for the
way it haunts a listener. But some sections of the poem are impressive
in a way that cannot be adequately explained by alliteration or assonance. Look, for example, at lines 28–33. The passage begins with a
series of pleasant-sounding vowel and consonant combinations. Line 29
picks up and echoes in "ruins" the "r" of "rings" and the "u" of
"through." It echoes in "time" the "m" and "i" of "mind." Lines 30–31
use similar "f . . . e" patterns in "frozen leaves" and "frightened trees."
But the lines are pleasantly musical beyond these patterns, and the

music is appropriate to Dylan's description of the world into which he is escaping. When the poet looks back, however, he sees less pleasant things, and his language changes accordingly. From the attractive "smoke rings of my mind," the imagery of the poem turns to "the twisted reach of crazy sorrow"; the sound of the language becomes vaguely unpleasant and cacophonous in the consonants of "twisted reach" and "crazy." Sound mirrors sense in the change from euphony to cacophony, moving from the pleasant to the unpleasant.

After listening to Bob Dylan sing the song, make a careful line-by-line analysis of it and discuss the extent to which the poet is in full control of the sound of his verse, weaving complicated patterns of euphony and cacophony as the imagery of the song demands.

John Milton, whose ear was probably as fine as that of any poet who has ever lived, used euphonic and cacophonic effects often, but nowhere more effectively than in the passage of *Paradise Lost* (I, 876–83) that describes the opening of the gates of Hell to let Satan fly up to earth to tempt Adam and Eve. Notice how the euphony of the lines turns to cacophony as the gates swing open and the harmony of creation is disturbed by the discord of Hell.

> . . . then in the key-hole turns
> Th' intricate wards, and every Bolt and Bar
> Of massy iron or solid Rock with ease
> Unfast'ns: on a sudden op'n fly
> With impetuous recoil and jarring sound
> Th' infernal doors, and on their hinges grate
> Harsh Thunder, that the lowest bottom shook
> Of *Erebus*.

Erebus: according to Hesiod, the first child of Chaos; here a dark, vast envelope of space and matter.

Read "General William Booth Enters into Heaven" carefully, and comment on the various sounds used by Lindsay and their appropriateness to the sense of the poem. Then listen to a recording of the poet reading the poem. Lindsay addressed his poetry to an American audience of the late nineteenth century that had little use for verse, so to a certain extent he had to perform to get their attention. Is his too much a performance piece to be a good poem?

General William Booth Enters into Heaven

To be sung to the tune of "The Blood of the Lamb" with indicated instruments.

I

(Bass drum beaten loudly.)
Booth led boldly with his big bass drum—
(Are you washed in the blood of the Lamb?)
The Saints smiled gravely and they said: "He's come."
(Are you washed in the blood of the Lamb?)
Walking lepers followed, rank on rank,   5
Lurching bravos from the ditches dank,
Drabs from the alleyways and drug fiends pale—
Minds still passion-ridden, soul-powers frail:—
Vermin-eaten saints with moldy breath,
Unwashed legions with the ways of Death—   10
(Are you washed in the blood of the Lamb?)

(Banjos.)
Every slum had sent its half-a-score
The round world over. (Booth had groaned for more.)
Every banner that the wide world flies
Bloomed with glory and transcendent dyes.   15
Big-voiced lasses made their banjos bang;
Tranced, fanatical they shrieked and sang:—
"Are you washed in the blood of the Lamb?"
Hallelujah! It was queer to see
Bull-necked convicts with that land make free.   20
Loons with trumpets blowed a blare, blare, blare
On, on upward thro' the golden air!
(Are you washed in the blood of the Lamb?)

2

(Bass drum slower and softer.)
Booth died blind and still by faith he trod,
Eyes still dazzled by the ways of God.   25

Booth led boldly, and he looked the chief,
Eagle countenance in sharp relief,
Beard a-flying, air of high command
Unabated in that holy land.

    (*Sweet flute music.*)
Jesus came from out the court-house door,   30
Stretched his hands above the passing poor.
Booth saw not, but led his queer ones there
Round and round the mighty court-house square.
Then, in an instant all that blear review
Marched on spotless, clad in raiment new.   35
The lame were straightened, withered limbs uncurled
And blind eyes opened on a new, sweet world.

    (*Bass drum louder.*)
Drabs and vixens in a flash made whole!
Gone was the weasel-head, the snout, the jowl!
Sages and sibyls now, and athletes clean,   40
Rulers of empires, and of forests green!

    (*Grand chorus of all instruments. Tambourines to the
    foreground.*)
The hosts were sandalled, and their wings were fire!
(Are you washed in the blood of the Lamb?)
But their noise played havoc with the angel-choir.
(Are you washed in the blood of the Lamb?)   45
Oh, shout Salvation! It was good to see
Kings and Princes by the Lamb set free.
The banjos rattled and the tambourines
Jing-jing-jingled in the hands of Queens.

    (*Reverently sung, no instruments.*)
And when Booth halted by the curb for prayer   50
He saw his Master thro' the flag-filled air.
Christ came gently with a robe and crown
For Booth the soldier, while the throng knelt down.
He saw King Jesus. They were face to face,

And he knelt a-weeping in that holy place.   55
Are you washed in the blood of the Lamb?

—Vachel Lindsay

1. *General William Booth*: founder of the Salvation Army. 2. *washed in the blood of the Lamb*: baptized a Christian. 6. *bravos*: assassins, murderers. 7. *drabs*: whores. 40. *sibyls*: prophetesses.

KINESTHESIA

Assonance, alliteration, euphony, and cacophony are all ways in which the sounds of words affect our ears; but when we read poetry aloud ourselves, the sound values influence us in another way. As we say words—any words—the muscles of our mouth and tongue and diaphram tense and relax in different places. In some words the feeling of those tensed and relaxed muscles, our sense of *kinesthesia,* contributes to the connotative meaning of the words when we say them. The word "sneer," for example, causes the muscles of our face to tense in a manner that actually produces a sneer. We are aware of this sneer because of our sense of kinesthesia, and the feeling of the word actually contributes to its meaning. A similar case could be made for the word "explosion"; the sudden expiration of breath on the "o" sound following the "pl" amounts to an explosion of breath reproducing the sense of the word. We feel this explosion when we say the word, and a line like "The eastern world, it is explodin'" may be said to have kinesthetic effect.

Such effects are not much discussed by critics of poetry, although they would go far to explain the success of certain individual lines. Read the last line of Tennyson's "The Eagle" again: "And like a thunderball he falls." Say it over a few times, and notice the position of your tongue as you proceed through the accented vowels "i," "u," and "a." If necessary, sound the vowels alone, one after the other; put your finger between your teeth and feel the position of your tongue. Quite clearly it falls from a place directly below the front roof of the mouth to the back bottom of the throat. As we read the line, our sense of kinesthesia tells us that our tongue is falling, and subconsciously the motion of our tongue reinforces the sense of the line in a way that makes it particularly memorable.

Read the lines following, again from Milton's *Paradise Lost* (I, 44–47), in which the poet describes the fall of Satan and his company from heaven:

> . . . Him the Almighty Power
> Hurl'd headlong flaming from th' Ethereal Sky
> With hideous ruin and combustion down
> To bottomless perdition. . . .

The sentence is long enough to begin with, but Milton fills it with "h" sounds that take more breath than most to say. The result is that by the time we reach the end of the sentence, we—like Satan and company who, Milton tells us, have been falling for nine days—are pretty much out of breath. We feel in our lungs something that enhances the meaning of the lines. It is also possible that the rhythm of these lines enhances their effect: the staggering blow of Christ is felt in the accent on "Him," achieved by distorting the syntax of the sentence, and is repeated again in the three accented syllables of "Hurl'd headlong flaming." The angels fall for a couple of lines, then strike the bottom of hell with a thud and bounce on the word "perdition."

These are ways in which the feeling of a word as one reads it actually parallels sense. It might be that there are kinesthetic patterns to poetry just as there are patterns of meaning and sound. Perhaps the appeal of some lines is to be explained by the fact that they do actually "feel so groovy to say." "Mister Tambourine Man" may be just such a phrase, as may be the following piece, which is apparently an attempt to reproduce kinesthetically on the lips what a leaky water faucet must feel:

Water Faucet

Smooothooooze
Dribble
Dribbledribble

Drop.

—anonymous

Few poets rely heavily on kinesthetic effects, however, at least consciously, and few critics even bother to consider them. Either they are too subtle to be discussed at any length, or they are relatively unimportant in most poetry.

RHYME

More than any other poetic device, rhyme is associated by most people with poetry—so much so that they are frequently annoyed by poetry that does not rhyme, and in writing their own verse they are willing to engage in virtually any distortion of rhythm or normal English syntax for the sake of a rhyme. In terms of twisted word order, meaningless imagery, and awkward metrical patterns, rhyme is responsible for more bad poetry than any other poetic device—which may account for the tendency of modern poets to avoid it entirely. Yet rhyme was a late development in English versification, and poetry can and does exist very well without it. Indeed, one could intelligently argue that rhyme is essentially foreign to English verse; as we have noted, Old English poetry did not rhyme at all. The device of rhyme was introduced from the French (originally from the Latin), where it was used for ornamentation and where the highly inflected nature of the language made rhyme an easy matter. Because inflectional endings rhyme, Latin poetry that rhymed not only at the end of a line, but two, three, or even four places in the middle of lines could be written—and was. English is not so inflected, however, and rhymes are more difficult. The English poet, unless he is incredibly facile with words, has two choices: he may engage in the distortions we mentioned earlier for the sake of perfect rhymes, or he may use *half rhymes* or *slant rhymes*—"over" and "lover," for example—or *eye rhymes*—"through" and "enough" or "watch" and "catch." Although the poet sometimes uses half rhymes to avoid the typewriter bells that frequently ring at the end of perfectly rhymed lines, or for some other poetic effect, the wealth of imperfect rhyme in English poetry points up the fact that finding an exact rhyme that fits a line's sense without distorting its syntax is not as easy as it sometimes appears. The other side of the coin, of course, is that imperfect rhyme is not nearly so noticeable (or obtrusive) as it first appears. It is used extensively in hymns and in songs, where it slips by without much objection.

Subterranean Homesick Blues

Johnny's in the basement
mixing up the medicine;
I'm on the pavement
thinking about the government.
The man in the trench coat,   5
badge out, laid off,
says he's got a bad cough;
wants to get it paid off.
Look out, kid—
it's somethin' you did;—   10
God knows when—
but you're doin' it again!
You better duck down the alley-way
lookin' for a new friend;
the man in the coon-skin cap   15
by the big pen
wants eleven dollar bills:
You only got ten.

Maggie comes fleet foot
Face full of black soot   20
Talkin' at the heat put
Plants in the bed but
The phone's tapped any-way
Maggie says that many say
They must bust in early May   25
Orders from the D. A.
Look out kid
Don't matter what you did
Walk on your tip toes
Don't try "No Doz"   30
Better stay away from those
that carry around a fire hose

Keep a clean nose
Watch the plain clothes
You don't need a weather man   35
To know which way the wind blows.

Get sick, get well
Hang around a ink well
Ring bell, hard to tell
If anything is goin' to sell   40
Try hard, get barred
Get back, write braille
Get jailed, jump bail
Join the army if you fail.
Look out kid, you're gonna get hit   45
But users, cheaters
Six time losers
Hang around the theatres
Girl by the whirlpool
Lookin' for a new fool   50
Don't follow leaders
Watch the parkin' meters.

Ah get born, keep warm
Short pants, romance, learn to dance
Get dressed, get blessed   55
Try to be a success
Please her, please him, buy gifts
Don't steal, don't lift
Twenty years of schoolin'
And they put you on the day shift.   60
Look out kid they keep it all hid
Better jump down a manhole
Light yourself a candle, don't wear sandals
Try to avoid the scandals
Don't wanna be a bum   65
You better chew gum
The pump don't work
'Cause the vandals took the handles.

                                                        —*Bob Dylan*

The pattern of rhymes in this poem is very rough, although rhymes themselves are plentiful. At the beginning of the second stanza, Dylan rhymes "foot," "soot," and "put," then half-rhymes "but." Those four rhymes are followed by four more: "way," "say," "May," and "A." It would appear that the stanzas follow an *a a a a b b b b* pattern, at least for the initial eight lines. But the first stanza does nothing of the sort: even if we allow the poet to rhyme "medicine" and "basement," which really do not sound much alike, the pattern for that stanza is obviously *a a a a b c c c*. The last stanza begins something like this: *a b c c d d*, although the first four lines of that stanza contain extensive internal rhyme. Clearly the poet is more interested in piling up rhymes of various kinds than he is in being regular in his usage. In English poets of the past—notably John Skelton—such an arrangement was considered reprehensible, but in this poem the irregular profusion is largely responsible for what Dylan, with his pronunciation, would call its "suckcess." Just why?

Given another subject and another poem—say an elegy on the death of a friend—this irregular incessant rhyme would quite literally destroy the poem. But Dylan is not writing an elegy. "Subterranean Homesick Blues" is not about death, unless it's the death of spirit that accompanies confusion and alienation; it is about life in the twentieth century as experienced by a young man originally from Minnesota who later migrated to New York. Dylan is creating a kaleidoscopic view of life in modern America, and the dangers and pitfalls and exploitations that confront a kid trying to grow up in it. In a very few lines of idiomatic poetry he manages to say just about everything that Paul Goodman said a few years ago in his widely popular book, *Growing Up Absurd*: youth is exploited economically, socially, educationally; it is put down, bought off, and most of all bribed-threatened-cajoled into staying in line. Such an existence is depressing, infuriating, but most of all confusing, because kids get it from all sides at once. It is the element of confusion that Dylan manages to capture so well in his driving tempo and jangling rhymes, which complement each other. The rhymes of the poem are functional, something beyond pattern and ornamentation. Sense is paralleled by sound in the poem.

Look again at the rhymes of "Subterranean Homesick Blues." Some are one-syllable, or *masculine* rhymes, like "pool" and "fool." Others, like "laid off" and "paid off," are two-syllable, or *feminine* rhymes. (The names probably derive from the old belief that odd numbers were mas-

culine and even numbers feminine.) But the difference between the
two is more than the difference between one and two syllables. Feminine
rhyme seems to have an inherent lightness to it that is absent from
masculine rhyme. Perhaps doubling the rhyme quadruples the effect of
the rhyme. Thus, "vandals took the handles" is light although not
necessarily comic. Poems that use triple rhyme are usually downright
funny, as these couplets from Byron's *Don Juan* should demonstrate.

> For instance—passion in a lover's glorious,
> But in a husband is pronounced uxorious.

> He learn'd the arts of riding, fencing, gunnery,
> And how to scale a fortress—or a nunnery.

> But—oh! ye lords of ladies intellectual,
> Inform us truly, have they not hen-peck'd you all?

Here is a poem by a Southern poet of the last century about a small
river in northeastern Georgia. It makes extensive use of alliteration, assonance and rhyme, in an attempt to create a sound equivalent to that
of the river at various stages of its length. Although in the process of
painting this sound picture it makes some stunningly stupid statements
—"And flee from folly on every side," or "The hickory told me manifold/
Fair tales of shade . . ."—the poet is relatively successful in his attempt.
What uses of rhyme, assonance, and alliteration contribute to the poem?
To what extent should we be willing to accommodate inadequacies of
sense for the sake of sound effects?

Song of the Chattahoochee

> Out of the hills of Habersham,
>   Down the valleys of Hall,
> I hurry amain to reach the plain,
> Run the rapid and leap the fall,
> Split at the rock and together again,   5
> Accept my bed, or narrow or wide,
> And flee from folly on every side
> With a lover's pain to attain the plain
>   Far from the hills of Habersham,
>   Far from the valleys of Hall.   10

All down the hills of Habersham,
  All through the valleys of Hall,
The rushes cried *Abide, abide,*
The willful waterweeds held me thrall,
The laving laurel turned my tide,   15
The ferns and the fondling grass said *Stay,*
The dewberry dipped for to work delay,
And the little reeds sighed *Abide, abide,*
  Here in the hills of Habersham,
  Here in the valleys of Hall.   20

High o'er the hills of Habersham,
  Veiling the valleys of Hall,
The hickory told me manifold
Fair tales of shade, the poplar tall
Wrought me her shadowy self to hold,   25
The chestnut, the oak, the walnut, the pine,
Overleaning, with flickering meaning and sign,
Said, *Pass not, so cold, these manifold*
  Deep shades of the hills of Habersham,
  These glades in the valleys of Hall.   30

And oft in the hills of Habersham,
  And oft in the valleys of Hall,
The white quartz shone, and the smooth brook-stone
Did bar me of passage with friendly brawl,
And many a luminous jewel lone   35
—Crystals clear or a-cloud with mist,
Ruby, garnet and amethyst—
Made lures with the lights of streaming stone
  In the clefts of the hills of Habersham,
  In the beds of the valleys of Hall.   40

But oh, not the hills of Habersham,
  And oh, not the valleys of Hall
Avail: I am fain for to water the plain.
Downward the voices of Duty call—
Downward, to toil and be mixed with the main,   45
The dry fields burn, and the mills are to turn,

And a myriad flowers mortally yearn,
And the lordly main from beyond the plain
  Calls o'er the hills of Habersham,
  Calls through the valleys of Hall.   50

                          —Sidney Lanier

1. *Habersham*: a county in northeastern Georgia. 2. *Hall*: a county slightly southwest of Habersham.

In scansion of English poetry, rhyme scheme is designated by assigning each rhyme sound with a letter, using an *x* for lines that are obviously unrhymed. The last stanza of "Song of the Chattahoochee" would be designated *a b c b c d d c a b*, a very complicated stanzaic pattern. Four-line stanzas have a tendency to rhyme in an *a b a b* pattern; long poems tend toward *a a b b c c d d e e f f*, or couplet, arrangement. Triplets, as one would suspect, consist of three similar rhymes in a row; they usually appear among a series of couplets to break the monotony. There is no commonly used method of indicating internal rhymes, or for distinguishing half and slant rhymes from perfect rhyme. Look at some of the other poems in this book and practice designating the rhyme scheme and—more important—discussing the appropriateness of the rhyme scheme to the poem's theme. Is it significant, for example, that Frost's "Design" uses a very tight rhyme pattern?

METER AND RHYTHM

Rhyme designates one essential characteristic of a stanzaic pattern; the other characteristic is *meter,* or *rhythm,* and it is high time we turned our attention to that important subject. Rhythm is one quality all poetry shares—even "free verse," which tends to be less regular than most poetry in most respects. All language has a rhythm of a sort: some syllables fall easily off the lips, others take longer to say; some syllables receive an accent, others simply do not; some sequences of letters move faster and louder than others. Conversational English prose, however, usually ignores the possibilities for patterning this natural rhythm—except especially poetic prose (such as that of Thomas Wolfe) or highly rhetorical speech (such as that of a revival sermon)—but poetry consistently imposes some pattern, more or less exact depending on the purposes of the poet, on the language it uses.

There are any number of theoretical explanations for rhythm in poetry, none of them particularly satisfactory. According to one, the poet's insight acts to impose order on raw experience: given an apparently capricious and disordered world, the poet draws from everyday experiences a series of insights, interrelationships, and patterns that he communicates to his audience in a poem. Art, then, is experience that has been ordered by the artist; the poet as artist imposes the pattern of order on the experience communicated in his poem. And this pattern is embodied not only in the cognitive meaning of the words, but—more important—in the pattern of the rhythm of the language he uses. The major defects of this theory are two: first, rhythm was apparent in poetry long before poets *consciously* viewed their function in terms of ordering experience, which would make the explanation somewhat after the fact; second, it is obvious to even the most casual observer that too much order-in-terms-of-patterned language becomes monotonous, and poets frequently achieve some of their most impressive effects with the irregularities of their rhythms, with the disorder of their order. The two sides of the issue may be best examined in Morse Peckham's *Man's Rage for Chaos* (Chilton, 1965).

Another explanation holds that order *is* inherent in nature and experience, and that the poet is reproducing in his art a rhythmic regularity he sees and feels in the natural world around him. This naturalist-biological explanation sees rhythm in poetry as a verbal correlative of the natural rhythm exemplified by the movement of the planets, the human heartbeat, the turning of the seasons. Such a view of man, his nature, and his love of poetry elevates verse to the highest form of literary expression; it is most sensitive to man's natural state and his innate desires. Like the first explanation, however, it suggests falsely that the poetry that is most rhythmical would naturally be the poetry that pleases most. The fact of the matter is that the regularity of an amplified human heartbeat would either put a man to sleep or drive him insane in a matter of days.

Perhaps the real explanation of rhythm in poetry is historical, profoundly unphilosophical, and quite simple: as we have noted before, in early societies poetry was sung, or at least accompanied by rhythmic musical instruments while being chanted. Music has a rhythm of its own—a very regular rhythm in what we loosely call classical music, a somewhat looser rhythm in jazz pieces and chants. The rhythm of the music was naturally transferred to the words of the lyric. Many medieval and French poems owe their forms to the musical patterns of the songs to which they were sung. And a glance at any modern rock song shows how musical accompaniment influences the rhythm of the language of a poem. Of course, words were written down long before music, and lyrics became divorced from their accompaniment. But poetry retained the rhythm of the music to which it was first set.

Whatever the reason for the existence of meter, the fact is that there is considerable rhythm in poetry, rhythm that forms an important part of the poet's use of words as sounds. What makes rhythm a complicated subject to discuss is first, that it requires a sensitivity to language that some people simply don't seem to have in order to identify the rhythm of a line or two of poetry, and second, that there are a number of different ways of measuring rhythm. The Japanese *haiku* counts syllables: five in the first line, seven in the second, five in the third. Most scholars agree that the earliest English poetry counted accented syllables only: two to the half line, four to the full line, with accented syllables bound together by assonance and alliteration. Classical poets *scanned* (that is, measured) poetry *quantitatively*: that is, on the basis of how long it took to say each syllable. Medieval poets, whose Latin was not all it should have been, misunderstood the classical treatises and thought scansion was *qualitative*: that is, based on accentual patterns. They introduced into western literature the kind of qualitative scansion that still forms the basis for most English verse. (If you take the time to think about it, you will notice that usually a syllable that is long qualitatively is also long quantitatively, so their mistake is perhaps understandable.) Thus it is that most discussions of poetry in English identify pattern on the basis of accented and unaccented syllables, and it is with a discussion of this kind of scansion that we begin an examination of rhythm.

Qualitative scansion divides all syllables into two basic types, accented and unaccented, although this division may be something of a fiction, since accent is frequently a relative matter, and normally unaccented syllables may be given some kind of stress within a given phrase. The approach is simple, however, and "works" for most poetry. Hence, we would scan a line of English prose as follows:

$$\text{/ } \cup \cup \text{ / } \cup \text{/} \cup \text{/ } \cup \text{ / } \cup \text{/}$$

Hence, we would scan a line of English prose as follows.
An accented syllable, as is obvious, is designated with a /; an unaccented syllable is designated with a ∪. Out of the possible combinations of *accented* and *unaccented* syllables (or *longs* and *shorts,* as they are frequently called), any variety of units or poetic feet can be constructed. The most popular of these are the following:

IAMB (∪/): I think that I shall nev er see

ANAPEST (∪∪/): For I'm wear y with hunt in' and fain
would lay down.

TROCHEE (/∪): Once u pon a midnight dreary

DACTYL (/∪∪): Half a league, half a league half a league
onward

These feet account for about 95 per cent of all English feet, although occasionally in lines of mainly iamb*ic* or trocha*ic* or anapes*tic* or dactyl*ic* feet a few others occur:

SPONDEE (//): someday

AMPHIBRACH (∪/∪): condition

AMPHIMACHER (/∪/): element

PYRRHUS (∪∪): Tomor row and tomor row and tomorrow

These feet are exceptional (probably designed to cover breakdowns in the qualitative scansion system); there is no such thing as a spond*aic* line or a phyrr*ic* line.

Lines of qualitatively scanned poetry are designated by an adjective describing the predominant foot followed by a noun indicating the number of feet in the line. For example, iambic pentameter is a line containing five iambic feet. The Greek prefixes are used to create the metrical designation: MONOMETER (one foot), DIMETER (two feet),

TRIMETER (three feet), TETRAMETER (four feet), PENTAMETER (five feet), HEXAMETER (six feet), HEPTAMETER (seven feet). Monometer and dimeter are uncommon. Longer lines, like larger molecules, are unstable and tend to dissociate: the ballad stanza is essentially a heptameter couplet broken into four instead of two lines, with four, three, four, three feet in each line.

One need not look far or long before discovering the defects of qualitative scansion. The most obvious is that there are some lines like "Tomorrow and tomorrow and tomorrow" (probably intended as iambic pentameter) that do not fit well into the system; others contain large numbers of imperfect or defective feet—feet with more or fewer short syllables than they should have. Another problem is the tendency of poets to invert feet, especially at the beginning of poems, thereby confusing the pattern.

> / ∪ ∪ / ∪ / ∪ /
> Mark but this flea, and mark in this
>
> > (Donne, "The Flea")
>
> / ∪ ∪ / ∪ / ∪ / ∪ /
> Something there is that does not love a wall
>
> > (Frost, "Mending Wall")

In fact, the first stanza of any poem is notoriously unreliable as a guide to its metrical pattern.

In some instances punctuation or rhetorical considerations give an accent to a syllable that would not receive one according to an abstract metrical pattern.

> // / ∪ ∪ /
> O rose, thou art sick.

The syllable "O" picks up a secondary accent (as indicated) because of the rhetoric of the apostrophe, whereas normally it would be short. Or an accent may be said to hover somewhere around the two syllables "O rose," in which case it is marked as indicated. Neither scansion is very precise.

And finally, there are lines that simply resist the scansion a qualitative system would impose on them, like the third line of this stanza from Samuel Johnson's "On the Death of Mr. Robert Levet."

> Well tried through many a varying year,
>   See Levet to the grave descend,
> Officious, innocent, sincere,
>   Of every friendless name the friend.

The poem is written in iambic tetrameter, but the third line clearly breaks into a three-foot unit composed of one amphibrach, one dactyl, and one iamb:

$$\cup \;\; / \;\; \cup \qquad / \;\; \cup \;\; \cup \qquad \cup \;\; /$$
Officious, innocent, sincere,

Faced with these difficulties, modern methods of metrical analysis have become either incredibly complicated or very simple. Hopkins created for himself a system of poetics which is for all practical purposes unintelligible; Eliot has been accused of writing in something resembling simple Early English four-stress verse.

What is especially problematical about reducing lines to abstract patterns of /'s and ∪'s, however, is that such a system is inadequate; rhythm is more than meter, more than qualitative values. Patterns of qualitative scansion have no means for marking pauses within a line, the pause that usually comes somewhere toward the middle of any long line of verse (the *caesura*), or quantitative aspects of the words themselves. Consider the refrain line from Bob Dylan's song, "Sad-Eyed Lady of the Lowlands." Metrically, the line would probably scan

$$/ \;\;\; \cup \;\; / \;\; \cup \;\; / \;\; \cup \;\; / \;\; \cup$$
Sad-eyed lady of the lowlands.

Given Dylan's pronunciation, it would scan

$$/ \;\;\; / \;\; / \;\; \cup \;\; \cup \;\; \cup \;\; / \;\; /$$
Sad-eyed lady of the lowlands.

But neither scansion indicates what makes the line most effective: its phrasing, the changes in the tempo, the drawing out of the vowel sounds in "sad" and "eyed" and "lady" and "low" with the quickening of the phrase "of the" to provide a contrast.

Or consider the line from "Dover Beach" that describes the breaking of successive waves on the beach: "Begin, and cease, and then again begin." The metrics would be simple iambic pentameter. The commas after "begin" and "cease," however, force pauses at these points, and the last three feet are very regular. There is a sharp pause between the "e" of "cease" and the "a" of "and." The rhythm of the line looks something like this:

Begin, and cease, and then again begin,

The sound here parallels the sense because of the rhythm. As the waves break and cease, the sound ceases; when the waves begin again, the sound begins its regular pulse again. It is the rhythm, not the meter of the poem, that makes the line impressive. And traditional systems of scansion are incapable of indicating this rhythm.

The length of time it takes to say a syllable, the phrasing of a line, the caesural pause, the variety of tempo and accent: all of these are aspects of rhythm about which accentual scansion tells us little. Accentual terminology does allow us to say some things about a poet's use of rhythm. We might say that anapestic tetrameter has a galloping rhythm that would make it inappropriate for a religious meditation. But when we want to discuss the finer points of a poet's use of rhythm and sound patterns, we must move beyond mere accentual considerations to a careful examination of all aspects of rhythm. This is especially true of modern poetry, which is less concerned with forcing words to fit accentual patterns than with the creation of appropriate rhythmic effects in what is largely a free verse.

Read Don L. Lee's poem and, if possible, listen to the poet himself reading it. Does the poem scan accentually at all? Is the rhythm patterned in any way? How does the poet change rhythm and tempo to suit his mood? Is there any way you could indicate all the variations the poet manages in rhythm, tempo, accent, and quantity?

But He Was Cool

or: he even stopped for green lights

super-cool
ultrablack
a tan/purple
had a beautiful shade.

he had a double-natural   5
that wd put the sisters to shame.
his dashikis were tailor made
& his beads were imported sea shells
  (from some blk/country i never heard of)
he was triple-hip.   10

his tikis were hand carved
out of ivory
& came express from the motherland.
he would greet u in swahili
& say good-by in yoruba.   15
wooooooooooooo-jim he bes so cool & ill tel li gent
   cool-cool is so cool he was un-cooled by
     other niggers' cool
   cool-cool ultracool was bop-cool/ice box
     cool so cool cold cool   20
   his wine didn't have to be cooled, him was
     air conditioned cool
   cool-cool/real cool made me cool—now
     ain't that cool
   cool-cool so cool him nick-named refrigerator.   25

cool-cool so cool
he didn't know,
after detroit, newark, chicago &c.,
we had to hip
   cool-cool/ super-cool/ real cool   30
  that
to be black
is
to be
very-hot.   35
          —*Don L. Lee*

In the past two chapters we have been discussing poetry in terms
of words as meanings and words as sounds, developing both a facility
in the sensitive reading of poetry and a familiarity with the critical
terminology useful in talking intelligently and fluently about it. By

now you should be able to identify similes and metaphors in a poem, point out patterns of imagery, evaluate allusions, and treat both the sound of a poem and the relationship between sound and sense. Insofar as these matters are concerned, you will be left largely on your own for the rest of this text, perhaps for the remainder of your experience with poetry—for what concerns us in the rest of this book are matters quite different: generic classifications, the special problems posed by longer poems or groups of poems, and the possibilities of making value judgments about poetry. It might be a good idea, therefore, for you to review the work of the last two chapters and bring together as much of what you have learned about poetry as sound and sense in the reading, analysis, and discussion of this poem by Dylan Thomas.

Fern Hill

Now as I was young and easy under the apple boughs
About the lilting house and happy as the grass was green,
    The night above the dingle starry,
        Time let me hail and climb
    Golden in the heydays of his eyes,   5
And honored among wagons I was prince of the apple towns
And once below a time I lordly had the trees and leaves
        Trail with daisies and barley
    Down the rivers of the windfall light.

And as I was green and carefree, famous among the barns   10
About the happy yard and singing as the farm was home,
    In the sun that is young once only,
        Time let me play and be
    Golden in the mercy of his means,
And green and golden I was huntsman and herdsman, the calves   15
Sang to my horn, the foxes on the hills barked clear and cold,
        And the sabbath rang slowly
    In the pebbles of the holy streams.

All the sun long it was running, it was lovely, the hay
Fields high as the house, the tunes from the chimneys, it was air   20
    And playing, lovely and watery
        And fire green as grass.

And nightly under the simple stars
As I rode to sleep the owls were bearing the farm away,
All the moon long I heard, blessed among stables, the nightjars   25
    Flying with the ricks, and the horses
        Flashing into the dark.

And then to awake, and the farm, like a wanderer white
With the dew, come back, the cock on his shoulder: it was all
    Shining, it was Adam and maiden,   30
        The sky gathered again
    And the sun grew round that very day.
So it must have been after the birth of the simple light
In the first, spinning place, the spellbound horses walking warm
    Out of the whinnying green stable   35
        On to the fields of praise.

And honored among foxes and pheasants by the gay house
Under the new made clouds and happy as the heart was long,
    In the sun born over and over,
        I ran my heedless ways,   40
    My wishes raced through the house high hay
And nothing I cared, at my sky blue trades, that time allows
In all his tuneful turning so few and such morning songs
    Before the children green and golden
        Follow him out of grace,   45

Nothing I cared, in the lamb white days, that time would take me
Up to the swallow thronged loft by the shadow of my hand,
    In the moon that is always rising,
        Not that riding to sleep
    I should hear him fly with the high fields   50
And wake to the farm forever fled from the childless land.
Oh as I was young and easy in the mercy of his means,
        Time held me green and dying
    Though I sang in my chains like the sea.

                        —*Dylan Thomas*

   2. *lilting*: rhythmic, swinging. 3. *dingle*: a deep, narrow cleft between two
hills. 25. *nightjars*: nocturnal European birds. 26. *ricks*: stacks of hay or straw.

4
Genres

The literary term used to designate the class or subclass of literature into which a particular work falls is *genre*. Poetry is a generic term, as are prose and drama; but so too are lyric and epic (kinds of poetry), comedy and tragedy (kinds of drama), and novel, short story, and novella (kinds of fiction). On a still finer scale, epic poetry may be classified into folk epic, literary epic, romance, or Breton Lay; lyric poetry into ballad, ode, sonnet, dramatic monologue, complaint, or any one of a host of other classifications. Genre, then, is a loosely used term, and may designate a kind of literature in either a broad or a narrow sense.

The idea of literary genres is an old one, a leftover from critical thought of the pre-Romantic period. It presupposes a fixed number of types of literature, each with its own formal characteristics, style, and appropriate subject matter. When the poet writes he selects a particular form and uses the style, language, stanzaic patterns, subject, and other conventions appropriate to it. A good poet is one who is proficient in all traditional genres. The type of mentality that reads Aristotle's definition of tragedy and then sets it up as the rule by which all tragedies must be written is the same mentality responsible for the notion of literary genres. But precisely *because* the majority of English poets have shared this idea of generic classifications, and have written their poems with the conventions of various genres in mind, it is useful to know something of the forms, the language, and the stanzaic requirements of a few of the more popular genres. A knowledge of the conventions of the literary ballad will help us explain how a bad ballad, say Housman's "The True Lover," came to be bad: the poet was mechanically following conventions that he might perhaps have better ignored. Certainly a knowledge of the requirements of various genres helps explain why some poems that seem to be nothing more than trite convention came into being. And if we ourselves believe in this method of composition, an awareness of the conventions of literary genres might help us write some poetry of our own.

But in the twentieth century few people really hold a rigid generic attitude toward poetry. Most modern poets look upon genres as forms within which they may be as innovative as they like, as requirements that they can ignore almost at will. Many poets are willing to make up genres of their own, compose poems that cross genres or do not fit any genre, or ignore conventions to the point where such generic designations become almost (but not quite) meaningless. On the whole, this is probably a saner attitude than viewing generic requirements as rules demanding strict conformity. Like most terms in English, genres tend to be more descriptive than prescriptive; like Aristotle's definition of tragedy, genres describe an extant body of work rather than some airy theoretical conception in the mind of the critic that poets must thenceforth follow. As the body of works described grows, the critic must change his definition in order to account for developments in the genre he describes. If Aristotle were writing about tragedy in the 1970's, it is doubtful that he would have written anything like what he wrote in 350 B.C.; generic terms defined in the eighteenth or nineteenth centuries need redefinition in terms of developments in poetry during the twentieth century. Just because Paul Simon's "The Boxer" does not conform to a nineteenth-century definition of dramatic monologues does not prevent it from being a dramatic monologue in the twentieth century, and *Death of a Salesman* cannot be rejected as tragedy just because it does not conform to Aristotle's dictum about nobility of characters.

There are dozens of genres used regularly by English poets today, and dozens more used by poets of the past. At various points in literary history some genres have experienced a greater popularity than others, and fads come and go. The dream vision, for example, very popular in the Middle Ages, nearly disappeared—but now it appears to have regained a considerable degree of popularity, especially in the poetry of rock ("The Strangest Dream," "I Dreamed I Saw St. Augustine," "I dreamed I saw Joe Hill last night"). A survey of all generic types is beyond the scope of this text, but some genres are more important than others because of the influence they now exert on poets and composers. In the following section we will investigate the conventions of half-a-dozen or so genres in an attempt to see how those conventions can function as a framework within which to develop intelligent literary criticism and within which a poet can innovate creatively.

BALLADS

The term *ballad* may be used to refer either to a type of narrative poem or to a stanzaic pattern. Paradoxically, ballads in the narrative sense are not ipso facto ballads in the stanzaic sense, and vice versa. The ballad stanza is in effect an iambic heptameter couplet dissociated into four lines of alternating tetrameter and trimeter, rhymed *x a x a*. Frequently the rhyme is only approximate, and just as frequently the meter is only roughly iambic. In many cases the last line is a refrain or involves some form of variation or incremental repetition. The first stanza of "Barbara Allan" will illustrate a typical ballad stanza.

$$\smile \smile / \smile \smile / \smile / \smile / \smile \smile /$$
It was in and about the Martinmas time,
$$\smile \smile / \smile / \smile / \smile / \smile$$
When the green leaves were a falling,
$$\smile \smile / \smile / \smile \smile / \smile / \smile$$
That Sir John Graeme in the west country
$$\smile \smile / \smile / \smile \smile / \smile$$
Fell in love with Barbara Allan.

In the broad generic sense, ballad refers to any poem composed for singing or recitation and primarily concerned with the narration of one dramatic, concrete episode. In a narrower sense, ballad refers to compositions of folk origins, popular in England, America, Australia, and especially along the Scottish border during the latter Middle Ages, sung by wandering minstrels (or—in the sixteenth century—published on large single sheets of paper called *broadsides*), dealing with a wide range of social and political issues, usually of a gloomy or unfortunate nature. Apart from being dramatic and concrete narratives, ballads have several distinctive traits: sketchy characterization, frequent use of dialogue, understatement, repetition, abrupt transition, oversimplification of plot and character, and a general preference for themes of love, death, and domestic tragedy. In the film *Tom Jones,* for example, a ballad singer passes by Tom as he awaits his forthcoming hanging, singing a ballad about "poor Tommy." In its subject, stanzaic pattern, composition, performance, and tone this ballad is typical. Ballads can and have migrated from area to area, even from continent to continent, and after some modification been recorded as virtually new poems. Numerous versions, all from various times and geographies, exist of most popular ballads, including "Barbara Allan" and "Lord Randall."

The literary ballad is to the folk ballad what the literary epic is to the folk epic: an imitation to be read, not sung, written by a "professional" poet rather than an unlettered bard. Literary ballads usually use the folk ballad stanza as well as the other conventions of the folk ballad, but for some reason literary ballads invariably prove inferior to their folk counterparts. They lack the qualities of sparseness, spontaneity, authenticity, and eerie otherworldliness that mark good folk ballads. Housman's "The True Lover" almost seems a parody instead of a sincere attempt at immitation, and Keats' "Belle Dame Sans Merci" is simply too literary.

The following selection contains both folk and literary ballads in both the ballad and other stanzas, dating from the late medieval period to the twentieth century, on a wide assortment of lords, lovers, and labor leaders. Construct the details of the episode with which each poet is dealing, explore the possibilities left open by the sparseness of detail and explanation, and form some evaluation of the poem's success. Ballads, perhaps more than any other form of poetry, should be heard as well as read, for when read their defects are more apparent and their virtues less obvious than when they are heard.

The House of the Rising Sun

There is a house in New Orleans,
They call the Rising Sun.
It has been the ruin of many a poor girl,
And me, oh Lord, was one.

If I had listened to what mama said,   5
I'd be at home today.

But being so young and foolish, poor girl,
Let a gambler lead me astray.

My mother is a tailor,
She sews those new blue jeans.   10
My sweetheart is a drunkard, Lord,
Down in New Orleans.

The only thing a drunkard needs
Is a suitcase and a trunk.
The only time he's satisfied   15
Is when he's on a drunk.

He'll fill his glasses to the brim,
He passes them around,
And the only pleasure he gets out of life
Is bumming from town to town.   20

Go tell my baby sister,
Never do like I have done.
To shun that house in New Orleans
They call The Rising Sun.

It's one foot on the platform,   25
And the other one on the train.
I'm going back to New Orleans
To wear the ball and chain.

I'm going back to New Orleans,
My race is almost run.   30
I'm going back to spend my life
Beneath that Rising Sun.

                                                        —*anonymous*

   Title: There is no specific house in New Orleans called The Rising Sun, although the sign as a symbol for a bawdy house is frequent in America and
England.

   Read this ballad over several times, or listen to it performed on
record. Notice, incidentally, that recorded versions vary significantly

and are similar to the one printed here only in broad outline. The ballad is spoken in the first person by a young girl who ran away from home, was seduced and abandoned in the finest melodramatic manner by a good-for-nothing gambler, and is now returning to New Orleans and the House of the Rising Sun. Many of the details are not especially clear: the house itself has been the ruin of many women, but does that necessarily make it a bawdy house? The suggestion is strong, but not so strong as to be conclusive. And the ball and chain of line 28: are they metaphorical (suggesting that try as she may, the girl cannot escape her way of life) or literal (suggesting that she has been arrested and is being sent to a New Orleans jail)? And the rising sun beneath which she will spend the rest of her life: is that the sign of the house or is that the heavenly body under which she will be buried after her race is run? Or is it perhaps both at once?

But ballads always have an aura of mystery to them, a vague indefinite quality to their narrative that allows the listener to sketch in details for himself. In its paucity of definite detail "The House of the Rising Sun" is typical of its genre, and we should expect rather than criticize the vagueness we find in it. Notice, though, the scope of the poem, the amount of information it does convey in thirty-two short lines. We meet the girl, her mother and sister, her lover, and the Rising Sun, and get a very good idea of the way all these elements have come together in the life of the speaker. The poem has scope but lacks precision. Notice also the colloquial simplicity, the roughness of the meter, the tragedy implicit in the story: all these are also to be expected in a ballad, and we should not be especially critical of expressions like "me, oh Lord, was" or "Never do like I have done" because they are grammatically incorrect or poetically unpolished. This is what ballads are like, as the remaining poems in this section should make abundantly clear.

Barbara Allan

It was in and about the Martinmas time,
    When the green leaves were a-falling,
That Sir John Graeme in the west country
    Fell in love with Barbara Allan.

He sent his man down through the town,   5
    To the place where she was dwelling,
"O haste and come to my master dear,
    Gin ye be Barbara Allan."

O slooly, slooly rose she up,
    To the place where he was lying,   10
And when she drew the curtain by—
    "Young man, I think you're dying."

"O it's I'm sick, and very, very sick,
    And 'tis a' for Barbara Allan."
"O the better for me ye's never be,   15
    Tho' your heart's blood were a-spilling.

"O dinna ye mind, young man," said she,
    "When ye was in the tavern a-drinking,
That ye made the healths gae round and round,
    And slighted Barbara Allan."   20

And slowly, slowly raise she up,
    And slowly, slowly left him;
And singing, said she cou'd not stay,
    Since death of life had reft him.

She had not gane a mile but twa,   25
    When she heard the dead-bell ringing,
And every jow that the dead-bell geid,
    It cry'd, Woe to Barbara Allan.

"O mother, mother, make my bed,
    O make it saft and narrow,   30
Since my love died for me today,
    I'll die for him tomorrow.

                                —anonymous

---

1. *Martinmas*: St. Martin's Day, November 11. 26. *dead-bell*: the death bell, which tolled to mark a death in the community.

Edward, Edward

"Why dois your brand sae drap wi' bluid,
             Edward, Edward?
Why dois your brand sae drip wi' bluid?
   And why sae sad gang yee, O?"
"O, I hae killed my hauke sae guid,   5
             Mither, mither,
O, I hae killed my hauke sae guid,
   And I had nae mair bot hee, O."

"Your haukis bluid was nevir sae reid,
             Edward, Edward,   10
Your haukis bluid was nevir sae reid,
   My deir son I tell thee, O."
"O, I hae killed my reid-roan steid,
             Mither, mither,
O, I hae killed my reid-roan steid,   15
   That erst was sae fair and frie, O."

"Your steid was auld, and ye hae gat mair,
             Edward, Edward,
Your steid was auld, and ye hae gat mair,
   Sum other dule ye drie, O."   20
"O, I hae killed my fadir deir,
             Mither, mither,
O, I hae killed my fadir deir,
   Alas, and wae is mee, O!"

"And whatten penance wul ye drie for that,   25
             Edward, Edward?
And whatten penance wul ye drie for that?
   My deir son, now tell me, O."
"Ile set my feit in yonder boat,
             Mither, mither,   30
Ile set my feit in yonder boat,
   And Ile fare ovir the sea, O."

"And what wul ye doe wi' your towirs and your ha',
             Edward, Edward,
And what wul ye doe wi' your towirs and your ha',   35
   That were sae fair to see, O?"
"Ile let thame stand tul they doun fa',
   For here nevir mair maun I bee, O."

"And what wul ye leive to your bairns and your wife,
             Edward, Edward?   40
And what wul ye leive to your bairns and your wife,
   When ye gang ovir the sea, O?"
"The warldis room, late them beg thrae life,
             Mither, mither,
The warldis room, late them beg thrae life,   45
   For thame nevir mair wul I see, O."

"And what wul ye leive to your ain mither deir?
             Edward, Edward?
And what wul ye leive to your ain mither deir?
   My deir son, now tell me, O."   50
"The curse of hell frae me sall ye beir,
             Mither, mither,
The curse of hell frae me sall ye beir,
   Sic counseils ye gave to me, O."

                                        —anonymous

   1. *brand*: sword. 4. *gang*: go. 13. *reid-roan*: reddish-brown. 20. *dule ye drie*:
grief you suffer. 27. *drie*: do. 38. *maun*: must. 39. *bairns*: children. 54. *sic*: such.

Pretty Polly

I courted Pretty Polly the live long night,
I courted Pretty Polly the live long night,
Then left her next morning before it was light.

O Polly, pretty Polly, come away with me,
O Polly, pretty Polly, come away with me,   5
Before we get married some pleasure to see.

He led her over the fields and the valleys so wide
He led her over the fields and the valleys so wide
Until pretty Polly, she fell by his side.

Oh Willie, oh Willie, I'm afraid of your ways   10
Oh Willie, oh Willie, I'm afraid of your ways
I'm afraid you will lead my poor body astray.

Polly, pretty Polly, you're guessing just right
Polly, pretty Polly, you're guessing just right
I dug on your grave the best part of last night.   15

She threw her arms around him and trembled with fear
She threw her arms around him and trembled with fear
How can you kill the poor girl that loves you so dear?

There's no time to talk and there's no time to stand
There's no time to talk and there's no time to stand   20
Then he drew his knife all in his right hand.

He stabbed her to the heart and her heart's blood did flow
He stabbed her to the heart and her heart's blood did flow
And into the grave pretty Polly did go.

Then he threw a little dirt over her and started for home   25
Then he threw a little dirt over her and started for home
Leaving no one behind but the wild birds to mourn.

—*anonymous*

The Wife of Usher's Well

There lived a wife at Usher's Well,
    And a wealthy wife was she;
She had three stout and stalwart sons,
    And sent them o'er the sea.

They hadna been a week from her,   5
   A week but barely ane,
Whan word came to the carline wife
   That her three sons were gane.

They hadna been a week from her,
   A week but barely three,   10
Whan word came to the carlin wife
   That her sons she'd never see.

"I wish the wind may never cease,
   Nor [fashes] in the flood,
Till my three sons come hame to me,   15
   In earthly flesh and blood."

It fell about the Martinmas,
   When nights are lang and mirk,
The carlin wife's three sons came hame,
   And their hats were o' the birk.   20

It neither grew in syke nor ditch,
   Nor yet in ony sheugh;
But at the gates o Paradise,
   That birk grew fair eneugh.

"Blow up the fire, my maidens!   25
   Bring water from the well!
For a' my house shall feast this night,
   Since my three sons are well."

And she has made to them a bed,
   She's made it large and wide,   30
And she's ta'en her mantle her about,
   Sat down at the bed-side.

Up then crew the red, red cock,
   And up and crew the gray;
The eldest to the youngest said,   35
   " 'Tis time we were away."

The cock he hadna craw'd but once,
    And clapp'd his wings at a',
When the youngest to the eldest said,
    "Brother, we must awa'.   40

"The cock doth craw, the day doth daw,
    The channerin' worm doth chide;
Gin we be mist out o' our place,
    A sair pain we maun bide.

"Fare ye weel, my mother dear!   45
    Fareweel to barn and byre!
And fare ye weel, the bonny lass
    That kindles my mother's fire!"

                                        —anonymous

7. *carline*: peasant. 14. *fashes*: fishes. 20. *birk*. birch. 21. *syke*: rivulet. 22. *sheugh*: trench. 42. *channerin' worm*: gnawing worm. 46. *byre*: cowhouse.

Ballad of the Goodly Fere

Simon Zelotes speaketh it somewhile after the Crucifixion

Ha' we lost the goodliest fere o' all
For the priests and the gallows tree?
Aye, lover he was of brawny men,
O' ships and the open sea.

When they came wi' a host to take Our Man   5
His smile was good to see,
"First let these go!" quo' our Goodly Fere,
"Or I'll see ye damned," says he.

Aye, he sent us out through the crossed high spears,
And the scorn of his laugh rang free,   10
"Why took ye not me when I walked about
Alone in the town?" says he.

Oh we drank his "Hale" in the good red wine
When we last made company,
No capon priest was the Goodly Fere   15
But a man o' men was he.

I ha' seen him drive a hundred men
Wi' a bundle o' cords swung free,
When they took the high and holy house
For their pawn and treasury.   20

They'll no get him a' in a book I think
Though they write it cunningly;
No mouse of the scrolls was the Goodly Fere
But aye loved the open sea.

If they think they ha' snared our Goodly Fere   25
They are fools to the last degree.
"I'll go to the feast," quo' our Goodly Fere,
"Though I go to the gallows tree."

"Ye ha' seen me heal the lame and the blind,
And wake the dead," says he,   30
"Ye shall see one thing to master all:
'Tis how a brave man dies on the tree."

A son of God was the Goodly Fere
That bade us his brothers be.
I ha' seen him cow a thousand men.   35
I ha' seen him upon the tree.

He cried no cry when they drave the nails
And the blood gushed hot and free,
The hounds of the crimson sky gave tongue
But never a cry cried he.   40

I ha' seen him cow a thousand men
On the hills o' Galilee,
They whined as he walked out calm between,
Wi' his eyes like the gray o' the sea.

Like the sea that brooks no voyaging   45
With the winds unleashed and free,
Like the sea that he cowed at Gennesaret
Wi' twey words spoke' suddenly.

A master of men was the Goodly Fere,
A mate of the wind and sea,   50
If they think they ha' slain our Goodly Fere
They are fools eternally.

I ha' seen him eat o' the honey-comb
Sin' they nailed him to the tree.

—*Ezra Pound*

7. *Fere*: companion. 17ff.: Cf. Mark 11:15, 16. 47. *Gennesaret*: Cf. Matthew 8:24ff.

Isle of Sirens

There's a story of beautiful women
On an island in the sea
Who call to men sailing by;
And as we stayed on our course, I could hear them callin' me,
And Lord, I can't stand that beautiful cry!   5
"Keep course," cried the captain,
"Ignore them, let them be.
Straight ahead," cried the captain,
"Sail on by and stay free,
Remember laws of mutiny."   10

And as we moved the voices got louder,
They sang beautiful things in my ear.
I must go to that island of women,
I must see these beautiful creatures that I hear.
Love is wild and desires have no fear.   15
"Keep course," cried the captain,

"Straight ahead, you stubborn man;
We're all lonely," cried the captain,
"Take heed from an old man,
For you don't understand."   20

"Old man, your admonition
Makes no sense to me;
You know nothing of temptation
And desires are heaven to me."
And off he leapt into the sea.   25
"Keep course," cried the captain.

                                        —*Curtis Mayfield*

Sir Patrick Spence

The king sits in Dumferling toune,
   Drinking the blude-reid wine:
"O whar will I get guid sailor,
   To sail this schip of mine?"

Up and spak an eldern knicht,   5
   Sat at the kings richt kne:
"Sir Patrick Spence is the best sailor
   That sails upon the se."

The king has written a braid letter,
   And signed it wi' his hand,   10
And sent it to Sir Patrick Spence,
   Was walking on the sand.

The first line that Sir Patrick red,
   A loud lauch lauched he;
The next line that Sir Patrick red,   15
   The teir blinded his ee.

"O wha is this has done this deid,
   This ill deid don to me,
To send me out this time o' the yeir,
   To sail upon the se?!   20

"Mak hast, mak hast, my mirry men all,
   Our guid schip sails the morne:"
"O say na sae, my master deir,
   For I feir a deadlie storme.

"Late late yestreen I saw the new moone,   25
   Wi' the auld moone in hir arme,
And I feir, I feir, my deir master,
   That we will cum to harme."

O our Scots nobles were richt laith
   To weet their cork-heild schoone;   30
Bot lang owre a' the play wer playd,
   Thair hats they swam aboone.

O lang, lang, may their ladies sit,
   Wi' thair fans into their hand,
Or eir they se Sir Patrick Spence   35
   Cum sailing to the land.

O lang, lang, may the ladies stand,
   Wi' thair gold kems in their hair,
Waiting for their ain deir lords,
   For they'll se thame na mair.   40

Have owre, have owre to Aberdour,
   It's fiftie fadom deip,
And thair lies guid Sir Patrick Spence,
   Wi' the Scots lords at his feit.

                                  —anonymous

   3. *guid*: good. 9. *braid*: broad? 30. *cork-heild schoone*: cork-heeled shoes.

The True Lover

The lad came to the door at night,
   When lovers crown their vows,
And whistled soft and out of sight
   In shadow of the boughs.

"I shall not vex you with my face   5
   Henceforth, my love, for aye;
So take me in your arms a space
   Before the east is grey.

"When I from hence away am past
   I shall not find a bride,   10
And you shall be the first and last
   I ever lay beside."

She heard and went and knew not why;
   Her heart to his she laid;
Light was the air beneath the sky   15
   But dark under the shade.

"Oh do you breathe, lad, that your breast
   Seems not to rise and fall,
And here upon my bosom prest
   There beats no heart at all?"   20

"Oh loud, my girl, it once would knock,
   You should have felt it then;
But since for you I stopped the clock
   It never goes again."

"Oh lad, what is it, lad, that drips   25
   Wet from your neck on mine?
What is it falling on my lips,
   My lad, that tastes of brine?"

"Oh like enough 'tis blood, my dear,
   For when the knife has slit   30
The throat across from ear to ear
   'Twill bleed because of it."

Under the stars the air was light
   But dark below the boughs,
The still air of the speechless night,   35
   When lovers crown their vows.

                                   —A. E. Housman

Ballad of the Landlord

Landlord, landlord,
My roof has sprung a leak.
Don't you 'member I told you about it
Way last week?

Landlord, landlord,   5
These steps is broken down.
When you come up yourself
It's a wonder you don't fall down.

Ten Bucks you say I owe you?
Ten Bucks you say is due?   10
Well, that's Ten Bucks more'n I'll pay you
Till you fix this house up new.

What? You gonna get eviction orders?
You gonna cut off my heat?
You gonna take my furniture and   15
Throw it in the street?

Um-huh! You talking high and mighty.
Talk on—till you get through.
You ain't gonna be able to say a word
If I land my fist on you.   20

Police! Police!
Come and get this man!
He's trying to ruin the government
And overturn the land!

Copper's whistle!   25
Patrol bell!
Arrest.

Precinct Station.
Iron cell.
Headlines in press: 30

MAN THREATENS LANDLORD

.

.   .

TENANT HELD NO BAIL

.

.   .

JUDGE GIVES NEGRO 90 DAYS IN COUNTY JAIL

—Langston Hughes

La Belle Dame Sans Merci

O what can ail thee, knight at arms,
    Alone and palely loitering?
The sedge has withered from the lake,
    And no birds sing!

O what can ail thee, knight at arms,   5
    So haggard and so woe-begone?
The squirrel's granary is full,
    And the harvest's done.

I see a lily on thy brow,
    With anguish moist and fever dew;   10
And on thy cheeks a fading rose
    Fast withereth too.—

I met a lady in the meads,
    Full beautiful, a faery's child;
Her hair was long, her foot was light,   15
    And her eyes were wild.

I made a garland for her head,
    And bracelets, too, and fragrant zone;
She looked at me as she did love,
    And made sweet moan.   20

I set her on my pacing steed,
    And nothing else, saw all day long;

For sidelong would she bend, and sing
   A faery's song.

She found me roots of relish sweet,   25
   And honey wild, and manna dew;
And sure in language strange she said,
   "I love thee true."

She took me to her elfin grot,
   And there she wept and sighed full sore;   30
And there I shut her wild, wild eyes
   With kisses four.

And there she lullèd me asleep,
   And there I dreamed, ah woe betide!
The latest dream I ever dreamt,   35
   On the cold hillside.

I saw pale kings, and princes too,
   Pale warriors, death-pale were they all,
Who cried, "La Belle Dame sans Merci
   Thee hath in thrall!"   40

I saw their starved lips in the gloam
   With horrid warning gaped wide—
And I awoke and found me here,
   On the cold hill's side.

And this is why I sojourn here,   45
   Alone and palely loitering;
Though the sedge is withered from the lake,
   And no birds sing.

                                                —John Keats

   13. *meads*: meadows. 18. *fragrant zone*: girdle. 29. *grot*: grotto.

Joe Hill

I dreamed I saw Joe Hill last night,
Alive as you or me.
Says I, "But Joe, you're ten years dead,"
"I never died," said he.

"The copper bosses killed you, Joe,   5
They shot you, Joe," says I.
"Takes more than guns to kill a man,"
Says Joe, "I didn't die."

And standing there as big as life
And smiling with his eyes,   10
Says Joe, "What they can never kill
Went on to organize."

From San Diego up to Maine,
In every mine and mill
Where working men defend their rights,   15
It's there you'll find Joe Hill.

                              —*Earl Robinson–Alfred Hayes*

Joe Hill

Joe Hill came over from Sweden's shore
Looking for some work to do;
And The Statue of Liberty waved him by
As Joe come a sailing through, Joe Hill;
As Joe come a sailing through.   5

Oh, his clothes were coarse, and his hopes were high,
As he headed for the Promised Land.
And it took a few weeks on the out-of-work streets
Before he began to understand,
Before he began to understand.   10

Then he got hired by a Bowery bar,
Sweeping up a saloon.
As his rag would sail o'er the barroom rail,
It sounded like he whistled on a tune.
You could almost hear him whistling on a tune.   15

And Joe rolled on from job to job,
From the docks to the railroad line.
And no matter how hungry the hand that wrote,
In his letters he was always doing fine,
In his letters he was always doing fine.   20

The years went by like the sun going down,
Slowly turned the page.
And when Joe looked back at the sweat on his tracks,
He had nothing to show but his age,
He had nothing to show but his age.   25

So he headed out for the California shore.
There things were just as bad.
So he joined the Industrial Workers of the World,
'Cause The Union was the only friend he had,
'Cause The Union was the only friend he had.   30

The strikes were bloody; and the strikes were black,
As hard as they were long.
In the dark of the night, Joe would stay awake and write.
In the morning he would wake them with a song,
In the morning he would wake them with a song.   35

He wrote his words to the tunes of the day,
To be passed along the union vine.
And the strikes were led; and the songs were spread.
And Joe Hill was always on the line,
And Joe Hill was always on the line.   40

Then in Salt Lake City, a murder was made.
There was hardly a clue to find.
Yes, the proof was poor but the sheriff was sure

That Joe was the killer of the crime,
That Joe was the killer of the crime.   45

Joe raised his hands, but they shot him down.
He had nothing but guilt to give.
It's a doctor I need, and they left him to bleed.
But he made it 'cause he had the will to live,
But he made it 'cause he had the will to live.   50

The trial was held in a building of wood.
There the killer would be named.
And the days weighed more than the cold copper ore,
'Cause he feared that he was being framed,
'Cause he feared that he was being framed.   55

Strange are the ways of the western law;
Strange are the ways of fate.
For the government crawled to the mine owners' call,
And the judge was appointed by The State,
And the judge was appointed by The State.   60

Now Utah justice can be had
But not for a Union Man.
And Joe was warned by some early morn
There'd be one less singer in the land,
There'd be one less singer in the land.   65

Oh, William Spry was Governor Spry,
And a life was his to hold.
On the last appeal fell a Governor's tear—
May the Lord have mercy on your soul,
May the Lord have mercy on your soul.   70

President Wilson held up the day,
But even he would fail.
For nobody heard the soul searching words
Of the soul in the Salt Lake City jail,
Of the soul in the Salt Lake City jail.   75

For thirty-six years he lived out his days,
And he more than played his part.
For the songs that he made, he was carefully paid
By a rifle bullet buried in his heart,
By a rifle bullet buried in his heart.   80

Yes, they lined Joe Hill up against the wall,
Blindfold over his eyes.
It's the life of the rebel that he chose to live;
It's the death of the rebel that he died,
It's the death of the rebel that he died.   85

In his time in the cell he wrote to his friends,
His wishes all were plain—
My body can't be found on this Utah ground,
So they laid him on a fast departing train,
So they laid him on a fast departing train.   90

The rebel rode to Chicago Town.
There were 30,000 people to mourn.
And just about the time that Joe lay dying
A legend was just a-being born,
A legend was just a-being born.   95

Now, some say Joe was guilty as charged;
Some say he wasn't even there.
And I guess nobody will ever know,
'Cause the court records all have disappeared,
'Cause the court records all have disappeared.   100

Now wherever you go in this fair land,
In every union hall,
In the dusty dark these words are marked
In between all the cracks upon the wall,
In between all the cracks upon the wall.   105

It's the very last lines that Joe Hill wrote
When he knew that his days were through:
"Boys, this is my last and final wish,

Good luck to all of you,
Good luck to all of you." 110

—Phil Ochs

28. *Industrial Workers of the World*: "The Union," an organization of the early twentieth century that suffered strong persecution in the United States because of its alleged communist ties.

ELEGIES

The classical *elegy* was a long formal lyric poem on virtually any serious subject "written in an elegiac [i.e., elevated] manner." More recent usage has tended to restrict the term only to poems on the subject of death, usually, but not necessarily, the death of a single individual close to the poet. Of course the best-known elegies in English are Milton's "Lycidas," written for his friend and fellow student Edward King; Tennyson's "In Memoriam," for Arthur Hallam; and Whitman's "When Lilacs Last in the Dooryard Bloom'd," for Abraham Lincoln. The formal elegy moves from an initial lament through a series of metaphysical transformations to some kind of resolution or even rejoicing at its conclusion, a movement easily managed when the Christian and pagan religions held strong sway, but more difficult after the demise of Heaven and the Elysian Fields. Paul Simon's song "So Long, Frank Lloyd Wright" finds a note of affirmation in the composer's memories of the architect; George Harrison's elegy for all modern mankind, "While My Guitar Gently Weeps," finds its resolution in the not-very-comforting thought that "With every mistake we must surely be learning." Modern elegies are generally less formal than older English or classical elegies and do not break as easily into tripartite sections. Resolution is frequently constructed on fame or honor or dignity—or absent entirely. Modern poets in their rage for simplicity also tend to ignore a raft of other elegiac conventions, such as addresses to mythical deities and muses and a ritual plucking of laurel by the poet, since such conventions strike a modern reader as posed.

Discuss the following elegies. Pay particular attention to the way imagery, tone, and rhythm effect the attitude of the listener toward the subject. Note too what comfort each poem offers to mitigate the remorse of death.

To an Athlete Dying Young

The time you won your town the race
We chaired you through the market-place;
Man and boy stood cheering by,
And home we brought you shoulder-high.

To-day, the road all runners come,   5
Shoulder-high we bring you home,
And set you at your threshold down,
Townsman of a stiller town.

Smart lad, to slip betimes away
From fields where glory does not stay   10
And early though the laurel grows
It withers quicker than the rose.

Eyes the shady night has shut
Cannot see the record cut,
And silence sounds no worse than cheers   15
After earth has stopped the ears:

Now you will not swell the rout
Of lads that wore their honours out,
Runners whom renown outran
And the name died before the man.   20

So set, before its echoes fade,
The fleet foot on the sill of shade,
And hold to the low lintel up
The still-defended challenge-cup.

And round that early-laurelled head   25
Will flock to gaze the strengthless dead.
And find unwithered on its curls
The garland briefer than a girl's.

                                                            —*A. E. Housman*

2. *chaired*: carried on one's shoulders. 23. *lintel*: a horizontal support above a
door or window.

Housman's elegy is short, but it is very polished and elegant, and it breaks cleanly into three distinct divisions: the initial two stanzas present the subject by drawing a comparison between a victory parade and a funeral; the middle three stanzas present three different but related reasons why the athlete should not mind dying; and the final two stanzas manage some genuine affirmation in the form of the challenge-cup and the garland. Notice the way in which Housman moves from the past tense in stanza one to the present for the main portion of the poem to the future in the last, affirmative stanza. The change of tenses works to associate sorrow with the present and affirmation with the future, thereby emphasizing the development of his argument. Probably the calm, reserved tone of the poem produced by the measured, polished lines lends its own affirmative dignity to the effect of the imagery, argument, and tense sequence. Most impressive, however, is the classical simplicity of the poem: there is no riotous profusion of similes and metaphors, no intricately Latinate diction, no self-indulgent emotionalism—just a clean, decorous, elegantly simple poem. And like the simple laurel wreath of victory that the athlete once wore to mark his triumph in the foot race he won on earth, this simple poem is a very appropriate mark of triumph in the race of life.

Elegy in a Country Churchyard

The Curfew tolls the knell of parting day,
   The lowing herd wind slowly o'er the lea,
The plowman homeward plods his weary way
   And leaves the world to darkness and to me.

Now fades the glimmering landscape on the sight,   5
   And all the air a solemn stillness holds,
Save where the beetle wheels his droning flight,
   And drowsy tinklings lull the distant folds;

Save that from yonder ivy-mantled tower
   The moping owl does to the moon complain   10
Of such, as wandering near her secret bower,
   Molest her ancient solitary reign.

Beneath those rugged elms, that yew-trees's shade,
   Where heaves the turf in many a mould'ring heap,
Each in his narrow cell for ever laid,   15
   The rude Forefathers of the hamlet sleep.

The breezy call of incense-breathing Morn,
   The swallow twitt'ring from the straw-built shed,
The cock's shrill clarion, or the echoing horn,
   No more shall rouse them from their lowly bed.   20

For them no more the blazing hearth shall burn,
   Or busy housewife ply her evening care:
No children run to lisp their sire's return,
   Or climb his knees the envied kiss to share.

Oft did the harvest to their sickle yield,   25
   Their furrow oft the stubborn glebe has broke;
How jocund did they drive their team afield!
   How bowed the woods beneath their sturdy stroke!

Let not Ambition mock their useful toil,
   Their homely joys, and destiny obscure;   30
Nor Grandeur hear with a disdainful smile
   The short and simple annals of the poor.

The boast of heraldry, the pomp of power,
   And all that beauty, all that wealth e'er gave,
Awaits alike th' inevitable hour.   35
   The paths of glory lead but to the grave.

Nor you, ye Proud, impute to These the fault,
   If Memory o'er their Tomb no Trophies raise,
Where through the long-drawn aisle and fretted vault
   The pealing anthem swells the note of praise.   40

Can storied urn or animated bust
   Back to its mansion call the fleeting breath?
Can Honor's voice provoke the silent dust,
   Or Flattery sooth the dull cold ear of Death?

Perhaps in this neglected spot is laid 45
   Some heart once pregnant with celestial fire;
Hands that the rod of empire might have swayed,
   Or waked to ecstasy the living lyre.

But Knowledge to their eyes her ample page
   Rich with the spoils of time did ne'er unroll; 50
Chill Penury repressed their noble rage,
   And froze the genial current of the soul.

Full many a gem of purest ray serene,
   The dark unfathomed caves of ocean bear:
Full many a flower is born to blush unseen, 55
   And waste its sweetness on the desert air.

Some village-Hampden, that with dauntless breast
   The little Tyrant of his fields withstood;
Some mute inglorious Milton here may rest,
   Some Cromwell guiltless of his country's blood. 60

Th' applause of list'ning senates to command
   The threats of pain and ruin to despise,
To scatter plenty o'er a smiling land,
   And read their history in a nation's eyes,

Their lot forbade: nor circumscribed alone 65
   Their growing virtues, but their crimes confined;
Forbade to wade through slaughter to a throne,
   And shut the gates of mercy on mankind,

The struggling pangs of conscious truth to hide,
   To quench the blushes of ingenuous shame, 70
Or heap the shrine of Luxury and Pride
   With incense kindled at the Muse's flame.

Far from the madding crowd's ignoble strife,
   Their sober wishes never learned to stray;
Along the cool sequestered vale of life 75
   They kept the noiseless tenor of their way.

Yet ev'n these bones from insult to protect,
   Some frail memorial still erected nigh,
With uncouth rhymes and shapeless sculpture decked,
   Implores the passing tribute of a sigh.   80

Their name, their years, spelt by th' unlettered muse,
   The place of fame and elegy supply:
And many a holy text around she strews,
   That teach the rustic moralist to die.

For who to dumb Forgetfulness a prey,   85
   This pleasing anxious being e'er resigned,
Left the warm precincts of the cheerful day,
   Nor cast one longing ling'ring look behind?

On some fond breast the parting soul relies,
   Some pious drops the closing eye requires;   90
Ev'n from the tomb the voice of Nature cries,
   Ev'n in our Ashes live their wonted Fires.

For thee, who mindful of th' unhonored Dead
   Dost in these lines their artless tale relate,
If chance, by lonely contemplation led,   95
   Some kindred Spirit shall inquire thy fate,

Haply some hoary-headed Swain may say,
   "Oft have we seen him at the peep of dawn
Brushing with hasty steps the dews away
   To meet the sun upon the upland lawn.   100

"There at the foot of yonder nodding beech
   That wreathes its old fantastic roots so high,
His listless length at noontide would he stretch,
   And pore upon the brook that babbles by.

"Hard by yon wood, now smiling as in scorn,   105
   Mutt'ring his wayward fancies he would rove,
Now drooping, woeful wan, like one forlorn,
   Or crazed with care, or crossed in hopeless love.

"One morn I missed him on the customed hill,
   Along the heath and near his favorite tree; 110
Another came; nor yet beside the rill,
   Nor up the lawn, nor at the wood was he;

"The next with dirges due in sad array
   Slow through the church-way path we saw him borne.
Approach and read (for thou can'st read) the lay, 115
   Graved on the stone beneath yon agèd thorn."

THE EPITAPH

Here rests his head upon the lap of earth
   A youth to fortune and to fame unknown.
Fair Science frowned not on his humble birth,
   And Melancholy marked him for her own. 120

Large was his bounty, and his soul sincere,
   Heaven did a recompense as largely send:
He gave to Misery all he had, a tear,
   He gained from Heaven ('twas all he wished) a friend.

No farther seek his merits to disclose, 125
   Or draw his frailties from their dread abode
(There they alike in trembling hope repose),
   The bosom of his Father and his God.

—*Thomas Gray*

23. *lisp*: announce. 26. *glebe*: ecclesiastical pasture lands. 39. *fretted*: ornamented with a boarder of interlaced, angular design. 57. *Hampden*: a leader of Parliament in the Puritan revolt against King Charles led by Cromwell in the early 1640's. 97. *haply*: perhaps; *swain*: a country lad.

Elegy for Jane

                                   My student, thrown by a horse

I remember the neckcurls, limp and damp as tendrils;
And her quick look, a sidelong pickerel smile;
And how, once startled into talk, the light syllables leaped for her,

And she balanced in the delight of her thought,
A wren, happy, tail into the wind,   5
Her song trembling the twigs and small branches.
The shade sang with her;
The leaves, their whispers turned to kissing,
And the mould sang in the bleached valleys under the rose.

Oh, when she was sad, she cast herself down into such a pure   10
    depth,
Even a father could not find her:
Scraping her cheek against straw,
Stirring the clearest water.

My sparrow, you are not here,
Waiting like a fern, making a spiney shadow.   15
The sides of wet stones cannot console me,
Nor the moss, wound with the last light.

If only I could nudge you from this sleep,
My maimed darling, my skittery pigeon.
Over this damp grave I speak the words of my love: 20
I, with no rights in this matter,
Neither father nor lover.

—Theodore Roethke

Buffalo Bill's

Buffalo Bill's
defunct
            who used to
            ride a watersmooth-silver
                                    stallion
and break onetwothreefourfive pigeonsjustlikethat
                                            Jesus

he was a handsome man
                        and what i want to know is
how do you like your blueeyed boy
Mister Death

—e. e. cummings

While My Guitar Gently Weeps

I look at you all see the love there that's sleeping
While my guitar gently weeps
I look at the floor and I see it needs sweeping
Still my guitar gently weeps
I don't know why nobody told you how to unfold your love 5
I don't know how someone controlled you
They bought and sold you.

I look at the world and I notice it's turning
While my guitar gently weeps
With every mistake we must surely be learning 10
Still my guitar gently weeps
I don't know how you were diverted
You were perverted too
I don't know how you were inverted
No one alerted you. 15

I look at you all see the love there that's sleeping
While my guitar gently weeps
Look at you all . . .
Still my guitar gently weeps.

—George Harrison

When Lilacs Last in the Dooryard Bloom'd

1

When lilacs last in the dooryard bloom'd,
And the great star early droop'd in the western sky in the night,
I mourn'd, and yet shall mourn with ever-returning spring.

Ever-returning spring, trinity sure to me you bring,
Lilac blooming perennial and drooping star in the west, 5
And thought of him I love.

2

O powerful western fallen star!
O shades of night—O moody, tearful night!
O great star disappear'd—O the black murk that hides the star!
O cruel hands that hold me powerless—O helpless soul of me!   10
O harsh surrounding cloud that will not free my soul.

3

In the dooryard fronting an old farm-house near the white-wash'd
    palings,
Stands the lilac-bush tall-growing with heart-shaped leaves of rich
    green,
With many a pointed blossom rising delicate, with the perfume
    strong I love,
With every leaf a miracle—and from this bush in the dooryard,   15
With delicate-color'd blossoms and heart-shaped leaves of rich
    green,
A sprig with its flower I break.

4

In the swamp in secluded recesses,
A shy and hidden bird is warbling a song.

Solitary the thrush,   20
The hermit withdrawn to himself, avoiding the settlements,
Sings by himself a song.

Song of the bleeding throat,
Death's outlet song of life, (for well dear brother I know,
If thou wast not granted to sing thou would'st surely die.)   25

5

Over the breast of the spring, the land, amid cities,
Amid lanes and through old woods, where lately the violets peep'd
    from the ground, spotting the gray debris,
Amid the grass in the fields each side of the lanes, passing the
    endless grass,
Passing the yellow-spear'd wheat, every grain from its shroud in
    the dark-brown fields uprisen,

Passing the apple-tree blows of white and pink in the orchards,   30
Carrying a corpse to where it shall rest in the grave,
Night and day journeys a coffin.

6

Coffin that passes through lanes and streets,
Through day and night with the great cloud darkening the land,
With the pomp of the inloop'd flags with the cities draped in black,   35
With the show of the States themselves as of crape-veil'd women
     standing,
With processions long and winding and the flambeaus of the night,
With the countless torches lit, with the silent sea of faces and the
     unbared heads,
With the waiting depot, the arriving coffin, and the sombre faces,
With dirges through the night, with the thousand voices rising
     strong and solemn,   40
With all the mournful voices of the dirges pour'd around the coffin,
The dim-lit churches and the shuddering organs—where amid these
     you journey,
With the tolling tolling bells' perpetual clang,
Here, coffin that slowly passes,
I give you my sprig of lilac.   45

7

(Nor for you, for one alone,
Blossoms and branches green to coffins all I bring,
For fresh as the morning, thus would I chant a song for you O
     sane and sacred death.

All over bouquets of roses,
O death, I cover you over with roses and early lilies,   50
But mostly and now the lilac that blooms the first,
Copious I break, I break the sprigs from the bushes,
With loaded arms I come, pouring for you,
For you and the coffins all of you O death.)

8

O western orb sailing the heaven,   55
Now I know what you must have meant as a month since I walk'd,

As I walk'd in silence the transparent shadowy night,
As I saw you had something to tell as you bent to me night after
    night,
As you droop'd from the sky low down as if to my side, (while the
    other stars all look'd on,)
As we wander'd together the solemn night, (for something I know
    not what kept me from sleep,)   60
As the night advanced, and I saw on the rim of the west how full
    you were of woe,
As I stood on the rising ground in the breeze in the cool transparent
    night,
As I watch'd where you pass'd and was lost in the netherward
    black of the night,
As my soul in its trouble dissatisfied sank, as where you sad orb,
Concluded, dropt in the night, and was gone.   65

9

Sing on there in the swamp,
O singer bashful and tender, I hear your notes, I hear your call,
I hear, I come presently, I understand you,
But a moment I linger, for the lustrous star has detain'd me,
The star my departing comrade holds and detains me.   70

10

O how shall I warble myself for the dead one there I loved?
And how shall I deck my song for the large sweet soul that has
    gone?
And what shall my perfume be for the grave of him I love?

Sea-winds blown from east and west,
Blown from the Eastern sea and blown from the Western sea, till
    there on the prairies meeting,   75
These and with these and the breath of my chant,
I'll perfume the grave of him I love.

11

O what shall I hang on the chamber walls?
And what shall the pictures be that I hang on the walls,
To adorn the burial-house of him I love?   80

Pictures of growing spring and farms and homes,

With the Fourth-month eve at sundown, and the gray smoke lucid and bright,

With floods of the yellow gold of the gorgeous, indolent, sinking sun, burning, expanding the air,

With the fresh sweet herbage under foot, and the pale green leaves of the trees prolific,

In the distance the flowing glaze, the breast of the river, with a wind-dapple here and there,   85

With ranging hills on the banks, with many a line against the sky, and shadows,

And the city at hand with dwellings so dense, and stacks of chimneys,

And all the scenes of life and the workshops, and the workmen homeward returning.

12

Lo, body and soul—this land,

My own Manhattan with spires, and the sparkling and hurrying tides, and the ships,   90

The varied and ample land, the South and the North in the light, Ohio's shores and flashing Missouri,

And ever the far-spreading prairies cover'd with grass and corn.

Lo, the most excellent sun so calm and haughty,

The violet and purple morn with just-felt breezes,

The gentle soft-born measureless light   95

The miracle spreading bathing all, the fulfill'd noon,

The coming eve delicious, the welcome night and the stars,

Over my cities shining all, enveloping man and land.

13

Sing on, sing on you gray-brown bird,

Sing from the swamps, the recesses, pour your chant from the bushes,

Limitless out of the dusk, out of the cedars and pines.   100

Sing on dearest brother, warble your reedy song,

Loud human song, with voice of uttermost woe.

O liquid and free and tender!
O wild and loose to my soul—O wondrous singer!   105
You only I hear—yet the star holds me, (but will soon depart,)
Yet the lilac with mastering odor holds me.

14
Now while I sat in the day and look'd forth,
In the close of the day with its light and the fields of spring, and
the farmers preparing their crops,
In the large unconscious scenery of my land with its lakes and
forests,   110
In the heavenly aerial beauty, (after the perturb'd winds and the
storms,)
Under the arching heavens of the afternoon swift passing, and the
voices of children and women,
The many-moving sea-tides, and I saw the ships how they sail'd,
And the summer approaching with richness, and the fields all busy
with labor,
And the infinite separate houses, how they all went on, each with
its meals of minutia of daily usages,   115
And the streets how their throbbings throbb'd, and the cities pent
—lo, then and there,
Falling upon them all and among them all, enveloping me with
the rest,
Appear'd the cloud, appear'd the long black trail,
And I knew death, its thought, and the sacred knowledge of death.

Then with the knowledge of death as walking one side of me,   120
And the thought of death close-walking the other side of me,
And I in the middle as with companions, and as holding the hands
of companions,
I fled forth to the hiding receiving night that talks not,
Down to the shores of the water, the path by the swamp in the
dimness,
To the solemn shadowy cedars and ghostly pines so still.   125

And the singer so shy to the rest receiv'd me,
The gray-brown bird I know receiv'd us comrades three,
And he sang the carol of death, and a verse for him I love.

From deep secluded recesses,
From the fragrant cedars and the ghostly pines so still,   130
Came the carol of the bird.

And the charm of the carol rapt me,
As I held as if by their hands my comrades in the night,
And the voice of my spirit tallied the song of the bird.

Come lovely and soothing death,   135
Undulate round the world, serenely arriving, arriving,
In the day, in the night, to all, to each,
Sooner or later delicate death.

Prais'd be the fathomless universe,
For life and joy, and for objects and knowledge curious,   140
And for love, sweet love—but praise! praise! praise!
For the sure-enwinding arms of cool-enfolding death.

Dark mother always gliding near with soft feet,
Have none chanted for thee a chant of fullest welcome?
Then I chant it for thee, I glorify thee above all,   145
I bring thee a song that when thou must indeed come, come
    unfalteringly.

Approach strong deliveress,
When it is so, when thou hast taken them I joyously sing the dead,
Lost in the loving floating ocean of thee,
Laved in the flood of thy bliss O death.   150

From me to thee glad serenades,
Dances for thee I propose saluting thee, adornments and feastings
    for thee,
And the sights of the open landscape and the high-spread sky are
    fitting,
And life and the fields, and the huge and thoughtful night.

The night in silence under many a star,   155
The ocean shore and the husky whispering wave whose voice I
    know,

And the soul turning to thee O vast and well-veil'd death,
And the body gratefully nestling close to thee.

Over the tree-tops I float thee a song,
Over the rising and sinking waves, over the myriad fields and the
   prairies wide,   160
Over the dense-pack'd cities all and the teeming wharves and ways,
I float this carol with joy, with joy to thee O Death.

                                    15

To the tally of my soul,
Loud and strong kept up the gray-brown bird,
With pure deliberate notes spreading filling the night.   165

Loud in the pines and cedars dim,
Clear in the freshness moist and the swamp-perfume,
And I with my comrades there in the night.

While my sight that was bound in my eyes unclosed,
As to long panoramas of visions.   170

And I saw askant the armies,
I saw as in noiseless dreams hundreds of battle-flags,
Borne through the smoke of the battles and pierc'd with missiles I
   saw them,
And carried hither and yon through the smoke, and torn and
   bloody,
And at last but a few shreds left on the staffs, (and all in silence,) 175
And the staffs all splinter'd and broken.

I saw battle-corpses, myriads of them,
And the white skeletons of young men, I saw them,
I saw the debris and debris of all the slain soldiers of the war,
But I saw they were not as was thought,   180
They themselves were fully at rest, they suffer'd not,
The living remain'd and suffer'd, the mother suffer'd,
And the wife and the child and the musing comrade suffer'd,
And the armies that remain'd suffer'd.

16

Passing the visions, passing the night, 185
Passing, unloosing the hold of my comrades' hands,
Passing the song of the hermit bird and the tallying song of my
soul,
Victorious song, death's outlet song, yet varying ever-altering song,
As low and wailing, yet clear the notes, rising and falling, flooding
the night,
Sadly sinking and fainting, as warning and warning, and yet again
bursting with joy, 190
Covering the earth and filling the spread of the heaven,
As that powerful psalm in the night I heard from recesses,
Passing, I leave thee lilac with heart-shaped leaves,
I leave thee there in the door-yard, blooming, returning with
spring.

I cease from my song for thee, 195
From my gaze on thee in the west, fronting the west, communing
with thee,
O comrade lustrous with silver face in the night.

Yet each to keep and all, retrievements out of the night,
The song, the wondrous chant of the gray-brown bird,
And the tallying chant, the echo arous'd in my soul, 200
With the lustrous and drooping star with the countenance full
of woe,
With the holders holding my hand nearing the call of the bird,
Comrades mine and I in the midst, and their memory ever to keep,
for the dead I loved so well,
For the sweetest, wisest soul of all my days and lands—and this for
his dear sake,
Lilac and star and bird twined with the chant of my soul, 205
There in the fragrant pines and the cedars dusk and dim.
                                        —*Walt Whitman*

EPIGRAMS

Originally *epigram* meant simply "inscription," and usually referred to an epitaph. Modern epigrams are not, of course, inscriptions, nor are they usually epitaphs, but they retain the characteristics of both: they are short, concise, polished, usually topical poems, a few lines of rhetorical balance and parallelism. Frequently the epigram is used as a tool of satire, a usage that developed during the English Renaissance period, although many poets of that and later periods used the epigram for other purposes. We may sometimes call the style of a long poem *epigramatic,* in that it may contain short, concise, memorable lines or couplets that might well stand alone as epigrams. For example, Pope's well-known couplet about hope springing eternal is an epigram lifted out of its original context in a very long poem. Few songs are short enough to be legitimate epigrams, although James Brown's "Say it Loud: 'I'm Black and I'm Proud'" is an obvious exception, as is Phil Ochs' brief jingle from his *Rehearsals for Retirement* album.

Where Were You in Chicago?

Where were you in Chicago? You know I didn't see you there;
I didn't see them break your head, or breathe the teargassed air.
Where were you in Chicago when the fight was being fought?
Oh where were you in Chicago? Because I was in Detroit!
                                                     —*Phil Ochs*

Here are a few other epigrams from various English and American poets. As you can see, epigrams are not hard to write, although something as clean as Dryden's "Epigram on Milton" takes considerable work. As an exercise, you might try a few yourself.

On King Charles

We have a pretty witty king
    And whose word no man relys on:
He never said a foolish thing,
    And never did a wise one.
                                        —*John Wilmot, Earl of Rochester*

The Debt

This is the debt I pay
Just for one riotous day,
Years of regret and grief,
Sorrow without relief.

Pay it I will to the end—   5
Until the grave, my friend,
Gives me a true release—
Gives me the clasp of peace.

Slight was the thing I bought,
Small was the debt I thought,   10
Poor was the loan at best—
God! but the interest!

                                        —*Paul Laurence Dunbar*

Presence and Absence

When what is lov'd, is Present, love doth spring;
But being absent, Love lies languishing.

                                        —*Robert Herrick*

On a Perfumed Lady

You say y'are sweet; how sho'd we know
Whether that you be sweet or no?
From powders and perfumes keep free;
Then we shall smell how sweet you be.

                                        —*Robert Herrick*

The Golf Links

The golf links lie so near the mill
      That almost every day
The laboring children can look out
      And see the men at play.

                                        —*Sarah Cleghorn*

An Old Colt

For all night-sinnes, with others wives, unknowne,
Colt, now, doth daily penance in his owne.

—Ben Jonson

To Doctor Empirick

When men a dangerous disease did scape,
Of old, they gave a cock to Æsculape;
Let me give two: that doubly am got free,
From my diseases danger, and from thee.

—Ben Jonson

2. *Aesculape*: Roman god of medicine and healing.

Epigram on Milton

Three poets, in three distant ages born,
Greece, Italy, and England did adorn.
The first in loftiness of thought surpassed,
The next in majesty, in both the last:
The force of Nature could no farther go;   5
To make a third, she joined the former two.

—John Dryden

Gemini

Because poor PUER's both unsure and vain,
Those who befriend him suffer his disdain,
While those who snub him gain his deference.
He loves his enemies, in a certain sense.

It is the power of Heaven to withdraw   5
Which fills PUELLA with religious awe.
She worships the remoteness of a wraith.
If God should die for her, she'd lose her faith.

—Richard Wilbur

1. *puer*: boy. 6. *puella*: girl. 7. *wraith*: a visible spirit.

Ana {Mary / Army} gram

How well her name an *Army* doth present,
In whom the Lord of Hosts did pitch his tent!

                                                        —*George Herbert*

Little Lyric (Of Great Importance)

I wish the rent
Was heaven sent.

                                                        —*Langston Hughes*

Gone Boy

Playboy of the dawn,
Solid gone!
Out all night
Until 12—1—2 a.m.

Next day
When he should be gone
To work—
Dog-gone!
He ain't gone.

                                                        —*Langston Hughes*

from Essay on Criticism

A perfect judge will read each work of wit
With the same spirit that its author writ:
Survey the whole, nor seek slight faults to find
Where nature moves, and rapture warms the mind;
Nor lose, for that malignant dull delight,
The gen'rous pleasure to be charmed with wit.
But in such lays as neither ebb nor flow,

5

Correctly cold, and regularly low,
That, shunning faults, one quiet tenor keep,
We cannot blame indeed—but we may sleep.   10
In wit, as nature, what affects our hearts
Is not th' exactness of peculiar parts;
'Tis not a lip or eye we beauty call,
But the joint force and full result of all.
Thus when we view some well proportioned dome   15
(The world's just wonder, and ev'n thine, O Rome!)
No single parts unequally surprise;
All comes united to th' admiring eyes;
No monstrous height or breadth or length appear;
The whole at once is bold, and regular.   20
    Whoever thinks a faultless piece to see,
Thinks what ne'er was, nor is, nor e'er shall be.
In ev'ry work regard the writer's end,
Since none can compass more than they intend;
And if the means be just, the conduct true,   25
Applause, in spite of trivial faults, is due.
As men of breeding, sometimes men of wit,
T' avoid great errors must the less commit,
Neglect the rules each verbal critic lays,
For not to know some trifles is a praise.   30
Most critics, fond of some subservient art,
Still make the whole depend upon a part;
They talk of principles, but notions prize,
And all to one loved folly sacrifice.
    Once on a time La Mancha's knight, they say,   35
A certain bard encount'ring on the way,
Discoursed in terms as just, with looks as sage,
As e'er could Dennis, of the Grecian stage;
Concluding all were desp'rate sots and fools
Who durst depart from Aristotle's rules.   40
Our author, happy in a judge so nice,
Produced his play, and begged the knight's advice;
Made him observe the subject and the plot,
The manners, passions, unities—what not?
All which exact to rule were brought about,   45
Were but a combat in the lists left out.
"What! leave the combat out?" exclaims the knight.

"Yes, or we must renounce the Stagirite."
"Not so, by heav'n!" he answers in a rage;
"Knights, squires, and steeds must enter on the stage." 50
"So vast a throng the stage can ne'er contain."
"Then build a new, or act it in a plain."
   Thus critics of less judgment than caprice,
Curious, not knowing, not exact but nice,
Form short ideas, and offend in arts 55
(As most in manners) by a love to parts.
   Some to conceit alone their taste confine,
And glitt'ring thoughts struck out at ev'ry line;
Pleased with a work where nothing's just or fit,
One glaring chaos and wild heap of wit. 60
Poets, like painters, thus unskilled to trace
The naked nature and the living grace,
With gold and jewels cover ev'ry part,
And hide with ornaments their want of art.
True wit is nature to advantage dressed, 65
What oft was thought, but ne'er so well expressed;
Something whose truth convinced at sight we find,
That gives us back the image of our mind.
As shades more sweetly recommend the light,
So modest plainness sets off sprightly wit; 70
For works may have more wit than does 'em good,
As bodies perish through excess of blood.
   Others for language all their care express,
And value books, as women men, for dress.
Their praise is still, "The style is excellent."— 75
The sense they humbly take upon content.
Words are like leaves; and where they most abound,
Much fruit of sense beneath is rarely found.
False eloquence, like the prismatic glass,
Its gaudy colors spreads on ev'ry place; 80
The face of nature we no more survey:
All glares alike, without distinction gay.
But true expression, like th' unchanging sun,
Clears and improves whate'er it shines upon;
It gilds all objects, but it alters none. 85
Expression is the dress of thought, and still
Appears more decent as more suitable;

A vile conceit in pompous words expressed
Is like a clown in regal purple dressed;
For diff'rent styles with diff'rent subjects sort,   90
As sev'ral garbs with country, town, and court.
Some by old words to fame have made pretense,
Ancients in phrase, mere moderns in their sense;
Such labored nothings, in so strange a style,
Amaze th' unlearn'd, and make the learned smile.   95
Unlucky as Fungoso in the play,
These sparks with awkward vanity display
What the fine gentleman wore yesterday;
And but so mimic ancient wits, at best,
As apes our grandsires, in their doublets dressed.   100
In words as fashions the same rule will hold,
Alike fantastic if too new or old:
Be not the first by whom the new are tried,
Nor yet the last to lay the old aside.
    But most by numbers judge a poet's song,   105
And smooth or rough with them is right or wrong:
In the bright Muse though thousand charms conspire,
Her voice is all these tuneful fools admire;
Who haunt Parnassus but to please their ear,
Not mend their minds; as some to church repair,   110
Not for the doctrine, but the music there.
These equal syllables alone require,
Though oft the ear the open vowels tire;
While expletives their feeble aid do join,
And ten low words oft creep in one dull line;   115
While they ring round the same unvaried chimes,
With sure returns of still-expected rimes:
Where'er you find "the cooling western breeze,"
In the next line it "whispers through the trees";
If crystal streams "with pleasing murmurs creep,"   120
The reader's threatened (not in vain) with "sleep";
Then, at the last and only couplet fraught
With some unmeaning thing they call a thought,
A needless Alexandrine ends the song,
That, like a wounded snake, drags its slow length along.   125
Leave such to tune their own dull rimes, and know

What's roundly smooth or languishingly slow;
And praise the easy vigor of a line
Where Denham's strength and Waller's sweetness join.
True ease in writing comes from art, not chance,   130
As those move easiest who have learned to dance.
'Tis not enough no harshness gives offense;
The sound must seem an echo to the sense.
Soft is the strain when zephyr gently blows,
And the smooth stream in smoother numbers flows;   135
But when loud surges lash the sounding shore,
The hoarse, rough verse should like the torrent roar.
When Ajax strives some rock's vast weight to throw,
The line too labors, and the words move slow;
Not so when swift Camilla scours the plain,   140
Flies o'er the unbending corn, and skims along the main.
Hear how Timotheus' varied lays surprise,
And bid alternate passions fall and rise!
While, at each change, the son of Libyan Jove
Now burns with glory and then melts with love;   145
Now his fierce eyes with sparkling fury glow,
Now sighs steal out and tears begin to flow:
Persians and Greeks like turns of nature found,
And the world's victor stood subdued by sound!
The pow'r of music all our hearts allow,   150
And what Timotheus was, is Dryden now.

                                                    —*Alexander Pope*

35. *La Mancha's knight*: Don Quixote. The episode Pope describes is not from
the original, but from a spurious continuation. 38. *Dennis*: a popular critic
(1657–1734). 57. *conceit*: metaphor, usually overly clever or ingenious. 76. *upon
content*: on trust. 90. *sort*: consort, harmonize, are appropriate. 96. *Fungoso*: the
foppish butt of many of Jonson's jokes in *Every Man Out Of His Humor*. 105.
numbers: versification. Note how Pope makes the lines exemplify the defects of
sound they condemn, just as many of his previous lines exemplified the defects
of sense they attacked. 124. *Alexandrine*: a line of six iambic feet—like the line
following. 129. *Denham . . . and Waller*: minor poets influential in the development of the heroic couplet in which Pope is writing. 138. *Ajax*: a Greek hero,
characterized in English literature from the Renaissance on as exceptionally strong
and exceptionally thick-witted. 140. *Camilla*: a woman who fought against the
Trojans after they arrived in Italy (cf. *Aeneid* VII. 808 ff.). 142. *Timotheus*: a
musician of Alexander the Great. The reference may be to Dryden's "Alexander's
Feast." 151. *Dryden*: a major British poet, contemporary of Pope.

DRAMATIC MONOLOGUES

A *dramatic monologue* is exactly what the name implies: a poem recording the speech, usually informal, of a single fictional character (not the poet himself) who reveals to the reader something of his personality, his past, and the situation in which he finds himself when he speaks the poem. It is never introduced, like Tennyson's "Lotos-Eaters," with "He said"; ordinarily it does not contain description by anyone except the character giving the monologue. For the duration of the poem the poet steps outside of himself and assumes the personality of the speaker; he writes a poem that records what purports to be the actual speech of the Duke of Ferrara, Isaac, Gerontion, or whomever the poet is impersonating.

Stricter definitions of the genre require that we meet the speaker at a crucial point in his life, a moment when he himself reaches some new self-awareness or reveals his character dramatically to someone else. The reader is able to identify a listener in many cases: we learn in "My Last Duchess," for example, that Ferrara is talking to an emmisary of the father of his next duchess, and that they are negotiating about arrangements for the marriage. Browning's "The Bishop Orders His Tomb" tells us about the speaker's past as well as his present, and makes it clear to us and eventually to the bishop himself that the two bastard sons to whom he is speaking will most certainly not bury him in the splendor he initially describes. The dramatic monologues of the nineteenth century, especially those of Browning, are probably the high point of the art's development; other artists who use the form are rarely so compact or so clever at conveying information by hints and suggestions. Frost, Eliot, Robinson, Lowell and many other contemporary poets have found the genre useful, and composers Leonard Cohen and Paul Simon both write songs that might be considered dramatic monologues: "The Story of Isaac," "Overs," "the Boxer." Ochs and Dylan, whose lyrics frequently treat character in crisis, do not usually create fictional characters—the narrators of "Visions of Johanna" and "Rehearsals for Retirement" are most probably the poets themselves. Neither song, then, is a dramatic monologue.

Dover Beach

The sea is calm to-night.
The tide is full, the moon lies fair
Upon the straits;—on the French coast the light
Gleams and is gone; the cliffs of England stand,
Glimmering and vast, out in the tranquil bay.   5
Come to the window, sweet is the night-air!
Only, from the long line of spray
Where the sea meets the moon-blanch'd land,
Listen! you hear the grating roar
Of pebbles which the waves draw back, and fling,   10
At their return, up the high strand,
Begin, and cease, and then again begin,
With tremulous cadence slow, and bring
The eternal note of sadness in.

Sophocles long ago   15
Heard it on the Ægean, and it brought
Into his mind the turbid ebb and flow
Of human misery; we
Find also in the sound a thought,
Hearing it by this distant northern sea.   20

The Sea of Faith
Was once, too, at the full, and round earth's shore
Lay like the folds of a bright girdle furl'd.
But now I only hear
Its melancholy, long, withdrawing roar,   25
Retreating, to the breath
Of the night-wind, down the vast edges drear
And naked shingles of the world.

Ah, love, let us be true
To one another! for the world, which seems   30
To lie before us like a land of dreams,
So various, so beautiful, so new,
Hath really neither joy, nor love, nor light,

Nor certitude, nor peace, nor help for pain;
And we are here as on a darkling plain   35
Swept with confused alarms of struggle and flight,
Where ignorant armies clash by night.

—Matthew Arnold

15. *Sophocles*: Greek tragedian, author of *Oedipus Rex*.

The dramatic situation in which the speaker confronts us can be re-
constructed from hints in his speech by a little ingenuity on our part.
A man is looking out of a window (line 6) at Dover Beach (title) and
beyond it to France (line 3). He muses on the tranquility of the night,
the beauty of the cliffs and the bay and the glimmering lights on the
opposite coast, and listens pensively to the "tremulous cadence" of the
ocean. The tide is going out, and the waves pick up pebbles as they approach the shore, then fling them back along the sand as they break.
The sound of the grating pebbles is all that undercuts the magic of the
moonlight night along the spectacular cliffs of Dover.

But the pebbles are enough to set the speaker thinking; they bring in,
as he puts it, a note of sadness. Just what the speaker means by this
note of sadness is not yet clear (either to himself or to us), but it starts
him thinking of Sophocles, the Greek tragedian, whose primary concern was, as the speaker sees it, the ebb and flow of human sadness.
Perhaps the speaker is projecting his own views onto Sophocles; perhaps he sees in the Greek a man from a distant time and culture who
shares something of his own outlook on the human situation. In any
event, we begin to understand now the note of human sadness in line
14. Then the speaker develops his thought further by comparing the
sea before him and faith (lines 21ff.). By line 28 his thoughts have
wandered a long way, geographically and philosophically, from the beginning of the poem, and we are snapped back to reality in line 29.
The speaker addresses his love (we do not know whether it is his wife
or not) and suggests that in the face of a world in which ignorance,
confusion, and darkness prevail, a world without faith, all that is left is
for lovers to be true to one another. The closing image—the darking
plain upon which ignorant armies clash—finally defines for us what
Arnold meant by the note of sadness and the sea of faith: faith amounts
to certitude and love and joy and peace and light—all the things absent

now; the note of sadness is a note of regret at the loss of all these marks
of civilized society. The realization, which has dawned on the speaker
as gradually as it dawns on us, brings the poem to a rather dark conclusion.

Review the poem carefully. Note the significance of the glimmering
lights in line 4, the irony in the opening description of the beautiful,
sweet, pleasant evening, the impact of the "naked shingles" image. Note
too Arnold's careful use of language as sound in this poem; his use of
assonance, alliteration, kinesthesia, euphony, and cacophony. Note too
the way sound parallels sense. All of these considerations—sound, sense,
theme, structure—combine to make "Dover Beach" a great poem.

My Last Duchess

Ferrara

That's my last Duchess painted on the wall,
Looking as if she were alive. I call
That piece a wonder, now: Frà Pandolf's hands
Worked busily a day, and there she stands.
Will't please you sit and look at her? I said   5
"Frà Pandolf" by design, for never read
Strangers like you that pictured countenance,
The depth and passion of its earnest glance,
But to myself they turned (since none puts by
The curtain I have drawn for you, but I)   10
And seemed as they would ask me, if they durst,
How such a glance came there; so, not the first
Are you to turn and ask thus. Sir, 'twas not
Her husband's presence only, called that spot
Of joy into the Duchess' cheek: perhaps   15
Frà Pandolf chanced to say, "Her mantel laps
Over my lady's wrist too much," or "Paint
Must never hope to reproduce the faint
Half-flush that dies along her throat": such stuff
Was courtesy, she thought, and cause enough   20
For calling up that spot of joy. She had
A heart—how shall I say?—too soon made glad,
Too easily impressed: she liked whate'er

She looked on, and her looks went everywhere.
Sir, 'twas all one! My favor at her breast,   25
The dropping of the daylight in the West,
The bough of cherries some officious fool
Broke in the orchard for her, the white mule
She rode with round the terrace—all and each
Would draw from her alike the approving speech,   30
Or blush, at least. She thanked men—good! but thanked
Somehow—I know not how—as if she ranked
My gift of a nine-hundred-years-old name
With anybody's gift. Who'd stoop to blame
This sort of trifling? Even had you skill   35
In speech—(which I have not)—to make your will
Quite clear to such an one, and say, "Just this
Or that in you disgusts me; here you miss,
Or there exceed the mark"—and if she let
Herself be lessoned so, nor plainly set   40
Her wits to yours, forsooth, and made excuse,
—E'en then would be some stooping; and I choose
Never to stoop. Oh sir, she smiled, no doubt,
Whene'er I passed her; but who passed without
Much the same smile? This grew; I gave commands;   45
Then all smiles stopped together. There she stands
As if alive. Will't please you rise? We'll meet
The company below, then. I repeat,
The Count your master's known munificence
Is ample warrant that no just pretence   50
Of mine for dowry will be disallowed;
Though his fair daughter's self, as I avowed
At starting, is my object. Nay, we'll go
Together down, sir. Notice Neptune, though,
Taming a sea-horse, thought a rarity,   55
Which Claus of Innsbruck cast in bronze for me!

                      —*Robert Browning*

Ferrara: Ruler and kingdom of Renaissance Italy. 3. *Fra Pandolf*: a fictional painter. The painting sounds suspiciously like the "Mona Lisa" of Da Vinci. 56. *Klaus of Innsbruck*: a fictional sculptor. Such a statue exists today in the Palace of the Doges, Venice.

The Story of Isaac

The door it opened slowly
  My father he came in
  I was nine years old
And he stood so tall above me
  Blue eyes they were shining   5
  And his voice was very cold.
Said, "I've had a vision
  And you know I'm strong and holy
  I must do what I've been told."
So he started up the mountain   10
  I was running he was walking
  And his ax was made of gold.

The trees they got much smaller
  The lake a lady's mirror
  We stopped to drink some wine   15
Then he threw the bottle over
  Broke a minute later
  And he put his hand on mine.
Thought I saw an eagle
  But it might have been a vulture,   20
  I never could decide.
Then my father built an altar
  He looked once behind his shoulder
  He knew I would not hide.

You who build the altars now   25
  To sacrifice these children
  You must not do it any more.
A scheme is not a vision
  And you never have been tempted
  By a demon or a god.   30
You who stand above them now

Your hatchets blunt and bloody,
   You were not there before.
When I lay upon a mountain
   And my father's hand was trembling   35
   With the beauty of the word.

And if you call me brother now
   Forgive me if I inquire
   Just according to whose plan?
When it all comes down to dust   40
   I will kill you if I must
   I will help you if I can.
When it all comes down to dust
   I will help you if I must
   I will kill you if I can.   45
And mercy on our uniform
Man of peace or man of war—
   The peacock spreads his fan.

—Leonard Cohen

The Bishop Orders His Tomb at Saint Praxed's Church

Rome, 15—

Vanity, saith the preacher, vanity!
Draw round my bed: is Anselm keeping back?
Nephews—sons mine . . . ah God, I know not! Well—
She, men would have to be your mother once,
Old Gandolf envied me, so fair she was!   5
What's done is done, and she is dead beside,
Dead long ago, and I am Bishop since,
And as she died so must we die ourselves,
And thence ye may perceive the world's a dream.
Life, how and what is it? As here I lie   10
In this state-chamber, dying by degrees,
Hours and long hours in the dead night, I ask
"Do I live, am I dead?" Peace, peace seems all.
Saint Praxed's ever was the church for peace;
And so, about this tomb of mine. I fought   15
With tooth and nail to save my niche, ye know:

—Old Gandolf cozened me, despite my care;
Shrewd was that snatch from out the corner South
He graced his carrion with, God curse the same!
Yet still my niche is not so cramped but thence   20
One sees the pulpit o' the epistle-side,
And somewhat of the choir, those silent seats,
And up into the aery dome where live
The angels, and a sunbeam's sure to lurk:
And I shall fill my slab of basalt there,   25
And 'neath my tabernacle take my rest,
With those nine columns round me, two and two,
The odd one at my feet where Anselm stands:
Peach-blossom marble all, the rare, the ripe
As fresh-poured red wine of a mighty pulse.   30
—Old Gandolf with his paltry onion-stone,
Put me where I may look at him! True peach,
Rosy and flawless: how I earned the prize!
Draw close: that conflagration of my church
—What then? So much was saved if aught were missed!   35
My sons, ye would not be my death? Go dig
The white-grape vineyard where the oil-press stood,
Drop water gently till the surface sink,
And if ye find . . . Ah God, I know not, I! . . .
Bedded in store of rotten fig-leaves soft,   40
And corded up in a tight olive-frail,
Some lump, ah God, of *lapis lazuli*,
Big as a Jew's head cut off at the nape,
Blue as a vein o'er the Madonna's breast . . .
Sons, all have I bequeathed you, villas, all,   45
That brave Frascati villa with its bath,
So, let the blue lump poise between my knees,
Like God the Father's globe on both his hands
Ye worship in the Jesu Church so gay,
For Gandolf shall not choose but see and burst!   50
Swift as a weaver's shuttle fleet our years:
Man goeth to the grave, and where is he?
Did I say basalt for my slab, sons? Black—
'Twas ever antique-black I meant! How else
Shall ye contrast my frieze to come beneath?   55
The bas-relief in bronze ye promised me,

Those Pans and Nymphs ye wot of, and perchance
Some tripod, thyrsus, with a vase or so,
The Saviour at his sermon on the mount,
Saint Praxed in a glory, and one Pan   60
Ready to twitch the Nymph's last garment off,
And Moses with the tables . . . but I know
Ye mark me not! What do they whisper thee,
Child of my bowels, Anselm? Ah, ye hope
To revel down my villas while I gasp   65
Bricked o'er with beggar's mouldy travertine
Which Gandolf from his tomb-top chuckles at!
Nay, boys, ye love me—all of jasper, then!
'Tis jasper ye stand pledged to, lest I grieve
My bath must needs be left behind, alas!   70
One block, pure green as a pistachio-nut,
There's plenty of jasper somewhere in the world—
And have I not Saint Praxed's ear to pray
Horses for ye, and brown Greek manuscripts,
And mistresses with great smooth marbly limbs?   75
—That's if ye carve my epitaph aright,
Choice Latin, picked phrase, Tully's every word,
No gaudy ware like Gandolf's second line—
Tully, my masters? Ulpian serves his need!
And then how I shall lie through centuries,   80
And hear the blessed mutter of the mass,
And see God made and eaten all day long,
And feel the steady candle-flame, and taste
Good strong thick stupefying incense-smoke!
For as I lie here, hours of the dead night,   85
Dying in state and by such slow degrees,
I fold my arms as if they clasped a crook,
And stretch my feet forth straight as stone can point,
And let the bedclothes, for a mortcloth, drop
Into great laps and folds of sculptor's-work: 90
And as yon tapers dwindle, and strange thoughts
Grow, with a certain humming in my ears,
About the life before I lived this life,
And this life too, popes, cardinals and priests,
Saint Praxed at his sermon on the mount,   95
Your tall pale mother with her talking eyes,

And new-found agate urns as fresh as day,
And marble's language, Latin pure, discreet,
—Aha, ELUCESCEBAT quoth our friend?
No Tully, said I, Ulpian at the best! 100
Evil and brief hath been my pilgrimage.
All *lapis*, all, sons! Else I give the Pope
My villas! Will ye ever eat my heart?
Ever your eyes were as a lizard's quick,
They glitter like your mother's for my soul, 105
Or ye would heighten my impoverished frieze,
Piece out its starved design, and fill my vase
With grapes, and add a vizor and a Term,
And to the tripod ye would tie a lynx
That in his struggle throws the thyrsus down, 110
To comfort me on my entablature
Whereon I am to lie till I must ask
"Do I live, am I dead?" There, leave me, there!
For ye have stabbed me with ingratitude
To death—ye wish it—God, ye wish it! Stone— 115
Gritstone, a-crumble! Clammy squares which sweat
As if the corpse they keep were oozing through—
And no more *lapis* to delight the world!
Well go! I bless ye. Fewer tapers there,
But in a row: and, going, turn your backs 120
—Ay, like departing altar-ministrants,
And leave me in my church, the church for peace,
That I may watch at leisure if he leers—
Old Gandolf, at me, from his onion-stone,
As still he envied me, so fair she was! 125

—*Robert Browning*

1. *Vanity* . . .: Cf. Ecclesiates, i:2. 14. *St. Praxed's*: the church actually exists in Rome, although it is much smaller than this poem would suggest. 21. *epistle-side*: the right side as one faces the altar. 31. *onion-stone*: a cheap marble prone to peeling. 41. *frail*: basket. 42. *lapis lazuli*: a bluish semi-precious stone. 46. *Frascati*: a town in the hills near Rome. 54. *antique-black*: a more expensive stone than basalt, also black. 57. *wot*: know. 58. *thyrsus*: a staff surmounted with a cone or ivy vines. 60. Note the garish mixture of scenes the Bishop orders. 77. *Tully*: Cicero, whose Latin was impeccable. 79. *Ulpian*: Domitius Ulpian (170–228 A.D.), whose Latin was of a lower quality. 82. *God made and eaten*: the reference is to the celebration of mass. 99. *Elucescebat*: "he was illustrious." The Latin is that of Ulpian, not of Cicero. 108. *vizor*: mask; *term*: bust. 116. *gritstone*: sandstone.

Mr. Edwards and the Spider

I saw the spiders marching through the air,
Swimming from tree to tree that mildewed day
   In latter August when the hay
   Came creaking to the barn. But where
      The wind is westerly,   5
Where gnarled November makes the spiders fly
Into the apparitions of the sky,
They purpose nothing but their ease and die
Urgently beating east to sunrise and the sea;

What are we in the hands of the great God?   10
It was in vain you set up thorn and briar
   In battle array against the fire
   And treason crackling in your blood;
      For the wild thorns grow tame
And will do nothing to oppose the flame;   15
Your lacerations tell the losing game
You play against a sickness past your cure.
How will the hands be strong? How will the heart endure?

A very little thing, a little worm,
Or hourglass-blazoned spider, it is said,   20
   Can kill a tiger. Will the dead
   Hold up his mirror and affirm
      To the four winds the smell
And flash of his authority? It's well
If God who holds you to the pit of hell,   25
Much as one holds a spider, will destroy,
Baffle and dissipate your soul. As a small boy

On Windsor Marsh, I saw the spider die
When thrown into the bowels of fierce fire:
   There's no long struggle, no desire   30
   To get up on its feet and fly—
      It stretches out its feet
And dies. This is the sinner's last retreat;

Yet, and no strength exerted on the heat
Then sinews the abolished will, when sick   35
And full of burning, it will whistle on a brick.

But who can plumb the sinking of that soul?
Josiah Hawley, picture yourself cast
   Into a brick-kiln where the blast
    Fans your quick vitals to a coal—   40
      If measured by a glass,
How long would it seem burning! Let there pass
A minute, ten, ten trillion; but the blaze
Is infinite, eternal: this is death,
To die and know it. This is the Black Widow, death.   45
                       —*Robert Lowell*

Title: The speaker is the eighteenth-century Puritan Jonathan Edwards, and much of the poem is derived from phrases and images in his writings. Particularly important among these is the well known sermon "Sinners in the Hands of an Angry God." 38. *Josiah Hawley*s possibly Edwards' uncle, Joseph Hawley.

Gerontion

                          Thou hast nor youth nor age
                          But as it were after dinner sleep
                          Dreaming of both.

Here I am, an old man in a dry month,
Being read to by a boy, waiting for rain.
I was neither at the hot gates
Nor fought in the warm rain
Nor knee deep in the salt marsh, heaving a cutlass,   5
Bitten by flies, fought.
My house is a decayed house,
And the jew squats on the window sill, the owner,
Spawned in some estaminet of Antwerp,
Blistered in Brussels, patched and peeled in London.   10
The goat coughs at night in the field overhead;
Rocks, moss, stonecrop, iron, merds.
The woman keeps the kitchen, makes tea,
Sneezes at evening, poking the peevish gutter.
               I an old man,   15
A dull head among windy spaces.

Signs are taken for wonders. "We would see a sign!"
The word within a word, unable to speak a word,
Swaddled with darkness. In the juvescence of the year
Came Christ the tiger   20

In depraved May, dogwood and chestnut, flowering judas,
To be eaten, to be divided, to be drunk
Among whispers; by Mr. Silvero
With caressing hands, at Limoges
Who walked all night in the next room;   25

By Hakagawa, bowing among the Titians;
By Madame de Tornquist, in the dark room
Shifting the candles; Fräulein von Kulp
Who turned in the hall, one hand on the door.
                Vacant shuttles   30
Weave the wind. I have no ghosts,
An old man in a draughty house
Under a windy knob.

After such knowledge, what forgiveness? Think now
History has many cunning passages, contrived corridors   35
And issues, deceives with whispering ambitions,
Guides us by vanities. Think now
She gives when our attention is distracted
And what she gives, gives with such supple confusions
That the giving famishes the craving. Gives too late   40
What's not believed in, or if still believed,
In memory only, reconsidered passion. Gives too soon
Into weak hands, what's thought can be dispensed with
Till the refusal propagates a fear. Think
Neither fear nor courage saves us. Unnatural vices   45
Are fathered by our heroism. Virtues
Are forced upon us by our impudent crimes.
These tears are shaken from the wrath-bearing tree.

The tiger springs in the new year. Us he devours.
                Think at last   50
We have not reached conclusion, when I

Stiffen in a rented house. Think at last
I have not made this show purposelessly
And it is not by any concitation
Of the backward devils   55
I would meet you upon this honestly.
I that was near your heart was removed therefrom
To lose beauty in terror, terror in inquisition.
I have lost my passion: why should I need to keep it
Since what is kept must be adulterated?   60
I have lost my sight, smell, hearing, taste and touch:
How should I use them for your closer contact?

These with a thousand small deliberations
Protract the profit of their chilled delirium,
Excite the membrane, when the sense has cooled,   65
With pungent sauces, multiply variety
In a wilderness of mirrors. What will the spider do,
Suspend its operations, will the weevil
Delay? De Bailhache, Fresca, Mrs. Cammel, whirled
Beyond the circuit of the shuddering Bear   70
In fractured atoms. Gull against the wind, in the windy straits
Of Belle Isle, or running on the Horn,
White feathers in the snow, the Gulf claims,
And an old man driven by the Trades
To a sleepy corner.   75
              Tenants of the house,
Thoughts of a dry brain in a dry season.

                                            —*T. S. Eliot*

Title: Eliot coined the word from the Greek *geron*, an old man. Epigraph: *Measure for Measure* III. 1. 32–34. 3. *hot gates*: a literal translation of Thermopylae. 12. *merds*: French for dung. 17. *We would see*: Cf. John 4:48. 18. *Word within a word*: Cf. John 1:1. 54. *concitation*: action.

COMPLAINTS

A *literary complaint* is a lyric poem in which the poet quite literally complains about (1) his unrequited love, his cruel mistress, or his mistreatment by his lover; (2) his generally unfortunate state; or (3) the miserable condition of the world around him. These subjects take in a broad spectrum of poems, however, and some further restriction of the term is necessary. Usually a complaint is an apostrophe by the poet addressed to some particular individual or personification: the mistress in question, the god of love, Fortune or Fate, God himself, or even the poem itself. Usually the poet does more than merely lament: he gives us some insight, either overt or indirect, into the causes of his sorrow, frequently discusses remedies, and often makes a direct appeal to some-one—his mistress, love, Fortune, God—for help in resolving his situation. While the complaint was most popular during the Renaissance, when virtually every poet apparently had several cruel mistresses and wrote poems to all of them, the genre has been popular since then and is in use today. The expression of a complaint is invariably formalized, and the poetry sounds strangely emotionless and conventional, more stylized than naturalistic. Every age has its conventionalized rhetoric, and the use of such rhetoric in the complaint helps add this stylized quality. One would hardly say, for example, that "Bye Bye, Love" conveys a feeling of genuine emotion in either its diction or its melody. The rhymes are conventional, some of the expressions are trite to the point where they cease to have any emotional appeal at all. But such is the nature of the genre, and given the diction of the 1950's, "Bye Bye, Love" is a pretty good complaint. Perhaps the very act of expressing emotion in such conventional diction helps to sublimate the feeling into rhetoric and mitigate whatever emotional distress the poet or reader might suffer.

Bye Bye, Love

There goes my baby with someone new;
She sure looks happy; I sure am blue;
She was my baby 'till he stepped in;
Goodbye to romance that might have been;

Bye Bye, Love;   5
Bye Bye, happiness;
Hello loneliness
I think I'm gonna cry;
Bye Bye, Love;

Bye Bye, sweet caress; 10
Hello emptiness;
I feel like I could die;

I'm through with romance, I'm through with love
I'm through with counting the stars above;
And here's the reason that I'm so free: 15
My lovin' baby is through with me.

      —Felice and Boudleaux Bryant

Farewell Love

Farewell Love, and all thy Laws for ever,
Thy baited hooks shall tangle me no more;
Senec and Plato call me from thy lore,
To perfect wealth my wit for to endeavor.
In blinde error when I did perséver, 5
Thy sharp repulse, that pricketh aye so sore,
Hath taught me to set in trifles no store,
And 'scape forth, since liberty is lever.
Therefore farewell, go trouble younger hearts,
And in me claim no more authority; 10
With idle youth go use thy property,
And thereon spend thy many brittle darts.
 For hitherto, though I have lost all my time,
 Me lusteth no longer rotten boughs to climb.

      —Sir Thomas Wyatt

 4. *my wit . . . endeavor*: to turn my attention. 8. *lever*: preferable, dearer.
14. *Me lusteth*: I desire.

Farewell, False Love

Farewell, false love, the oracle of lies,
A mortal foe and enemy to rest;
An envious boy, from whom all cares arise,
A bastard vile, a beast with rage possessed;

A way of error, a temple full of treason,   5
In all effects contrary unto reason.

A poisoned serpent covered all with flowers,
Mother of sighs and murtherer of repose,
A sea of sorrows from whence are drawn such showers
As moisture lends to every grief that grows;   10
A school of guile, a net of deep deceit,
A gilded hook that holds a poisoned bait.

A fortress foiled which reason did defend,
A siren song, a fever of the mind,
A maze wherein affection finds no end,   15
A raging cloud that runs before the wind,
A substance like the shadow of the sun,
A goal of grief for which the wisest run.

A quenchless fire, a nurse of trembling fear,
A path that leads to peril and mishap;   20
A true retreat of sorrow and despair,
An idle boy that sleeps in pleasure's lap,
A deep distrust of that which certain seems,
A hope of that which reason doubtful deems.

Sith then thy trains my younger years betrayed,   25
And for my faith ingratitude I find,
And sith repentance hath my wrongs bewrayed
Whose course was ever contrary to kind—
False love, desire, and beauty frail, adieu!
Dead is the root whence all these fancies grew.   30

                                             —*Sir Walter Raleigh*

Behold, Love

Behold, love, thy power how she despiseth!
My great pain how little she regardeth!
    The holy oath, whereof she taketh no cure,
    Broken she hath; and yet she bideth sure

Right at her ease and little she dreadeth. 5
Weaponed thou art, and she unarmed sitteth;
To thee, disdainful her life she ledeth,
   To me spiteful without cause or measure,
      Behold, love.

I am in hold: if pity thee moveth, 10
Go bend thy bow, that stony heartés breaketh,
   And with some stroke revenge the displeasure
   Of thee and him, that sorrow doeth endure,
And, as his lord, thee lowly entreateth.
      Behold, love. 15

                    —*Sir Thomas Wyatt*

A Leave-Taking

LET us go hence, my songs; she will not hear.
Let us go hence together without fear;
Keep silence now, for singing-time is over,
And over all old things and all things dear.
She loves not you nor me as all we love her. 5
Yea, though we sang as angels in her ear,
   She would not hear.

Let us rise up and part; she will not know.
Let us go seaward as the great winds go,
Full of blown sand and foam; what help is here? 10
There is no help, for all these things are so,
And all the world is bitter as a tear.
And how these things are, though ye strove to show,
   She would not know.

Let us go home and hence; she will not weep. 15
We gave love many dreams and days to keep,
Flowers without scent, and fruits that would not grow,
Saying "If thou wilt, thrust in thy sickle and reap."
All is reaped now; no grass is left to mow;
And we that sowed, though all we fell on sleep, 20
   She would not weep.

Let us go hence and rest; she will not love.
She shall not hear us if we sing hereof,
Nor see love's ways, how sore they are and steep.
Come hence, let be, lie still; it is enough.   25
Love is a barren sea, bitter and deep;
And though she saw all heaven in flower above,
     She would not love.

Let us give up, go down; she will not care.
Though all the stars made gold of all the air,   30
And the sea moving saw before it move
One moon-flower making all the foam-flowers fair
Though all those waves went over us, and drove
Deep down the stifling lips and drowning hair,
     She would not care.   35

Let us go hence, go hence; she will not see.
Sing all once more together; surely she,
She too, remembering days and words that were,
Will turn a little toward us, sighing; but we,
We are hence, we are gone, as though we had not been there.   40
Nay, and though all men seeing had pity on me,
     She would not see.

                       —Algernon Charles Swinburne

The Negro's Complaint

Forc'd from home and all its pleasures,
   Afric's coast I left forlorn,
To increase a stranger's treasures,
   O'er the raging billows borne.
Men from England bought and sold me   5
   Paid my price in paltry gold;
But, though slave they have enroll'd me,
   Minds are never to be sold.

Still in thought as free as ever,
   What are England's rights, I ask,   10

Me from my delights to sever,
   Me to torture, me to task?
Fleecy locks and black complexion
   Cannot forfeit nature's claim;
Skins may differ, but affection
   Dwells in white and black the same.   15

Why did all-creating Nature
   Make the plant for which we toil?
Sighs must fan it, tears must water,
   Sweat of ours must dress the soil.   20
Think, ye masters, iron-hearted,
   Lolling at your jovial boards,
Think how many backs have smarted
   For the sweets your cane affords.

Is there, as ye sometimes tell us,   25
   Is there one who reigns on high?
Has he bid you buy and sell us,
   Speaking from his throne, the sky?
Ask him if your knotted scourges,
   Matches, blood-extorting screws,   30
Are the means which duty urges
   Agents of his will to use?

Hark! he answers!—Wild tornadoes,
   Strewing yonder sea with wrecks;
Wasting towns, plantations, meadows,   35
   Are the voice with which he speaks.
He, foreseeing what vexations
   Afric's sons should undergo,
Fix'd their tyrants' habitations
   Where his whirlwinds answer—No.   40

By our blood in Afric wasted,
   Ere our necks receiv'd the chain;
By the mis'ries that we tasted,
   Crossing in your barks the main;
By our suff'rings since ye brought us   45
   To the man-degrading mart;

All sustain'd by patience, taught us
    Only by a broken heart:

Deem our nation brutes no longer
    Till some reason ye shall find   50
Worthier of regard and stronger
    Than the color of our kind.
Slaves of gold, whose sordid dealings
    Tarnish all your boasted pow'rs,
Prove that you have human feelings,   55
    Ere you proudly question ours!

William Cowper

5. *England*: the poem was written in 1788 by an Englishman about slavery in that country and its colonies. 24. *cane*: sugar cane, harvested in the Caribbean with slave labor, which was used to produce the sweets consumed in England. 44. *barks*: ships.

Thou Art Indeed Just, Lord

> *Justus quidem tu es, Domine, si disputem tecum: verumtamen justa loquar ad te: Quare via impiorum prosperatur? etc.*

Thou art indeed just, Lord, if I contend
With thee; but, sir, so what I plead is just.
Why do sinners' ways prosper? and why must
Disappointment all I endeavor end?
Wert thou my enermy, O thou my friend,   5
How wouldst thou worse, I wonder, than thou dost
Defeat, thwart me? Oh, the sots and thralls of lust
Do in spare hours more thrive than I that spend,
Sir, life upon thy cause. See, banks and brakes
Now, leavèd how thick! lacèd they are again   10
With fretty chervil, look, and fresh wind shakes
Them; birds build—but not I build; no, but strain,
Time's eunuch, and not breed one work that wakes
Mine, O thou lord of life, send my roots rain.

—Gerard Manley Hopkins

Epigraph: Jeremiah 12:1, translated in lines 1–3 of the poem itself. 11. *fretty*: ornamented with an interlaced, angular design; *chervil*: a lacy plant much like parsley.

SONNETS

The sonnet was imported to England from Italy during the early Renaissance, around 1500 A.D. Although unusually demanding in its rhyme scheme, it has proven by far the most popular and enduring of all English genres. The early sonnet—the *Petrarchan* or *Italian sonnet* as it is called—is a poem of fourteen lines of iambic pentameter broken into two units: an octet (consisting of eight lines) and a sestet (the remaining six). The octet always rhymes *a b b a a b b a;* the sestet may rhyme in a variety of ways: *c d c c d c, c d e c d e, c d c d c.* The natural division falls between the octet and the sestet. Frequently, the one poses a paradox that the other resolves, or a question that is answered, or a problem that is solved. Obviously a verse form this tight, which gives a poet only four or five sounds on which to construct fourteen rhymes, is much more difficult in English, an uninflected language, than in Italian, where the inflectional endings can be used for rhymes. Less than a century after the sonnet's introduction into England, Shakespeare was busy popularizing the *English* or *Shakespearean sonnet,* which allows seven different sounds in its rhyme scheme: a series of three quatrains (four-line units) followed by a couplet, usually rhymed *a b a b c d c d e f e f g g.* The natural division of the Shakespearean sonnet is different from that of the Italian: it breaks cleanly into three major units that may be used to develop three parallel paradoxes (or pose three parallel questions) and a couplet that may then resolve, recapitulate, or answer. The major break is between line 12 and line 13, although the breaks between quatrains are usually observed, at least by some form of punctuation. On rare occasions an ambitious English poet attempts a *Spenserean sonnet,* which combines Italian and English rhymes in an *a b a b b c b c c d c d e e* pattern.

Part of the success of the sonnet is due to its amazing versatility, a versatility that makes the rules we have been discussing almost an exercise in pedantry. Poets vary rhyme schemes, ignore the obvious breaking points, experiment in meters other than pentameter and in feet other than iambic. It always surprises some people to discover that many poems by e. e. cummings, one of the freest of all modern English poets, are really sonnets in disguise. The following selections, coupled with a glance back and a glance ahead at some of the other sonnets in this book, should demonstrate some of the versatility of the form. Study the rhyme schemes, the organization of the material within the form, the

use of form to supplement and even to convey the major part of a
poem's meaning. Observe how a good poet like Wordsworth or Milton
is at home within the apparently narrow confines of fourteen lines. And
perhaps, merely as an exercise in appreciation of other poems, try composing a sonnet of your own.

My Galley Charged with Forgetfulness

My galley, chargèd with forgetfulness,
Thorough sharp seas in winter nights doth pass
'Tween rock and rock; and eke mine enemy, alas!
That is my Lord, steereth with cruelness;
And every oar a thought in readiness,   5
As though that death were light in such a case.
An endless wind doth tear the sail apace
Of forcèd sighs, and trusty fearfulness;
A rain of tears, a cloud of dark disdain,
Hath done the wearèd cords great hinderance,   10
Wreathèd with error and eke with ignorance.
The stars be hid that led me to this pain.
Drownèd is reason that should me comfort,
And I remain despairing of the port.
                                                      —*Sir Thomas Wyatt*

1. *charged*: laden. 3. *eke*: also.

The comparison between a despairing lover and a ship lost in a
storm at sea is traditional, and can be traced through the Middle Ages
to classical literature. This ship, "charged with forgetfulness" (i.e., laden
with neglect—his lady's neglect), is steered by the poet's cruel enemy,
his disdainful mistress, who guides him from one sorrow to another.
Wyatt works out his metaphor at considerable length: the ship's oars
are his thoughts, the storm is his sighs, the rain is his tears, the clouds
are his lady's disdain. Most significant, however, are the stars of line
12, probably the eyes of his lady. It was a convention of medieval and
Renaissance iconography that love proceeded from the eyes of the be-
loved through the eyes of the lover; thus it was probably the eyes of
his lady that first attracted Wyatt. They are now hid (presumably behind her disdainful behavior), and the poet is without guidance. The

eye as the source of knowledge is also a Neo-Platonic convention: to see is to know. The blinding, then, is metaphysical, as Wyatt goes on to point out in the final two lines of the sonnet: reason is drowned, it does not function. And unless reason functions, Wyatt the man and the lover can never hope to achieve the self-control that will bring him to port (that is, a state of emotional stability). The metaphor is complicated, but the metaphysics of the poem are even more complicated.

Look at the rhyme scheme of the sonnet. The obvious breaking points are after lines 4, 8, and 12, but Wyatt's punctuation and thought force breaks after lines 3, 6, 11, and 12. Just as the lover is somewhat disjointed, the sonnet is a bit disjointed. Contrast the divisions of thought in this poem with those in the next two sonnets by Shakespeare. Note how Shakespeare, in contrast to Wyatt, ends each quatrain with a colon or a period. But then, he does not have Wyatt's reasons for irregularity.

Sonnet 18

Shall I compare thee to a Summer's day?
Thou art more lovely and more temperate:
Rough winds do shake the darling buds of May,
And Summer's lease hath all too short a date:
Sometime too hot the eye of heaven shines,   5
And often is his gold complexion dimm'd,
And every fair from fair sometime declines,
By chance, or nature's changing course, untrimm'd;
But thy eternal Summer shall not fade,
Nor lose possession of that fair thou ow'st,   10
Nor shall Death brag thou wander'st in his shade,
When in eternal lines to time thou grow'st:
    So long as men can breathe, or eyes can see,
    So long lives this, and this gives life to thee.
                                    —*William Shakespeare*

Sonnet 73

That time of year thou mayest in me behold
When yellow leaves, or none, or few, do hang

Upon those boughs which shake against the cold,
Bare ruined choirs, where late the sweet birds sang.
In me thou seest the twilight of such day   5
As after sunset fadeth in the west,
Which by and by black night doth take away,
Death's second self, that seals up all in rest.
In me thou seest the glowing of such fire
That on the ashes of his youth doth lie,   10
As the death-bed whereon it must expire,
Consumed with that which it was nourished by.
  This thou perceiv'st, which makes thy love more strong,
  To love that well which thou must leave ere long.
                                        —*William Shakespeare*

On the Late Massacre in Piedmont

Avenge, O Lord, thy slaughtered saints, whose bones
  Lie scattered on the Alpine mountains cold;
  Even them who kept thy truth so pure of old
  When all our fathers worshipped stocks and stones,
Forget not; in thy book record their groans   5
  Who were thy sheep and in their ancient fold
  Slain by the bloody Piedmontese that rolled
  Mother with infant down the rocks. Their moans
The vales redoubled to the hills, and they
  To heaven. Their martyred blood and ashes sow   10
  O'er all the Italian fields where still doth sway
The triple tyrant: that from these may grow
  A hundredfold, who having learned thy way
  Early may fly the Babylonian woe.
                                        —*John Milton*

Title: The Waldenses, a heretical sect settled in northern Italy, had been
given freedom of worship until 1655, when it was abruptly terminated. The
massacre that resulted was vigorously protested by all the Protestant powers of
Europe. 4. *stocks and stones*: graven images. 12. *triple tyrant*: the Pope, so
named because of his three-crowned tiara. 14. *Babylonian*: an allusion to the
Babylonian captivity of the Jews and to the Babylonian Captivity of the Papacy,
when the Pope resided for nearly a century in France rather than Rome.

London, 1802

Milton! thou shouldst be living at this hour:
England hath need of thee: she is a fen
Of stagnant waters: altar, sword, and pen,
Fireside, the heroic wealth of hall and bower,
Have forfeited their ancient English dower   5
Of inward happiness. We are selfish men;
Oh! raise us up, return to us again;
And give us manners, virtue, freedom, power.
Thy soul was like a Star, and dwelt apart;
Thou hadst a voice whose sound was like the sea: 10
Pure as the naked heavens, majestic, free,
So didst thou travel on life's common way,
In cheerful godliness; and yet thy heart
The lowliest duties on herself did lay.

—*William Wordsworth*

The World Is Too Much with Us

The world is too much with us; late and soon,
Getting and spending, we lay waste our powers:
Little we see in Nature that is ours;
We have given our hearts away, a sordid boon!
This Sea that bares her bosom to the moon;   5
The winds that will be howling at all hours,
And are up-gathered now like sleeping flowers;
For this, for everything, we are out of tune;
It moves us not—Great God! I'd rather be
A Pagan suckled in a creed outworn;   10
So might I, standing on this pleasant lea,
Have glimpses that would make me less forlorn;
Have sight of Proteus rising from the sea;
Or hear old Triton blow his wreathèd horn.

—*William Wordsworth*

14. *Triton*: god of the sea, whose horn was a conch shell.

Leda and the Swan

A sudden blow: the great wings beating still
Above the staggering girl, her thighs caressed
By the dark webs, her nape caught in his bill,
He holds her helpless breast upon his breast.

How can those terrified vague fingers push   5
The feathered glory from her loosening thighs?
And how can body, laid in that white rush,
But feel the strange heart beating where it lies?

A shudder in the loins engenders there
The broken wall, the burning roof and tower   10
And Agamemnon dead.
                          Being so caught up,
So mastered by the brute blood of the air,
Did she put on his knowledge with his power
Before the indifferent beak could let her drop?
                                    —*William Butler Yeats*

Title: the subject of the poem is the rape of Leda by Jupiter, disguised as a
swan.

next to of course god

"next to of course god america i
love you land of the pilgrims' and so forth oh
say can you see by the dawn's early my
country 'tis of centuries come and go
and are no more what of it we should worry   5
in every language even deafanddumb
thy sons acclaim your glorious name by gorry
by jingo by gee by gosh by gum
why talk of beauty what could be more beaut-
iful than these heroic happy dead   10
who rushed like lions to the roaring slaughter

they did not stop to think they died instead
then shall the voice of liberty be mute?"

He spoke. And drank rapidly a glass of water

—e. e. cummings

Carrion Comfort

Not, I'll not, carrion comfort, Despair, not feast on thee;
Not untwist—slack they may be—these last strands of man
In me or, most weary, cry *I can no more*. I can;
Can something, hope, wish day come, not choose not to be.
But ah, but O thou terrible, why wouldst thou rude on me   5
Thy wring-world right foot rock? lay a lionlimb against me? scan
With darksome devouring eyes my bruisèd bones? and fan,
O in turns of tempest, me heaped there; me frantic to avoid thee
  and flee?
  Why? That my chaff might fly; my grain lie, sheer and clear.
Nay in all that toil, that coil, since (seems) I kissed the rod,   10
Hand rather, my heart lo! lapped strength, stole joy, would laugh,
  chéer.
Cheer whom though? the hero whose heaven-handling flung me,
  foot trod
Me? or me that fought him? O which one? is it each one? That
  night, that year
Of now done darkness I wretch lay wrestling with (my God!)
  my God.

—Gerard Manley Hopkins

Anthem for a Doomed Youth

What passing-bells for these who die as cattle?
  Only the monstrous anger of the guns.
  Only the stuttering rifles' rapid rattle
Can pattern out their hasty orisons.
  No mockeries for them; no prayers nor bells,   5

Nor any voice of mourning save the choirs,—
   The shrill, demented choirs of wailing shells;
And bugles calling for them from sad shires.

What candles may be held to speed them all?
   Not in the hands of boys, but in their eyes   10
Shall shine the holy glimmers of good-byes.
   The pallor of girls' brows shall be their pall;
Their flowers the tenderness of patient minds,
And each slow dusk a drawing-down of blinds.
                               —Wilfred Owen

The Outcast

For the dim regions whence my fathers came
My spirit, bondaged by the body, longs.
Words felt, but never heard, my lips would frame;
My soul would sing forgotten jungle songs.
I would go back to darkness and to peace,   5
But the great western world holds me in fee,
And I may never hope for full release
While to its alien gods I bend my knee.
Something in me is lost, forever lost,
Some vital thing has gone out of my heart,   10
And I must walk the way of life a ghost
Among the sons of earth, a thing apart.

For I was born, far from my native clime,
Under the white man's menace, out of time.
                                —Claude McKay

5
Sustained Performances

Frequently poets group individual lyrics together to create larger units of greater or lesser cohesiveness, juxtaposing one poem against another, repeating themes and motifs, linking lyrics together with verbal or imagistic echoes, providing their readers with a sustained poetic performance that may run into hundreds, even thousands of lines. One way of bringing separate lyrics together in a loosely cohesive larger unit is to arrange the poems of a single volume so that they tell a story, or explore various aspects of a single theme, or develop a central idea. Edgar Lee Masters' *Spoon River Anthology,* for example, contains a series of lyrics depicting characters who all live in a fictional town along the Spoon River. Over the course of the volume a portrait emerges not only of the various people Masters characterizes, but of the town as a whole. A. E. Housman arranged the lyrics of his first volume of poetry, *A Shropshire Lad,* to tell the story of a young man, Terence Hearsay, who grew up in and later left the area around Shropshire. We meet friends of Terence, watch his character mature and develop, and understand something of the depression he feels when he is torn from the context that has given meaning to his life and sent to London. The unity of these two volumes is loose, of course, but they do have a cohesion that others lack.

Some poets prefer something more formal in the way of unifying structures. Tennyson's famous *In Memoriam* is really a long series of over a hundred independent lyrics that have been carefully organized, numbered, and printed together under one title. Sonnet cycles, series of sonnets that tell a story or develop philosophical meditations on a central theme, were popular during the Renaissance and are still being written today. Shakespeare and Sidney and Spenser all wrote sonnet sequences, as did Edna St. Vincent Millay, W. H. Auden, and George Meredith. Donne's *La Corona* is a series of seven sonnets, each linked to the next by repeated lines.

Or a poet may bring lyrics so close together that they act more as a unit than individually. He may print a single title, then subdivide his poem into sections, usually numbered and occasionally even marked with a subtitle or epigraph. But although the poems are printed under a single title, the various parts retain much of their own identity: the breaks between one section and another are usually abrupt and sharp, the verse form may change dramatically from section to section, the subjects of the sections may be significantly different. Even in cases like "The Quaker Graveyard," where the poet offers us a long poem with several subdivisions, it is best to analyze each unit as an individual lyric before drawing them together for discussion as a whole.

Sustained performances are unique and each requires a special set of guidelines for study—but all involve patterns of meaning that extend beyond the boundaries of individual lyrics or subsections of a large poem. *Sergeant Pepper's Lonely Hearts Club Band* requires a process of analysis not much different from that required by "The Quaker Graveyard" or a sonnet cycle, because *Sergeant Pepper* has a kind of unity absent on most rock albums. The individual lyrics are, of course, impressive, and they are the place to begin a discussion of that album; but a discussion of any one lyric must soon give way to a discussion of the meaning of the whole, just as a study of any one of Shakespeare's sonnets ought finally to lead to a treatment of the whole cycle. The techniques developed in treating *Sergeant Pepper* should prove quite useful in treating the sonnet cycle by Donne, "The Quaker Graveyard," and finally Wordsworth's "Ode," the most unified poem in this section.

Sergeant Pepper's Lonely Hearts Club Band

I

Sergeant Pepper's Lonely Hearts Club Band

It was twenty years ago today
That Sergeant Pepper taught the band to play.
They've been going in and out of style,
But they're guaranteed to raise a smile.

So may I introduce to you 5
The act you've known for all these years:
Sergeant Pepper's Lonely Hearts Club Band.
We're Sergeant Pepper's Lonely Hearts Club Band,
We hope you will enjoy the show.
We're Sergeant Pepper's Lonely Hearts Club Band. 10
Sit back and let the evening go,
Sergeant Pepper's Lonely,
Sergeant Pepper's Lonely,
Sergeant Pepper's Lonely Hearts Club Band.
It's wonderful to be here, 15
It's certainly a thrill,
You're such a lovely audience,
We'd like to take you home with us,
We'd love to take you home.
I don't really want to stop the show 20
But I thought you might like to know
That the singer's going to sing a song
And he wants you all to sing along.
So may I introduce to you
The one and only Billy Shears. 25
Sergeant Pepper's Lonely Hearts Club Band.

II

With a Little Help From My Friends

What would you think if I sang out of tune,
Would you stand up and walk out on me?
Lend me your ears and I'll sing you a song,
And I'll try not to sing out of key. 30
I get by with a little help from my friends,
I get high with a little help from my friends,
Going to try with a little help from my friends.
What do I do when my love is away?
(Does it worry you to be alone?) 35
How do I feel by the end of the day?
(Are you sad because you're on your own?)
No I get by with a little help from my friends.
Do you need anybody?
I need somebody to love. 40

Could it be anybody?
I want somebody to love.
Would you believe in a love at first sight?
Yes I'm certain that it happens all the time.
What do you see when you turn out the light?   45
I can't tell you, but I know it's mine.
Oh I get by with a little help from my friends.
Do you need anybody?
I just need somebody to love.
Could it be anybody?   50
I want somebody to love.
I get by with a little help from my friends,
Yes I get by with a little help from my friends,
With a little help from my friends.

                              III

                                    Lucy in the Sky with Diamonds

Picture yourself in a boat on a river   55
With tangerine trees and marmalade skies.
Somebody calls you, you answer quite slowly,
A girl with kaleidoscope eyes.
Cellophane flowers of yellow and green
Towering over your head,   60
Look for the girl with the sun in her eyes
And she's gone.
Lucy in the sky with diamonds,
Lucy in the sky with diamonds,
Lucy in the sky with diamonds.   65
Follow her down to a bridge by a fountain
Where rocking horse people eat marshmallow pies.
Ev'ryone smiles as you drift past the flowers
That grow so incredibly high.
Newspaper taxis appear on the shore   70
Waiting to take you away,
Climb in the back with your head in the clouds
And you're gone.
Lucy in the sky with diamonds,
Lucy in the sky with diamonds,   75
Lucy in the sky with diamonds.

Picture yourself on a train in a station
With plasticine porters with looking glass ties.
Suddenly someone is there at the turnstile,
The girl with kaleidoscope eyes.   80
Lucy in the sky with diamonds,
Lucy in the sky with diamonds,
Lucy in the sky with diamonds.

IV

Getting Better

It's getting better all the time.
I used to get mad at my school,   85
The teachers who taught me weren't cool,
Holding me down,
Turning me round,
Filling me up with your rules.
I've got to admit it's getting better,   90
It's a little better all the time.
I have to admit it's getting better,
It's getting better since you've been mine.
Me used to be angry young man,
Me hiding me head in the sand.   95
You gave me the word,
I finally heard,
I'm doing the best that I can.
I admit it's getting better,
It's a little better all the time.   100
Yes I admit it's getting better,
It's getting better since you've been mine.
Getting so much better all the time,
It's getting better all the time,
Better, better, better.   105
I used to be cruel to my woman,
I beat her and kept her apart from the things that she loved.
Man I was mean,
But I'm changing my scene,
And I'm doing the best that I can.   110
I admit it's getting better,
It's a little better all the time.

Yes I admit it's getting better,
It's getting better since you've been mine,
Getting so much better all the time.   115

V

Fixing a Hole

I'm fixing a hole where the rain gets in
And stops my mind from wandering
Where it will go.
I'm filling the cracks that ran through the door
And kept my mind from wandering   120
Where it will go.
And it really doesn't matter if I'm wrong, I'm right
Where I belong, I'm right
Where I belong.
See the people standing there   125
Who disagree and never win
And wonder why they don't get in my door.
I'm painting the room in a colourful way,
And when my mind is wandering
There I will go.   130
And it really doesn't matter if I'm wrong, I'm right
Where I belong, I'm right
Where I belong.
Silly people run around,
They worry me and never ask me   135
Why they don't get past my door.
I'm taking my time for a number of things
That weren't important yesterday,
And I still go.
I'm fixing a hole where the rain gets in   140
And stops my mind from wandering
Where it will go,
Where it will go.

VI

She's Leaving Home

Wedn'sday morning at five o'clock as the day begins,
Silently closing her bedroom door,   145

Leaving the note that she hoped would say more,
She goes downstairs to the kitchen clutching her handkerchief.
Quietly turning the backdoor key,
Stepping outside, she is free.
She (We gave her most of our lives)   150
Is leaving (Sacrificed most of our lives)
Home (We gave her ev'rything money could buy.)
She's leaving home after living alone for so many years.
(Bye, bye)

Father snores as his wife gets into her dressing gown,   155
Picks up the letter that's lying there,
Standing alone at the top of the stairs,
She breaks down and cries to her husband, "Daddy, our baby's gone.
Why would she treat us so thoughtlessly?
How could she do this to me?"   160
She (We never thought of ourselves.)
Is leaving (Never a thought for ourselves.)
Home (We struggled hard all our lives to get by.)
She's leaving home after living alone for so many years.
(Bye, bye)   165

Friday morning at nine o'clock she is far away,
Waiting to keep the appointment she made,
Meeting a man from the motor trade.
She (What did we do that was wrong?)
Is having (We didn't know it was wrong.)   170
Fun (Fun is the one thing that money can't buy.)
Something inside that was always denied for so many years.
She's leaving home,
Bye, bye.

VII

Being for the Benefit of Mr. Kite

For the benefit of Mister Kite   175
There will be a show tonight on trampoline.
The Hendersons will all be there
Late of Pablo Fanques fair, what a scene.
Over men and horses, hoops and garters,

Lastly through a hogshead of real fire.   180
In this way Mister K. will challenge the world.

The celebrated Mister K.
Performs his feat on Saturday at Bishopsgate.
The Hendersons will dance and sing
As Mister Kite flies through the ring. Don't be late.   185
Messrs. K. and H. assure the public
Their production will be second to none.
And of course Henry the horse dances the waltz.

The band begins at ten to six
When Mister K. performs his tricks without a sound,   190
And Mister H. will demonstrate,
Ten somersets he'll undertake on solid ground.
Having been some days in preparation,
A splendid time is guaranteed for all.
And tonight Mister Kite is topping the bill.   195

VIII

Within You Without You

We were talking about the space between us all
And the people who hide themselves behind a wall of illusion,
Never glimpse the truth. Then it's far too late
When they pass away.
We were talking about the love we all could share,   200
When we find it to try our best to hold it there with our love.
With our love we could save the world,
If they only knew.
Try to realize it's all within yourself, no one else can make you
    change,
And to see you're only very small   205
And life flows on within you and without you.
We were talking about the love that's gone so cold
And the people who gain the world and lose their soul. They don't
    know,
They can't see. Are you one of them?
When you've seen beyond yourself, then you may find peace of 210
    mind is waiting there,

And the time will come when you see we're all one
And life flows on within you and without you.

IX

When I'm Sixty-Four

When I get older, losing my hair,
Many years from now,
Will you still be sending me a valentine,   215
Birthday greetings, bottle of wine?
If I'd been out till quarter to three,
Would you lock the door?
Will you still need me,
Will you still feed me,   220
When I'm sixty-four?
You'll be older too.
And if you say the word
I could stay with you.

I could be handy mending a fuse   225
When your lights have gone;
You can knit a sweater by the fireside,
Sunday mornings go for a ride.
Doing the garden, digging the weeds—
Who could ask for more?   230
Will you still need me,
Will you still feed me,
When I'm sixty-four?
Ev'ry summer we can rent a cottage
In the Isle of Wight if it's not too dear.   235
We shall scrimp and save.
Grandchildren on your knee,
Vera, Chuck and Dave.

Send me a postcard, drop me a line
Stating point of view,   240
Indicate precisely what you mean to say,
Yours sincerely, wasting away.
Give me your answer, fill in a form,
Mine forever more.

Will you still need me,   245
Will you still feed me,
When I'm sixty-four?

X

Lovely Rita

Lovely Rita, meter maid,
Lovely Rita, meter maid,
Lovely Rita, meter maid,   250
Nothing can come between us.
When it gets dark I tow your heart away.
Standing by a parking meter,
When I caught a glimpse of Rita
Filling in a ticket in her little white book.   255
In a cap she looked much older
And the bag across her shoulder
Made her look a little like a military man.
Lovely Rita, meter maid,
May I enquire discreetly,   260
When are you free to take some tea with me?
Took her out and tried to win her;
Had a laugh and over dinner
Told her I would really like to see her again.
Got the bill and Rita paid it,   265
Took her home and nearly made it
Sitting on a sofa with a sister or two.
Oh, lovely Rita, meter maid,
Where would I be without you?
Give us a wink and make me think of you.   270
Lovely Rita, meter maid,
Lovely Rita, meter maid,
Lovely Rita, meter maid.

XI

Good Morning, Good Morning

Good morning good morning good morning good morning
Nothing to do to save his life,   275
Call his wife in.
Nothing to say but what a day,

How's your boy been?
Nothing to do, it's up to you.
I've got nothing to say but it's O.K.   280
Good morning good morning good morning
Going to work, don't want to go,
Feeling low down.
Heading for home you start to roam,
Then you're in town.   285
Ev'rybody knows there's nothing doing,
Ev'rything is close, it's like a ruin,
Ev'ryone you see is half asleep,
And you're on your own in the street.

After a while you start to smile,   290
Now you feel cool.
Then you decide to take a walk
By the old school.
Nothing has changed, it's still the same.
I've got nothing to say but it's O.K.   295
Good morning good morning good morning
People running round, it's five o'clock,
Ev'rywhere in town it's getting dark,
Ev'ryone you see is full of life,
It's time for tea and meet the wife.   300

Somebody needs to know the time,
Glad that I'm here.
Watching the skirts you start to flirt,
Now you're in gear.
Go to a show, you hope she goes.   305
I've got nothing to say but it's O.K.
Good morning good morning good morning

XII

Sergeant Pepper's Lonely Hearts Club Band
(Reprise)

We're Sergeant Pepper's Lonely Hearts Club Band,
We hope you have enjoyed the show.
We're Sergeant Pepper's Lonely Hearts Club Band,   310

We're sorry but it's time to go.
Sergeant Pepper's lonely.
Sergeant Pepper's lonely.
Sergeant Pepper's lonely.
Sergeant Pepper's lonely.   315
Sergeant Pepper's Lonely Hearts Club Band,
We'd like to thank you once again,
Sergeant Pepper's one and only Lonely Hearts Club Band,
It's getting very near the end.
Sergeant Pepper's lonely,   320
Sergeant Pepper's lonely,
Sergeant Pepper's Lonely Hearts Club Band.

XIII

A Day in the Life

I read the news today, oh boy,
About a lucky man who made the grade.
And though the news was rather sad,   325
Well I just had to laugh.
I saw the photograph.
He blew his mind out in a car.
He didn't notice that the lights had changed.
A crowd of people stood and stared.   330
They'd seen his face before.
Nobody was really sure
If he was from the House of Lords.

I saw a film today, oh boy.
The English army had just won the war.   335
A crowd of people turned away,
But I just had to look,
Having read the book.
I'd love to turn you on.

Woke up, fell out of bed,   340
Dragged a comb across my head,
Found my way downstairs and drank a cup,
And looking up I noticed I was late.
Found my coat and grabbed my hat,

Made the bus in seconds flat,   345
Found my way upstairs and had a smoke,
Somebody spoke and I went into a dream.

I read the news today, oh boy:
Four thousand holes in Blackburn, Lancashire,
And though the holes were rather small   350
They had to count them all.
Now they know how many holes it takes to fill the Albert hall.
I'd love to turn you on.

                                        —*The Beatles*

The more one listens to *Sergeant Pepper,* the more carefully one ana-
lyzes the imagery and the almost infinite variety of rhythm and rhyme,
the more one hears other albums by other rock groups, the more stunning
this album becomes. Musically and verbally it was impressive when it
first appeared; in retrospect it is even more impressive. There can be
little doubt that it will be listened to and studied for many years to
come, because of both the quality of its music and the variety of its
poetry.

The long-playing record imposes itself as a form upon The Beatles'
work, of course, and they must work within its context: the performance may not extend much beyond an hour, but at least forty minutes
of time must be filled. The public expects a series of single cuts on each
side; the first and the last cuts will have emphasis because of their posi-
tions. There will be a break at the end of the first side, which may
necessitate some form of recapitulation at the beginning of the second.
Within these predetermined confines, however, The Beatles are free to
develop a narrative (as The Who did with *Tommy*) or thematically related lyrics that work off each other. They compromise: the two "Sergeant Pepper" songs frame a series of distinct studies of great musical
and poetic variety, putting the whole album in the context of a stage
performance (the illusion is furthered by "A Little Help From My
Friends"). The last cut on the second side is parenthetical, outside the
performance context, a new perspective on all that has gone before.

The place to begin a consideration of the album is with the individual lyrics, some of which have already been the subject of considerable discussion. Only after one has grasped the songs individually

can one begin drawing patterns of meaning from the whole album. "Lucy In the Sky" is widely interpreted as an acid trip and an acrostic for LSD. Certainly both the tonal distortions of the music and the rich sensual imagery of the poem suggest the popular conception of such a trip. Moreover, the boat, the taxi, and the train all suggest "trip" in the literal sense, and the distortions in sense perception evidenced by the tall flowers past which one drifts, the intense awareness of color and taste in tangerine trees and marmalade skies, and the hallucinations hinted at by "rocking horse people" and Lucy's kaleidoscope eyes would seemingly settle the issue. But in an interview in the *Washington Post,* Paul McCartney claimed that the song derived from a picture drawn by John Lennon's little boy, Julian. Although he could not deny the appropriateness of the LSD interpretation, he claimed that in writing the poem they had never thought about that at all. It may, of course, be that the interview rather than the song was a put-on, but one is never sure. "Lucy In the Sky" is a powerful poem even if it is not an acid song: the title image suggests an awareness that the rest of the song develops, an awareness of the most common of things in the most uncommon of contexts, imbueing Lucy with mystical attraction. Perhaps the song is really about the awareness of the extraordinary within the ordinary—but then that is precisely what LSD is reported (perhaps erroneously) to open one's eyes to.

"For the Benefit of Mr. Kite" presents another problem. McCartney claimed it came straight off a wall poster; others remind us that kiff (pot) and hashish—Mssrs. K. and H. whose performance will be second to none—and horse are all slang terms for drugs, and argue for a drug interpretation. After all, H. turns somersets without ever leaving the ground, and K. flies through a ring. Perhaps the circus imagery is but an adjunct to describing a trip. Or perhaps the drug images and the circus images supplement each other, both functioning metaphorically to suggest a further, deeper theme: the loss of one's self (with related anxieties, self-analyses, and doubts) in the magic of a grand performance. Drugs take one away from reality for a moment just as the carnival atmosphere of a circus takes one away; one loses hold of reality in the noise and color and magic of the moment. And certainly Mister Kite's performance is a splendid, colorful, swirling, enchanting thing metrically as well as imagistically.

"A Day in the Life" is, with the possible exception of "Lucy in the Sky," the most haunting and the most ambiguous song on the album.

Madison Avenue has managed to make the phrase "turn on" virtually meaningless by applying it to everything from shades of cosmetics to chocolate malts, but the expression always did have a certain ambiguity to it. First, of course, it means drugs, and the man is having a smoke and the Beatles have admitted in various interviews to using various drugs and the B. B. C. was convinced enough of the line's meaning to ban the song from the network. But the other images in the song suggest that we are being asked to turn on to an awareness of the bankruptcy of life as we usually live it in the twentieth century, and to an awareness of what life might be. The man blew his mind out just when he finally made the grade, the war was won but nobody really cared. Life goes on, a collage of nearly missed buses and holes to be carefully counted. If "Lucy in the Sky" was a trip that turned us on to the magic of what is conventional, all that magic has disappeared in "A Day in the Life." The trip is over, and it was a bummer.

The comparison between these two songs brings us to a more important question: what kind of a statement does the album as a whole make? Everyone, including for a change McCartney himself, agrees that yes, it does have a unity, and it is obvious that the unity is intentional: "Sergeant Pepper's Lonely Hearts Club Band" introduces Billy Shears and "With A Little Help"; the record moves without a break from the end of "Sergeant Pepper's (Reprise)" to "A Day in the Life"; the drug motif repeats itself again and again in the "high" of "A Little Help," the weeds of "When I'm Sixty-Four," the tea of "Lovely Rita." Technically, the crescendo at the end of "A Day in the Life" is an analog of the barnyard cacophony at the end of "Good Morning," just as the emptiness of the imagery reflects the same banality implicit in the other. "Within You Without You" proclaims overtly what the previous lyrics suggested indirectly; it is a kind of summary of side one of the album before we begin side two. "When I'm Sixty-Four" balances "She's Leaving Home." And so on. But what kind of a statement does this unity make?

The context of the whole album is provided by the opening two songs: this is a performance by Sergeant Pepper (Ringo Star, alias Billy Shears—he wears the sergeant's stripes on his uniform) and his lonely hearts club band. Two things are important: the band is lonely, and it is performing. Perhaps the two are interrelated: performers are generally lonely people, lonely people perform when they pretend not to be lonely and in an attempt to escape their loneliness. What is especially significant, however, is that Sergeant Pepper and his band are aware of that fact that they are performing, that they are acting out an illusion—others are not as aware, but then again they are probably not as lonely. Some are off into a drug thing; others tell themselves that things are, after all, getting better all the time, or rationalize their disillusionment by excusing themselves. Some withdraw into self-isolation and others drown any misgivings they might have in the noise and excitement of a circus performance. "What we were talking about," says George Harrison bluntly in "Within You Without You," "is what is hypocritical and what is honest, and who hides behind what walls of illusion." But if the lyrics of this song outline inadequate responses people make when they are vaguely aware that something is wrong with their lives, the next three songs present us with a gallery of incredibly shallow individuals. The first proposes the most mundane of marriages to a mail-order bride; the second falls in love with a meter maid he happens to see writing up tickets; the third drives in self-impressed fashion aimlessly around town looking for pick-ups. What makes the whole despicable crowd especially disgusting (and The Beatles' comment especially morose) is the irrepressible high spirits of the music, which ironically mocks the words themselves and piles irony on top of irony. And then the band, Sergeant Pepper's Band, Sergeant Pepper's Lonely Hearts Club Band, breaks in with its initial statement, now made depressingly meaningful: "Sergeant Pepper's lonely." The "l" is lower case; the phrase ends with a period. The band is making a statement: "Sergeant Pepper is lonely," and that's what we've been talking about for the duration of this performance. By now we as listeners have begun to feel a trifle lonely too, and "A Day In the Life," with the alienated, impassive attitude of the observers and its resounding chord dying-out-to-nothing at the end is almost too much. But it is too much not simply because of the song itself, but because the entire weight of the whole album comes crashing down on that final chord. And the whole weight of *Sergeant Pepper* is a lot of weight.

La Corona

I

Deign at my hands this crown of prayer and praise,
Weav'd in my low devout melancholy,
Thou which of good, hast, yea art treasury,

All changing unchang'd Ancient of days;
But do not, with a vile crown of frail bays,   5
Reward my muse's white sincerity,
But what thy thorny crown gain'd, that give me,
A crown of Glory, which doth flower always;
The ends crown our works, but thou crown'st our ends,
For, at our end begins our endless rest;   10
The first last end, now zealously possessed,
With a strong sober thirst, my soul attends.
'Tis time that heart and voice be lifted high,
Salvation to all that will is nigh.

II

Annunciation
Salvation to all that will is nigh;   15
That All, which always is All everywhere,
Which cannot sin, and yet all sins must beare,
Which cannot die, yet cannot choose but die,
Loe, faithful Virgin, yields himself to lie
In prison, in thy womb; and though he there   20
Can take no sin, nor thou give, yet he'will wear
Taken from thence, flesh, which death's force may try.
Ere by the spheres time was created, thou
Wast in his mind, who is thy Son, and Brother;
Whom thou conceiv'st, conceiv'd; yea thou art now   25
Thy Maker's maker, and thy Father's mother;
Thou'hast light in dark; and shutst in little room,
Immensity cloisterd in thy dear womb.

III

Nativity
Immensity cloisterd in thy dear womb,
Now leaves his welbelov'd imprisonment,   30
There he hath made himself to his intent
Weak enough, now into our world to come;
But Oh, for thee, for him, hath th'Inn no room?
Yet lay him in this stall, and from the Orient,
Stars, and wisemen will travel to prevent   35
Th'effect of *Herod's* jealous general doom.
Seest thou, my Soul, with thy faith's eyes, how he

Which fills all place, yet none holds him, doth lie?
Was not his pity towards thee wondrous high,
That would have need to be pitied by thee?   40
Kiss him, and with him into Egypt go,
With his kind mother, who partakes thy woe.

IV

Temple

With his kind mother who partakes thy woe,
Joseph turn back; see where your child doth sit,
Blowing, yea blowing out those sparks of wit,   45
Which himself on the Doctors did bestow;
The Word but lately could not speak, and lo
It suddenly speaks wonders, whence comes it,
That all which was, and all which should be writ,
A shallow seeming child, should deeply know?   50
His Godhead was not soul to his manhood,
Nor had time mellowed him to this ripeness,
But as for one which hath a long task, 'tis good,
With the Sun to begin his business,
He in his ages morning thus began   55
By miracles exceeding power of man.

V

Crucifying

By miracles exceeding power of man,
He faith in some, envy in some begat,
For, what weak spirits admire, ambitious, hate;
In both affections many to him ran,   60
But Oh! the worst are most, they will and can,
Alas, and do, unto the immaculate,
Whose creature Fate is, now prescribe a Fate,
Measuring self-life's infinity to'a span,
Nay to an inch. Lo, where condemned he   65
Bears his own cross, with pain, yet by and by
When it bears him, he must bear more and die.
Now thou art lifted up, draw me to thee,
And at thy death giving such liberal dole,
Moist, with one drop of thy blood, my dry soul.   70

VI

Resurrection

Moist with one drop of thy blood, my dry soul
Shall (though she now be in extreme degree
Too stony hard, and yet too fleshly,) be
Freed by that drop, from being starv'd, hard, or foul,
And life, by this death abled, shall control   75
Death, whom thy death slew; nor shall to me
Fear of first or last death, bring misery,
If in thy little book my name thou enroll,
Flesh in that long sleep is not putrified,
But made that there, of which, and for which 'twas;   80
Nor can by other means be glorified.
May then sins sleep, and deaths soon from me pass,
That wak't from both, I again risen may
Salute the last, and everlasting day.

VII

Ascension

Salute the last and everlasting day,   85
Joy at the uprising of this Sun, and Son,
Ye whose just tears, or tribulation
Have purely washed, or burnt your drossy clay;
Behold the Highest, parting hence away,
Lightens the dark clouds, which he treads upon,   90
Nor doth he by ascending, show alone.
But first he, and he first enters the way.
O strong Ram, which hast batter'd heaven for me,
Mild Lamb, which with thy blood, hast mark'd the path;
Bright Torch, which shin'st, that I the way may see,   95
Oh, with thine own blood quench thine own just wrath,
And if thy holy Spirit, my Muse did raise,
Deign at my hands this crown of prayer and praise.

—*John Donne*

1. *Deign at*: accept from. 2. *melancholy*: pensiveness. 5. *bays*: laurel wreathes bestowed for excellency or achievement. 23. *spheres*: the nine spheres of the Ptolomaic universe, above and beyond which God had his dwelling place. 37. *doom*: judgment, decree. 45. *wit*: wisdom. 47. *The Word*: Cf. John 1:1. 76. *Death . . . slew*: Cf. "Death, be not Proud," Chapter II. 88. *drossy*: waste-like, earthy, impure. 93. *Rame*: an allusion to the ram sacrificed instead of Isaac by Abraham.

The Quaker Graveyard in Nantucket

For Warren Winslow, Dead at Sea

Let man have dominion over the fishes
the beasts and the whole earth, and
of the sea and the fowls of the air and
every creeping creature that moveth
upon the earth.

I

A brackish reach of shoal off Madaket,—
The sea was still breaking violently and night
Had steamed into our North Atlantic Fleet,
When the drowned sailor clutched the drag-net. Light
Flashed from his matted head and marble feet,   5
He grappled at the net
With the coiled, hurdling muscles of his thighs:
The corpse was bloodless, a botch of reds and whites,
Its open, staring eyes
Were lusterless dead-lights   10
Or cabin-windows on a stranded hulk
Heavy with sand. We weight the body, close
Its eyes and heave it seaward whence it came,
Where the heel-headed dogfish barks its nose
On Ahab's void and forehead; and the name   15
Is blocked in yellow chalk.
Sailors, who pitch this portent at the sea
Where dreadnaughts shall confess
Its hell-bent deity,
When you are powerless   20
To sand-bag this Atlantic bulwark, faced
By the earth-shaker, green, unwearied, chaste
In his steel scales: ask for no Orphean lute
To pluck life back. The guns of the steeled fleet
Recoil and then repeat   25
The hoarse salute.

II

Whenever winds are moving and their breath
Heaves at the roped-in bulwarks of this pier,

The terns and sea-gulls tremble at your death
In these home waters. Sailor, can you hear   30
The Pequod's sea wings, beating landward, fall
Headlong and break on our Atlantic wall
Off 'Sconset, where the yawing S-boats splash
The bellbouy, with ballooning spinnakers,
As the entangled, screeching mainsheet clears   35
The blocks: off Madaket, where lubbers lash
The heavy surf and throw their long lead squids
For blue-fish? Sea-gulls blink their heavy lids
Seaward. The winds' wings beat upon the stones,
Cousin, and scream for you and the claws rush   40
At the sea's throat and wring it in the slush
Of this old Quaker graveyard where the bones
Cry out in the long night for the hurt beast
Bobbing by Ahab's whaleboats in the East.

III

All you recovered from Poseidon died   45
With you, my cousin, and the harrowed brine
It fruitless on the blue beard of the god,
Stretching beyond us to the castles in Spain,
Nantucket's westward haven. To Cape Cod
Guns, cradled on the tide,   50
Blast the eelgrass about a waterclock
Of bilge and backwash, roil the salt and sand
Lashing earth's scaffold, rock
Our warships in the hand
Of the great God, where time's contrition blues   55
Whatever it was these Quaker sailors lost
In the mad scramble of their lives. They died
When time was open-eyed,
Wooden and childish; only bones abide
There, in the nowhere, where their boats were tossed 60
Sky-high, where mariners had fabled news
Of IS, the whited monster. What it cost
Them is their secret. In the monster's slick
I see the Quakers drown and hear their cry:
"If God himself had not been on our side,   65

If God himself had not been on our side,
When the Atlantic rose against us, why
Then it had swallowed us up quick."

IV

This is the end of the whaleroad and the whale
Who spewed Nantucket bones on the thrashed swell   70
And stirred the troubled waters to whirlpools
To send the Pequod packing off to hell:
This is the end of them, three-quarters fools,
Snatching at straws to sail
Seaward and seaward on the turntail whale,   75
Spouting out blood and water as it rolls,
Sick as a dog to these Atlantic shoals:
Clamavimus, O depths. Let the sea-gulls wail

For water, for the deep where the high tide
Mutters to its hurt self, mutters and ebbs.   80
Waves wallow in their wash, go out and out,
Leave only the death-rattle of the crabs,
The beach increasing, its enormous snout
Sucking the ocean's side.
This is the end of running on the waves;   85
We are poured out like water. Who will dance
The mast-lashed master of Leviathans
Up from this field of Quakers in their unstoned graves?

V

When the whale's viscera go and the roll
Of its corruption overruns this world   90
Beyond tree-swept Nantucket and Woods Hole
And Martha's Vineyard, Sailor, will your sword
Whistle and fall and sink into the fat?
In the great ash-pit of Jehoshaphat
The bones cry for the blood of the white whale,   95
The fat flukes arch and whack about its ears,
The death-lance churns into the sanctuary, tears
The gun-blue swingle, heaving like a flail,
And hacks the coiling life out: it works and drags

And rips the sperm-whale's midriff into rags,   100
Gobbets of blubber spill to wind and weather,
Sailor, and gulls go round the stoven timbers
Where the morning stars sing out together
And thunder shakes the white surf and dismembers
The red flag hammered in the mast-head. Hide,   105
Our steel, Jonas Messias, in Thy side.

VI

Our Lady of Walsingham

There once the penitents took off their shoes
And then walked barefoot the remaining mile;
And the small trees, a stream and hedgerows file
Slowly along the munching English lane,   110
Like cows to the old shrine, until you lose
Track of your dragging pain.
The stream flows down under the druid tree,
Shiloah's whirlpool gurgle and make glad
The castle of God. Sailor, you were glad   115
And whistled Sion by that stream. But see:

Our Lady, too small for her canopy,
Sits near the altar. There's no comeliness
At all or charm in that expressionless
Face with its heavy eyelids. As before,   120
This face, for centuries a memory,
Non est species, neque decor,
Expressionless, expresses God: it goes
Past castled Sion. She knows what God knows,
Not Calvary's Cross nor crib at Bethlehem   125
Now, and the world shall come to Walsingham.

VII

The empty winds are creaking and the oak
Splatters and splatters on the cenotaph,
The boughs are trembling and a gaff
Bobs on the untimely stroke   130
Of the greased wash exploding on a shoal-bell
In the old mouth of the Atlantic. It's well;

Atlantic, you are fouled with the blue sailors,
Sea-monsters, upward angel, downward fish:
Unmarried and corroding, spare of flesh   135
Mart once of supercilious, wing'd clippers,
Atlantic, where your bell-trap guts its spoil
You could cut the brackish winds with a knife
Here in Nantucket, and cast up the time
When the Lord God formed man from the sea's slime   140
And breathed into his face the breath of life,
And blue-lung'd combers lumbered to the kill.
The Lord survives the rainbow of His will.

—*Robert Lowell*

Subtitle. *Warren Winslow*: the poet's cousin, a naval officer, who was lost in World War II in the Atlantic off the southern end of Massachusetts. Epigraph: Genesis 1:26. 1. *Madaket*: a harbor on Nantucket. 4–16. based on the opening chapter of Thoreau's *Cape Cod*. 15. *Ahab*: captain of the Pequod, a ship in Melville's *Moby Dick,* a whaling novel that underlies the whole poem. 18. *dreadnaughts*: a type of British battleship. 22. *earth-shaker*: Poseidon, Greek god of the sea (Cf. lines 45 ff). 23. *Orphean Lute*: Orpheus, a Greek mythological character, went to Hades in search of his dead love Euridice. He so charmed Pluto with his lute playing that he was granted whatever he wished— his love Euridice, of course—on the condition that he not look back until he was safely out of the underworld. Just as the two approached earth, Orpheus glanced over his shoulder to be sure that Euridice was following him, and she was lost forever. 33. *'Sconset*: Siasconset, a town on eastern Nantucket; *yawing*: off course; *S-boats*: a class of racing sailboats. 34. *spinnakers*: large sails. 36. *lubbers*: here, surf-fishers. 42. *Quaker*: the Quakers were involved in the early American whaling industry, and acquired a reputation for crass materialism and commercialism. 62. *IS*: possibly a reference to Exodus 3:14 ("And God said to Moses, 'I AM THAT I AM'"). The whale in *Moby Dick* carries associations with the supernatural, although he is not the kind of god to which Christians are accustomed. 78. *Clamavimus*: "We have cried out." An adaptation of the beginning of Psalm 130, "Out of the depths have I cried," also known in English in the translation of Luther's hymn "Aus Tiefer Not." 87. *mast-lashed*: during storms at sea captains frequently lashed themselves to a mast to keep from being swept overboard. 91. *Wood's Hole*: a town in Cape Cod. 92. *Martha's Vineyard*: an island off Nantucket. 94. *Jehoshapat*: Cf. Joel 3. 103. *morning stars . . . together*: Cf. Job 38:7. Subtitle (VI). *Our Lady of Walsingham*: a shrine to the Virgin Mary in Norfolk, England. According to Lowell, many of the details of this section derive from E. I. Watkin's *Catholic Art and Culture* (New York: Sheed and Ward, 1944), pp. 213–14. 114. *Shiloah*: a town in Palestine famous for its brooks. 115. *castle*: Cf. line 47. 116. *Sion*: Zion, the holy city of Jerusalem; here perhaps a Protestant hymn tune. 122. *Non est . . . decor*: Isiah 53:2, "He hath no form nor comeliness." 143. Cf. Genesis 9:8–17 on Noah, God and the rainbow of His will.

Ode: Intimations of Immortality
from Recollections of Early Childhood

The Child is father of the Man;
And I could wish my days to be
Bound each to each by natural piety.

I

There was a time when meadow, grove, and stream,
The earth, and every common sight,
    To me did seem
      Appareled in celestial light,
The glory and the freshness of a dream.   5
It is not now as it hath been of yore—
    Turn whereso'er I may,
      By night or day,
The things which I have seen I now can see no more.

II

    The Rainbow comes and goes,   10
    And lovely is the Rose,
    The Moon doth with delight
Look round her when the heavens are bare,
    Waters on a starry night
    Are beautiful and fair;   15
  The sunshine is a glorious birth;
  But yet I know, where'er I go,
That there hath past away a glory from the earth.

III

Now, while the birds thus sing a joyous song,
    And while the young lambs bound   20
      As to the tabor's sound,
To me alone there came a thought of grief:
A timely utterance gave that thought relief,
    And I again am strong:
The cataracts blow their trumpets from the steep;   25
No more shall grief of mine the season wrong;
I hear the Echoes through the mountains throng,

The Winds come to me from the fields of sleep,
       And all the earth is gay;
           Land and sea   30
     Give themselves up to jollity,
       And with the heart of May
Doth every Beast keep holiday;—
       Thou Child of Joy,
Shout round me, let me hear thy shouts, thou happy Shepherd-boy!   35

IV

Ye blessèd Creatures, I have heard the call
     Ye to each other make; I see
The heavens laugh with you in your jubilee;
     My heart is at your festival,
     My head hath its coronal,   40
The fulness of your bliss, I feel—I feel it all.
     Oh evil day! if I were sullen
     While Earth herself is adorning,
        This sweet May-morning,
     And the Children are culling   45
        On every side,
    In a thousand valleys far and wide,
     Fresh flowers; while the sun shines warm,
And the Babe leaps up on his Mother's arm:—
     I hear, I hear, with joy I hear!   50
     —But there's a Tree, of many, one,
A single Field which I have looked upon,
Both of them speak of something that is gone:
     The Pansy at my feet
     Doth the same tale repeat: 55
Whither is fled the visionary gleam?
Where is it now, the glory and the dream?

V

Our birth is but a sleep and a forgetting;
The Soul that rises with us, our life's Star,
     Hath had elsewhere its setting,   60
       And cometh from afar:
     Not in entire forgetfulness,
     And not in utter nakedness,

But trailing clouds of glory do we come
    From God, who is our home: 65
Heaven lies about us in our infancy!
Shades of the prison-house begin to close
    Upon the growing Boy,
But He beholds the light, and whence it flows,
    He sees it in his joy;   70
The Youth, who daily farther from the east
    Must travel, still is Nature's Priest,
    And by the vision splendid
    Is on his way attended;
At length the Man perceives it die away,   75
And fade into the light of common day.

VI

Earth fills her lap with pleasures of her own;
Yearnings she hath in her own natural kind,
And, even with something of a Mother's mind,
    And no unworthy aim,   80
    The homely Nurse doth all she can
To make her Foster-child, her Inmate Man,
    Forget the glories he hath known,
And that imperial palace whence he came.

VII

Behold the Child among his new-born blisses,   85
A six years' Darling of a pigmy size!
See, where 'mid work of his own hand he lies,
Fretted by sallies of his mother's kisses,
With light upon him from his father's eyes!
See, at his feet, some little plan or chart,   90
Some fragment from his dream of human life,
Shaped by himself with newly-learned art;
    A wedding or a festival,
    A mourning or a funeral;
        And this hath now his heart,   95
    And unto this he frames his song:
        Then will he fit his tongue
To dialogues of business, love, or strife;
    But it will not be long

Ere this be thrown aside,   100
And with new joy and pride
The little Actor cons another part;
Filling from time to time his "humorous stage"
With all the Persons, down to palsied Age,
That Life brings with her in her equipage;   105
As if his whole vocation
Were endless imitation.

VIII

Thou, whose exterior semblance doth belie
Thy Soul's immensity;
Thou best Philosopher, who yet dost keep   110
Thy heritage, thou Eye among the blind,
That, deaf and silent, read'st the eternal deep,
Haunted for ever by the eternal mind,—
Mighty Prophet! Seer blest!
On whom those truths do rest,   115
Which we are toiling all our lives to find,
In darkness lost, the darkness of the grave;
Thou, over whom thy Immortality
Broods like the Day, a Master o'er a Slave,
A Presence which is not to be put by;   120
Thou little Child, yet glorious in the might
Of heaven-born freedom on thy being's height,
Why with such earnest pains dost thou provoke
The years to bring the inevitable yoke,
Thus blindly with thy blessedness at strife?   125
Full soon thy Soul shall have her earthly freight,
And custom lie upon thee with a weight,
Heavy as frost, and deep almost as life!

IX

O joy! that in our embers
Is something that doth live,   130
That nature yet remembers
What was so fugitive!
The thought of our past years in me doth breed
Perpetual benediction: not indeed

For that which is most worthy to be blest—   135
Delight and liberty, the simple creed
Of Childhood, whether busy or at rest,
With new-fledged hope still fluttering in his breast:—
        Not for these I raise
        The song of thanks and praise;   140
But for those obstinate questionings
        Of sense and outward things,
        Fallings from us, vanishings;
        Blank misgivings of a Creature
Moving about in worlds not realised,   145
High instincts before which our mortal Nature
Did tremble like a guilty Thing surprised:
        But for those first affections,
        Those shadowy recollections,
    Which, be they what they may,   150
Are yet the fountain light of all our day,
Are yet a master light of all our seeing;
    Uphold us, cherish, and have power to make
Our noisy years seem moments in the being
Of the eternal Silence: truths that wake,   155
        To perish never;
Which neither listlessness, nor mad endeavour,
        Nor Man nor Boy,
Nor all that is at enmity with joy,
Can utterly abolish or destroy!   160
        Hence in a season of calm weather
        Though inland far we be,
Our Souls have sight of that immortal sea
        Which brought us hither,
        Can in a moment travel thither,   165
And see the Children sport upon the shore,
And hear the mighty waters rolling evermore.

                        X
Then sing, ye Birds, sing, sing a joyous song!
        And let the young Lambs bound
        As to the tabor's sound!   170
We in thought will join your throng,

Ye that pipe and ye that play,
Ye that through your hearts to-day
Feel the gladness of the May!
What though the radiance which was once so bright   175
Be now for ever taken from my sight,
Though nothing can bring back the hour
Of splendour in the grass, of glory in the flower;
We will grieve not, rather find
Strength in what remains behind;   180
In the primal sympathy
Which having been must ever be;
In the soothing thoughts that spring
Out of human suffering;
In the faith that looks through death,   185
In years that bring the philosophic mind.

XI

And O, ye Fountains, Meadows, Hills, and Groves,
Forebode not any severing of our loves!
Yet in my heart of hearts I feel your might;
I only have relinquished one delight
To live beneath your more habitual sway.
I love the Brooks which down their channels fret,
Even more than when I tripped lightly as they;
The innocent brightness of a new-born Day
Is lovely yet;   195
The Clouds that gather round the setting sun
Do take a sober colouring from an eye
That hath kept watch o'er man's mortality;
Another race hath been, and other palms are won.
Thanks to the human heart by which we live,   200
Thanks to its tenderness, its joys, and fears,
To me the meanest flower that blows can give
Thoughts that do often lie too deep for tears.
                                    —*William Wordsworth*

Epigraph: the final lines of Wordsworth's "My Heart Leaps Up." 21. *tabor*: a small drum. 40. *coronal*: a garland worn on festive occasions.

6
Poems for Comparison

Judging poems is a risky business, because it is often difficult to distinguish between a poem we like and a poem that is good. The two terms are not synonymous; one tells us something about the reader and his tastes, the other says something about the poem itself. Unfortunately, however, personal taste, the preferences of an age, a poem's content, and personal associations peculiar to a reader or an audience often prevent an honest and objective appraisal of a poem. To be specific, a poem is not bad because I as a reader don't happen to like it; because I share the twentieth-century preference for understated rather than overstated poetry; because it criticises Richard Nixon who I think is a great man; or because it always reminds me of a girl I used to know who was a real bitch. All these considerations must be put aside before I can make an honest evaluation of a poem, and it should be within my powers as a critic to step outside of myself, at least as far as these matters are concerned, and look objectively at a poem. Such a perspective allows me to admit, say, that Shelley's "Ode to the West Wind" is a good poem and that Dylan's "Lay, Lady, Lay" is a good song, even though I may not happen to like them; conversely, it allows me to see that however much I personally like the poetry of A. E. Housman and the lyrics of Phil Ochs, they will never be "great" poetry by any objective standards.

Other considerations are more difficult to deal with. The nineteenth century, for example, literally wallowed in sentimentality, while the twentieth is usually pretty hard-nosed about its poetry. When I make a judgment to the effect that sentimentality is bad in poetry, and that Rod McKuen therefore writes bad songs, have I turned a personal preference into a critical judgment? Am I a prisoner of the twentieth century, sharing its prejudices and making judgments that some future generation will deem more a failure of my taste than a failure of the poet's artistic ability? Or is sentimentality simply bad? Or, to examine another possibility, if I accuse Ferlinghetti of a frightening failure of tone or a gross breach of decorum and taste in applying the term "*the king cat*" to Christ ("Someone During Eternity") am I exhibiting my personal religious attitudes, the prejudices of my age or peer group, or an objective critical judgment? In cases like these the critic has a difficult time rendering a judgment because it is hard to say exactly what amounts to a personal preference and what is objective criticism.

The argument can be pushed even further. If we condemn a poem because it indulges in a hopelessly garbled metaphor, or a self-contradictory simile, is it possible that we are in reality saying "I like unmixed metaphors and similes that don't contradict themselves"—that *all* our critical judgments are only preferences in disguise? In the final analysis, are all critical appraisals nothing more than "I like it" or "I don't like it," disguised behind some mumbo-jumbo about rhythm and sound and sense? Of course the end of such an argument is the critical premise that negates critical premises: "It is impossible to make an objective statement about a poem." But turning such a statement upon itself, we find that it too could amount only to a personal belief or preference; it is an objective critical statement that, according to itself, cannot be made. And because such a statement, by its own admission, must amount to nothing more than a personal opinion, those of us who do not hold that belief are perfectly free to make our own objective critical statements with some degree of confidence that they are indeed objective.

Probably critical appraisals can be honest if we only avoid (as much as possible) several critical fallacies: the *intentional fallacy,* which assumes that if a poet *intended* to do or say one thing, what he did or said must actually have fulfilled his expectations; *affective criticism,* which judges a poem on the basis of how it affects us as individual readers; and the *fallacy of content,* which assumes that a poem is good or bad literature depending on the importance or truth of its subject. As critics we must overlook doctrine and judge craft, because poetry is not ideas. In fact, philosophers like Plato exclude poets from their ideal Republics because poetry does not always teach truth and reality. Rupert Brooke is not a bad poet because he finds war ennobling any more than Wilfred Owen is automatically a good poet because he is critical of war. As critics we must first grant a poet his subject and his conventions, and judge him on the basis of his craft, the art of his work. Then—separately—we may judge the subject and the conventions of the poem: "Bye Bye, Love" is good song, granted the subject and conventions of American rock poetry of the late 1950's, but both the subject and the conventions appear banal from the point of view of the 1970's.

As critics we also have the right to demand. We have the right to expect that a poet will innovate, however slightly, within the conventions he has chosen, so that his poem will be something more than a pastiche of all that has gone before him. We have a right to expect the poet to be honest with himself and us, that he not pose—or, if he is putting us on, that he be aware of his pose himself, that he make us aware of it, that he have a good reason for posing. We have a right to expect the poet to exercise control over his poem, so that he does not distort syntax unduly for the sake of an unnecessary rhyme, so that his metaphors are clean when they should be clean, so that his ambiguities are the result of insight and thought rather than sloppy writing, so that the sound of the words contributes to rather than detracts from the sense of the poem. And finally, in great poetry at least, we have a right to demand that the poet not waste our time; not that every poem must deal with heavy subjects, but that when we finish lavishing time and attention on a poem we should come away with a sense of effort rewarded rather than a sense of disappointment, with a "that was good!" rather than a "So what?"

The following pairs of poems should allow you to exercise your critical judgment to decide what aspects of a poem are good or bad, what uses of imagery are better or worse, what treatments of a theme are effective or ineffective. In some cases the relative merits and demerits of the two poems are obvious on a first reading; take the time to work the details out in your mind and, perhaps, on paper, if only for the practice. In other cases the poems should provoke some real debate; keep the debate on a level above that of liking and disliking. And in a few cases the two poems are both well done, but show different possible exploitations of a metaphor or situation. Your problem in these instances is to evaluate the context of the poem, the presuppositions on which it is constructed, and arrive at some evaluation of poem-plus-convention. Exercise of judgment on this limited level should form the basis in theory and practice for evaluations of some of the poems that appear in chapter 7.

That the Night Come

She lived in storm and strife,
Her soul had such desire
For what proud death may bring
That it could not endure
The common good of life,   5
But lived as 'twere a king
That packed his marriage day
With banneret and pennon,
Trumpet and kettledrum,
And the outrageous cannon,   10
To bundle time away
That the night come.

—*William Butler Yeats*

My Candle Burns

My candle burns at both ends
It will not last the night;
But, oh, my foes and ah, my friends,
It gives a lovely light.

—*Edna St. Vincent Millay*

What exactly is the theme of these two poems? One is written in the first person, the other in the third; does the person have any effect on the impact of the poem and the ability of the poem to convey its theme? One is an epigram, the other a longer poem; does the poetic form have any effect on the poem's ability to convey theme? Analyze the two poems carefully for rhythm; which is more sophisticated? How would you describe the tone of the respective poems? Is one more appropriate than the other? All things considered—tone, point of view, verse rhythm, imagery—is one poem demonstrably superior to the other?

Departmental

An ant on the tablecloth
Ran into a dormant moth
Of many times his size.
He showed not the least surprise.
His business wasn't with such.   5
He gave it scarcely a touch,
And was off on his duty run.
Yet if he encountered one
Of the hive's enquiry squad
Whose work is to find out God   10
And the nature of time and space,
He would put him onto the case.
Ants are a curious race;
One crossing with hurried tread
The body of one of their dead   15
Isn't given a moment's arrest—
Seems not even impressed.
But he no doubt reports to any
With whom he crosses antennae,
And they no doubt report   20
To the higher up at court.
Then word goes forth in Formic:
"Death's come to Jerry McCormic,
Our selfless forager Jerry.
Will the special Janizary   25
Whose office it is to bury
The dead of the commissary
Go bring him home to his people.
Lay him in state on a sepal.
Wrap him for shroud in a petal.   30
Embalm him with ichor of nettle.
This is the word of your Queen."
And presently on the scene
Appears a solemn mortician;
And taking formal position   35
With feelers calmly atwiddle,

Seizes the dead by the middle,
And heaving him high in air,
Carries him out of there.
No one stands round to stare.   40
It is nobody else's affair.

It couldn't be called ungentle.
But how thoroughly departmental.

                                                —*Robert Frost*

   25. *Janizary*: a Turkish infantryman. 31. *ichor*: the etherial fluid reported to flow in the veins of the gods; here an embalming fluid.

The Unknown Citizen

> *To JS/07/M/378 This Marble Monument is Erected by the State*

He was found by the Bureau of Statistics to be
One against whom there was no official complaint,
And all the reports on his conduct agree
That, in the modern sense of an old-fashioned word, he was a saint,
For in everything he did he served the Greater Community.   5
Except for the War till the day he retired
He worked in a factory and never got fired,
But satisfied his employers, Fudge Motors Inc.
Yet he wasn't a scab or odd in his views,
For his Union reports that he paid his dues,   10
(Our report on his Union shows it was sound)
And our social Psychology workers found
That he was popular with his mates and liked a drink.
The Press are convinced that he bought a paper every day
And that his reactions to advertisements were normal in every way. 15
Policies taken out in his name prove that he was fully insured,
And his Health-card shows he was once in hospital but left it cured.
Both Producers Research and High-Grade Living declare
He was fully sensible to the advantage of the Installment Plan
And had everything necessary to the Modern Man,   20
A phonograph, a radio, a car and a frigidaire.
Our researchers into Public Opinion are content

That he held the proper opinions for the time of year;
When there was peace, he was for peace; when there was war, he
  went.
He was married and added five children to the population,   25
Which our Eugenist says was the right number for a parent of
  his generation,
And our teachers report that he never interfered with their
  education.
Was he free? Was he happy? The question is absurd:
Had anything been wrong, we should certainly have heard.

—*W. H. Auden*

Here are two poems of protest against the increasing depersonalization of life in modern America by two of her best poets. In what respects are their appraisals of the situation similar and different? Are the tones similar or different? What does the shorter line length contribute to the Frost poem? What is the effect of the feminine rhyme of the final couplet of that poem? How do you react to "Fudge Motors Inc." in "The Unknown Citizen?" Which poem is more direct? Which do you find the better poem?

Western Wind

O Western wind, when wilt thou blow
  That the small rain down can rain?
Christ, that my love were in my arms,
  And I in my bed again!

—*anonymous*

The Division

Rain on the windows, creaking doors,
  With blasts that besom the green,
And I am here, and you are there,
  And a hundred miles between!

O were it but the weather, Dear,   5
    O were it but the miles
That summed up all our severance,
    There might be room for smiles.

But that thwart thing betwixt us twain,
    Which nothing cleaves or clears,   10
Is more than distance, Dear, or rain,
    And longer than the years!

                                        —*Thomas Hardy*

These two poems use similar images to discuss similar themes; which
is more overt in its statement? Which is more ambiguous? "Western
Wind" has haunted poets and readers of poetry for centuries; "The
Division" is relatively unknown. Are the reputations justified? What is
there about rain and wind that make them appropriate images for a
poem about separated lovers? In *Poetry of Experience,* Archibald Mac-
Leish claims that "Western Wind" conveys a meaning that the emotion,
not the intelligence, knows. Is this a valid or even comprehensible statement? Can it also be made about "The Division?"

Love Minus Zero/No Limit

My love she speaks like silence
Without ideals of violence,
She doesn't have to say she's faithful
Yet she's true, like ice, like fire.
People carry roses   5
And make promises by the hours,
My love she laughs like the flowers.
Valentines can't buy her.

In the dime stores and bus stations
People talk of situations   10

Read books, repeat quotations
Draw conclusions on the wall.
Some speak of the future,
My love, she speaks softly,
She knows there's no success like failure   15
And that failure's no success at all.

The cloak and dagger dangles,
Madams light the candles.
In ceremonies of the horseman
Even the pawn must hold a grudge.   20
Statues made of match sticks
Crumble into one another,
My love, she does not bother,
She knows too much to argue or to judge.

The bridge at midnight trembles,   25
The country doctor rambles,
Bankers' nieces seek perfection
Expecting all the gifts that wise men bring.
The wind howls like a hammer,
The night blows cold an' rainy,   30
My love she's like some raven
At my window with a broken wing.

—Bob Dylan

Fire and Ice

Some say the world will end in fire,
Some say in ice.
From what I've tasted of desire
I hold with those who favor fire.
But if it had to perish twice,   5
I think I know enough of hate
To say that for destruction ice
Is also great
And would suffice.

—Robert Frost

Carefully examine the two poets' uses of the symbols fire and ice. Exactly what do these very basic elements signify in each poem? Is one signification any more traditional or even more trite than the other? Which usage is more ambiguous? Why? Is that ambiguity the result of insight on the poet's part, or merely of fuzzy thinking? Do these two uses of fire and ice as symbols exhaust the symbolic possibilities of either element? Granted that each poet uses the elements with different significations in poems about different subjects: which poet is more effective in his usage? Why?

Sonnet to My Mother

Most near, most dear, most loved and most far,
Under the window where I often found her
Sitting as huge as Asia, seismic with laughter,
Gin and chicken helpless in her Irish hand,
Irresistible as Rabelais but most tender for   5
The lame dogs and hurt birds that surround her,—
She is a procession no one can follow after
But be like a little dog following a brass band.
She will not glance up at the bomber nor condescend
To drop her gin and scuttle to a cellar,   10
But lean on the mahogany table like a mountain
Whom only faith can move, and so I send
O all my faith and all my love to tell her
That she will move from mourning into morning.
                                                     —*George Barker*

3. *seismic*: like an earthquake. 5. *Rabelais*: French satirist who specialized in broad, rolicking, sometimes bawdy humor. 12. *only faith can move*: Cf. Matthew 17:20.

My Mother's Hands

Such beautiful, beautiful hands!
   They're neither white nor small;
And you, I know, would scarcely think
   That they were fair at all.

I've looked on hands whose form and hue   5
   A sculptor's dream might be;
Yet are those wrinkled, aged hands
   Most beautiful to me.

Such beautiful, beautiful hands!
   Though heart were weary and sad,   10
These patient hands kept toiling on,
   That the children might be glad;
I always weep, as looking back
   To childhood's distant day,
I think how those hands rested not,   15
   When mine were at their play.

Such beautiful, beautiful hands!
   They're growing feeble now,
For time and pain have left their mark
   On hands, and heart, and brow.   20
Alas! alas! the nearing time,
   And the sad, sad day to me,
When 'neath the daisies, out of sight,
   These hands will folded be.

But oh, beyond this shadow land,   25
   Where all is bright and fair,
I know full well these dear old hands
   Will palms of victory bear;
Where crystal streams through endless years
   Flow over golden sands,   30
And where the old grow young again,
   I'll clasp my mother's hands.

                                        —*anonymous*

   What aspects of tone, meter, imagery, rhyme scheme, simile, and
metaphor make "Sonnet to my Mother" the superior poem?

Trees

I think that I shall never see
A poem lovely as a tree.

A tree whose hungry mouth is pressed
Against the earth's sweet flowing breast;

A tree that looks to God all day,   5
And lifts her leafy arms to pray;

A tree that may in summer wear
A nest of robins in her hair;

Upon whose bosom snow has lain;
Who intimately lives with rain.   10

Poems are made by fools like me,
But only God can make a tree.

                                              —*Joyce Kilmer*

Trees

To be a giant and keep quiet about it,
To stay in one's own place;
To stand for the constant presence of process
And always to seem the same;
To be steady as a rock and always trembling,   5
Having the hard appearance of death
With the soft, fluent nature of growth,
One's Being deceptively armored,
One's Becoming deceptively vulnerable;
To be so tough, and take the light so well,   10
Freely providing forbidden knowledge
Of so many things about heaven and earth
For which we should otherwise have no word—
Poems or people are rarely so lovely,

And even when they have great qualities   15
They tend to tell you rather than exemplify
What they believe themselves to be about,
While from the moving silence of trees,
Whether in storm or calm, in leaf and naked,
Night or day, we draw conclusions of our own,   20
Sustaining and unnoticed as our breath,
And perilous also—though there has never been
A critical tree—about the nature of things.

                                        —*Howard Nemerov*

"Trees," by Joyce Kilmer, is widely known and frequently read in American high schools. It was probably this poem that earned Kilmer the honor of having a rest stop on the New Jersey Turnpike named after him. Nemerov's "Trees" is virtually unknown, and no rest stops (or toll gates even) have been named in that poet's honor. Examine the two poems carefully. Both make similar comparisons involving the personification of trees; "A tree whose hungry mouth is pressed . . . A tree that looks to God all day," and "To be a giant and keep quiet about it, /To stay in one's own place." Both poems compare and contrast trees and poets: "Poems are made by fools like me, /But only God can make a tree," and "Poems or people are rarely so lovely." What critical statements can be made about each poem individually? Do they justify the relative reputations of the poems and their authors? Is one more insightful than the other? Exactly what insights does the better poem offer, and how does it go about conveying them? Is the dislike of superficiality a personal prejudice or an objective critical position?

The Demon Lover (A)

"O where have you been, my long, long love,
    This long seven years and more?"
"O I'm come to seek my former vows
    Ye granted me before."

"O hold your tongue of your former vows,   5
    For they will breed sad strife;

O hold your tongue of your former vows,
    For I am become a wife."

He turned him right and round about
    And the tear blinded his ee: 10
"I wad never hae trodden on Irish ground,
    If it had not been for thee.

"I might hae had a king's daughter,
    Far, far beyond the sea;
I might have had a king's daughter,   15
    Had it not been for the love o thee."

"If ye might have had a king's daughter,
    Yer sel ye had to blame;
Ye might have taken the king's daughter,
    For ye kend that I was nane.   20

"If I was to leave my husband dear,
    And my two babes also,
O what have you to take me to,
    If with you I should go?"

"I hae seven ships upon the sea—   25
    The eighth brought me to land—
With four-and-twenty bold mariners,
    And music on every hand."

She has taken up her two little babes,
    Kiss'd then baith cheek and chin: 30
"O fair ye weel, my ain two babes,
    For I'll never see you again."

She set her foot upon the ship,
    No mariners could she behold;
But the sails were o the taffetie,   35
    And the masts o the beaten gold.

They had not sailed a league, a league,
    A league but barely three,

When dismal grew his countenance,
    And drumlie grew his ee.   40

They had not sailed a league, a league,
    A league but barely three,
Until she espied his cloven foot,
    And she wept right bitterlie.

"O hold your tongue of your weeping," says he,   45
    "Of your weeping now let me be;
I will show you how the lilies grow
    On the banks of Italy."

"O what hills are yon, yon pleasant hills,
    That the sun shines sweetly on?"   50
"O yon are the hills of heaven," he said,
    "Where you will never win."

"O whaten mountain is yon," she said,
    "All so dreary wi frost and snow?"
"O yon is the mountain of hell," he cried,   55
    "Where you and I will go."

He strack the tap-mast wi his hand,
    The fore-mast wi his knee,
And he brake the gallant ship in twain,
    And sank her in the sea.   60

                          —*anonymous*

    10. *ee*: eye. 20. *kend*: knew. 40. *drumlie*: gloomy.

The Demon Lover (B)

"Well met, well met," said an old true love,
"Well met, well met," said he;
"I'm just returning from the salt, salt sea,
And it's all for the love of thee."

"Come in, come in, my old true love,   5
And have a seat with me.

It's been three-fourths of a long, long year
Since together we have been."

"Well I can't come in or I can't sit down,
For I haven't but a moment's time.   10
They say you're married to a house carpenter,
And your heart will never be mine.

"Now it's I could have married a king's daughter dear;
I'm sure she'd a married me;
But I've forsaken her crowns of gold,   15
And it's all for the love of thee.

"Now will you forsaken your house carpenter
And go along with me?
I'll take you where the grass grows green
On the banks of the deep blue sea."   20

She picked up her little babe,
And kisses gave it three.
Says, "Stay right here, my darling little babe,
And keep our poppa company."

Well he hadn't been on ship but about two weeks—   25
I'm sure it was not three—
Till his true love begin to weep and mourn
And to weep most bitterly,

Says, "Are you weeping for my silver or my gold?"
Says, "Are you weeping for my store?   30
Are you weeping for that house carpenter
Whose face you'll never see any more?"

"No, it's I'm not a-weeping for your silver or your gold,
Or neither for your store;
I am weeping for my darling little babe   35
Whose face I'll never see any more."

Well he hadn't been on ship but about three weeks—
I'm sure it was not four—
Till they sprung a leak in the bottom of the ship
And sunk for to rise no more.   40

—anonymous

    Here are two versions of the same ballad, the first printed in the early nineteenth century, the second in the early twentieth. Review the conventions of the ballad, then compare and contrast these two poems. Which do you find the better ballad? Why? Does the fact that the second version contains language and diction closer to modern American English influence your opinion in any way? Should it, if you are being an honest critic?

7
A Selection of Poems

LOVE

Love: that disposition or state of feeling with regard to a person which (arising from recognition of attractive qualities, from instincts of natural relationship, or from sympathy) manifests itself in solicitude for the welfare of the object, and usually also in delight in his presence and desire for his approval; warm affection, attachment.

i am a beggar always

i am a beggar always
who begs in your mind

(slightly smiling, patient, unspeaking
with a sign on his
breast   5
BLIND)yes i

am this person of whom somehow
you are never wholly rid(and who

does not ask for more than
just enough dreams to   10
live on)
       after all, kid

you might as well
toss him a few thoughts

a little love preferably,   15
anything which you can't
pass off on other people: for
instance a
plugged promise—

then he will maybe(hearing something   20
fall into his hat)go wandering
after it with fingers; till having

found
what was thrown away
                himself   25
taptaptaps out of your brain, hopes, life

to(carefully turning a
corner)never bother you any more.

                                 —e. e. cummings

Lay, Lady, Lay

Lay, lady, lay,
Lay across my big brass bed.
Lay, lady, lay,
Lay across my big brass bed.
Whatever colors you have in your mind   5
I'll show them to you
And you'll see them shine.

Lay, lady, lay,
Lay across my big brass bed.
Stay, lady, stay   10
With your man awhile.
Until the break of day
Let me see you make him smile.

His clothes are dirty, but his hands are clean
And you're the best thing that he's ever seen.   15

Stay, lady, stay,
Stay with your man awhile.
Why wait any longer for the world to begin?
You can have your cake and eat it too.
Why wait any longer for the one you love   20
When he's standing in front of you?

Lay, lady, lay,
across my big brass bed.
Stay, lady, stay
While the night is still ahead.   25
I long to see you in the morning light.
I long to reach for you in the night.
Stay, lady, stay,
Stay while the night is still ahead.

                                          —*Bob Dylan*

When You Are Old

When you are old and grey and full of sleep,
And nodding by the fire, take down this book,
And slowly read, and dream of the soft look
Your eyes had once, and of their shadows deep;

How many loved your moments of glad grace,   5
And loved your beauty with love false or true,
But one man loved the pilgrim soul in you,
And loved the sorrows of your changing face;

And bending down beside the glowing bars,
Murmur, a little sadly, how Love fled   10
And paced upon the mountains overhead
And hid his face amid a crowd of stars.
                                  —*William Butler Yeats*

California Dreamin'

All the leaves are brown,
And the sky is gray
I've been for a walk on a winter's day
I'd be safe and warm if I was in L.A.
California dreamin' on such a winter's day   5
Stopped into a church,
I passed along the way
I got down on my knees, and pretended to pray
You know the preacher likes the cold
He knows I'm going to stay   10
California dreamin' on such a winter's day.
If I didn't tell her I could leave today
California dreamin' on such a winter's day.
All the leaves are brown,
And the sky is gray   15
I've been for a walk on a winter's day
I'd be safe and warm if I was in L.A.
California dreamin' on such a winter's day.

—John Phillips

love note II: flags

Still, it is dear defiance now to carry
Fair flags of you above my indignation,
Top, with a pretty glory and a merry
Softness, the scattered pound of my cold passion.
I pull you down my foxhole. Do you mind?   5
You burn in bits of saucy color then.
I let you flutter out against the pained
Volleys. Against my power crumpled and wan.
You, and the yellow pert exuberance
Of dandelion days, unmocking sun;   10

The blowing of clear wind in your gay hair;
Love changeful in you (like a music, or
Like a sweet mournfulness, or like a dance,
Or like the tender struggle of a fan).

                                        —*Gwendolyn Brooks*

They Flee from Me

They flee from me that sometime did me seek,
    With naked foot stalking in my chamber.
I have seen them gentle, tame, and meek,
    That now are wild, and do not remember
    That sometime they put themself in danger   5
To take bread at my hand; and now they range
Busily seeking with a continual change.

Thanked be Fortune, it hath been otherwise
    Twenty times better; but once, in special,
In thin array, after a pleasant guise,   10
    When her loose gown from her shoulders did fall,
    And she me caught in her arms long and small,
Therewith all sweetly did me kiss,
And softly said, "Dear heart, how like you this?"

It was no dream; I lay broad waking.   15
    But all is turned thorough my gentleness,
Into a strange fashion of forsaking;
    And I have leave to go of her goodness,
    And she also to use newfangleness.
But since that I so kindely am served,   20
I would fain know what she hath deserved.

                                        —*Sir Thomas Wyatt*

8. *Fortune*: Semi-deific personification of the Renaissance and Middle Ages, always associated with change and instability. 19. *kindely*: kind as in nature; hence, "naturally."

Sonnet 116

Let me not to the marriage of true minds
Admit impediments. Love is not love
Which alters when it alteration finds,
Or bends with the remover to remove.
O no! it is an ever-fixèd mark   5
That looks on tempests and is never shaken;
It is the star to every wandering bark,
Whose worth's unknown, although his height be taken.
Love's not Time's fool, though rosy lips and cheeks
Within his bending sickle's compass come;   10
Love alters not with his brief hours and weeks,
But bears it out even to the edge of doom.
   If this be error and upon me proved,
    I never writ, nor no man ever loved.
                    —William Shakespeare

   7. *bark*: ship.

Honky Tonk Women

I met a gin-soaked, barroom queen in Memphis,
She tried to take me upstairs for a ride.
She had to heave me right across her shoulder
'Cause I just can't seem to drink you off my mind.
It's the Honky Tonk Women   5
Gimme the honky tonk blues.

I played a divorcee in New York City,
I had to put up some kind of a fight.
The lady then she covered me with roses,
She blew my nose and then she blew my mind.   10
It's the Honky Tonk Women
Gimme the honky tonk blues.
                    —Mick Jagger–Keith Richards

A Red, Red Rose

O, my luve is like a red, red rose,
    That's newly sprung in June.
O, my luve is like the melodie,
    That's sweetly play'd in tune.

As fair art thou, my bonie lass,   5
    So deep in luve am I,
And I will luve thee still, my dear,
    Till a' the seas gang dry.

Till a' the seas gang dry, my dear,
    And the rocks melt wi' the sun!   10
And I will luve thee still, my dear,
    While the sands o' life shall run.

And fare thee weel, my only luve,
    And fare thee weel a while!
And I will come again, my luve,   15
    Tho' it were ten thousand mile!

                    —*Robert Burns*

Crazy Jane Talks with the Bishop

I met the Bishop on the road
And much said he and I.
"Those breasts are flat and fallen now,
Those veins must soon be dry;
Live in a heavenly mansion,   5
Not in some foul sty."

"Fair and foul are near of kin,
And fair needs foul," I cried.
"My friends are gone, but that's a truth
Nor grave nor bed denied,   10
Learned in bodily lowliness
And in the heart's pride.

"A woman can be proud and stiff
When on love intent;
But Love has pitched his mansion in   15
The place of excrement;
For nothing can be sole or whole
That has not been rent."

—William Butler Yeats

Tonight Will Be Fine

Sometimes I find
I get to thinking of the past,
We swore to each other then
That our love would surely last
You kept right on loving   5
I went on a fast
Now I am too thin
And your love is too vast.

I choose the rooms
That I live in with care,   10
The windows are small
And the walls must be bare
There's only one bed
And there's only one prayer
And I listen all night   15
For your step on the stair.

Sometimes I see her
Undressing for me,
She's the soft naked lady
Love meant her to be   20
And she's moving her body
So brave and so free.
If I've got to remember
That's a fine memory.

But I know from your eyes   25
And I know from your smile
That tonight will be fine, will be fine
Will be fine, will be fine for a while.

                                             —*Leonard Cohen*

Porphyria's Lover

The rain set early in to-night,
    The sullen wind was soon awake,
It tore the elm-tops down for spite,
    And did its worst to vex the lake:
    I listened with heart fit to break.   5
When glided in Porphyria; straight
    She shut the cold out and the storm,
And kneeled and made the cheerless grate
    Blaze up, and all the cottage warm;
    Which done, she rose, and from her form   10
Withdrew the dripping cloak and shawl,
    And laid her soiled gloves by, untied
Her hat and let the damp hair fall,
    And, last, she sat down by my side
    And called me. When no voice replied,   15
She put my arm about her waist,
    And made her smooth white shoulder bare,
And all her yellow hair displaced,
    And, stooping, made my cheek lie there,
    And spread, o'er all, her yellow hair,   20
Murmuring how she loved me—she
    Too weak, for all her heart's endeavor,
To set its struggling passion free
    From pride, and vainer ties dissever,
    And give herself to me forever.   25
But passion sometimes would prevail,
    Nor could to-night's gay feast restrain
A sudden thought of one so pale
    For love of her, and all in vain:
    So, she was come through wind and rain.   30

Be sure I looked up at her eyes
    Happy and proud; at last I knew
Porphyria worshipped me: surprise
    Made my heart swell, and still it grew
    While I debated what to do.   35
That moment she was mine, mine, fair,
    Perfectly pure and good: I found
A thing to do, and all her hair
    In one long yellow string I wound
    Three times her little throat around,   40
And strangled her. No pain felt she;
    I am quite sure she felt no pain.
As a shut bud that holds a bee,
    I warily oped her lids: again
    Laughed the blue eyes without a stain.   45
And I untightened next the tress
    About her neck; her cheek once more
Blushed bright beneath my burning kiss:
    I propper her head up as before,
    Only, this time my shoulder bore   50
Her head, which droops upon it still:
    The smiling rosy little head,
So glad it has its utmost will,
    That all it scorned at once is fled,
    And I, its love, am gained instead!   55
Prophyria's love: she guessed not how
    Her darling one wish would be heard.
And thus we sit together now,
    And all night long we have not stirred,
    And yet God has not said a word!   60
                          —Robert Browning

Love and Life

All my past Life is mine no more,
    The flying hours are gone;
Like transitory Dreams giv'n o'er,
Whose Images are kept in store,
    By Memory alone.   5

The Time that is to come is not,
    How can it then be mine?
The present Moment's all my Lot,
And that, as fast as it is got,
    Phillis, is only thine.   10

Then talk not of Inconstancy,
    False Hearts, and broken Vows;
If I, by Miracle, can be
This live-long Minute true to thee,
    'Tis all that Heav'n allows.   15
               —*John Wilmot, Earl of Rochester*

Moonlight Drive

Let's swim to the moon
Let's climb through the tide
Penetrate the evening
That the city sleeps to hide
Let's swim out tonight, love   5
It's our turn to try
Parked beside the ocean
On our moonlight drive.

Let's swim to the moon
Let's climb through the tide   10
Surrender to the waiting worlds
That lap against our side
Nothing left open
And no time to decide
We've stepped into a river   15
On our moonlight drive.

Let's swim to the moon
Let's climb through the tide

You reach a hand to hold me
But I can't be your guide.   20
It's easy to love you
As I watch you glide
We're falling through wet forests
On our moonlight drive.

Come on, baby, gonna take a little ride   25
Goin' down by the ocean side
Gonna get real close
Get real tight
Baby, gonna drown tonight
Goin' down, down, down.   30

—*Jim Morrison*

WAR

War: hostile contention by means of armed forces, carried on between nations, states, or rulers, or between parties in the same nation against a foreign power, or against an opposing party in the state.

plato told

plato told

him:he couldn't
believe it(jesus

told him;he
wouldn't believe   5
it)lao

tsze
certainly told
him,and general
(yes   10

mam)
sherman;
and even
(believe it
or   15

not)you
told him:i told
him;we told him
(he didn't believe it,no

sir)it took   20
a nipponized bit of
the old sixth

avenue
el;in the top of his head:to tell

him   25
                                        —*e. e. cummings*

   23. *sixth avenue el*: shortly before the outbreak of World War II, the United
States government permitted the sale to Japan of New York City's Sixth Avenue
elevated subway as scrap metal.

White Boots Marchin' in a Yellow Land

The Pilot's playing poker in the cockpit of the plane;
The casualties are rising like the dropping of the rain.
And a mountain of machinery will fall before a man
When you're white boots marchin' in a yellow land.

Red blow the bugles of the dawn;   5
Morning has arrived; you must be gone.
And the lost patrol chase their chartered souls
Like old whores following tired armies.

It's written in the ashes of the village towns we've burned.
It's written in the empty beds of fathers unreturned.   10

And the chocolate in the children's eyes will never understand—
When you're white boots marchin' in a yellow land.

Train them well the men who will be fighting by your side,
And never turn your back if the battle turns the tide,
For the colors of a civil war are louder than commands—   15
When you're white boots marchin' in a yellow land.

Blow them from the forest and burn them from your sight
Tie their hands behind their backs and question through the
    night.
But when the firing squad is ready, they'll be spitting where
    they stand
At the white boots marchin' in a yellow land.   20

The comic and the beauty queen are dancing on the stage.
The raw recruits are lining up like coffins in a cage.
Oh! We're fighting in a war we lost before the war began.
We're the white boots marchin' in a yellow land.

Red blow the bugles of the dawn;   25
Morning has arrived; you must be gone.
And the lost patrol chase their chartered souls
Like old whores following tired armies.

                                        —*Phil Ochs*

The Soldier

If I should die, think only this for me:
    That there's some corner of a foreign field
That is for ever England. There shall be
    In that rich earth a richer dust concealed;
A dust whom England bore, shaped, made aware,   5
    Gave, once, her flowers to love, her ways to roam,
A body of England's, breathing English air,
    Washed by the rivers, blest by suns of home.
And think, this heart, all evil shed away,
    A pulse in the eternal mind, no less   10
    Gives somewhere back the thoughts by England given;

Her sights and sounds; dreams happy as her day;
   And laughter, learnt of friends; and gentleness,
      In hearts at peace, under an English heaven.
                           —*Rupert Brooke*

Epitaph on an Army of Mercenaries

These, in the day when heaven was falling,
   The hour when earth's foundations fled,
Followed their mercenary calling
   And took their wages and are dead.

Their shoulders held the sky suspended;   5
   They stood, and earth's foundations stay;
What God abandoned, these defended,
   And saved the sum of things for pay.
                         —*A. E. Housman*

On Being Asked for a War Poem

I think it better in times like these
A poet's mouth be silent, for in truth
We have no gift to set a statesman right;
He has had enough of meddling who can please
A young girl in the indolence of her youth,   5
Or an old man upon a winter's night.
                   —*William Butler Yeats*

Requiem for the Masses

Requiem eternam.

Mama, mama, forget your pies,
Have faith they won't get cold.

Then turn your eyes to the bloodshot skies,
Your flag is flying full,
At half mast for the matadors, 5
Who turned their backs to please the crowd,
And fell before the bull.

Red was the color of his blood flowing thin,
Pallid white was the color of his lifeless skin,
Blue was the color of the morning sky he saw from the ground
   where he died, 10
It was the last thing ever seen by him.

Kyrie eleison.
Requiem eternam.

Black and white were the figures that recorded him,
Black and white was the newsprint he was mentioned in, 15
Black and white was the question that so bothered him,
He never asked—he was taught not to ask—but was on his lips as
   they buried him.

Requiem eternam.

—*Terry Kirkman*

Title. *Requiem*: a funeral mass. This song draws heavily on various parts of that mass. 1. *Requiem eternam*: eternal rest, the first words of one introit. 12. *Kyrie eleison*: Lord, have mercy, the beginning of the Kyrie.

War Is Kind

Do not weep, maiden, for war is kind.
Because your lover threw wild hands toward the sky
And the affrighted steed ran on alone,
Do not weep.
War is kind. 5

   Hoarse, booming drums of the regiment,
   Little souls who thirst for fight,
   These men were born to drill and die.

The unexplained glory flies above them,
Great is the battle-god, great, and his kingdom—   10
A field where a thousand corpses lie.

Do not weep, babe, for war is kind.
Because your father tumbled in the yellow trenches,
Raged at his breast, gulped and died,
Do not weep.   15
War is kind.

Swift blazing flag of the regiment,
Eagle with crest of red and gold,
These men were born to drill and die.
Point for them the virtue of slaughter,   20
Make plain to them the excellence of killing
And a field where a thousand corpses lie.

Mother whose heart hung humble as a button
On the bright splendid shroud of your son,
Do not weep.   25
War is kind.

—Stephen Crane

The Knights

They have remained unaltered like nature,
not capable of a new inspiration,
happy to make outward renunciations
but without inward mutability.
They're in no hurry to understand,   5
they don't very much want to understand,
still ornamented in the idiot glitter
of old-fashioned armour, their old success.
And watching cowardice in place of courage
shoulder to shoulder in its careful ranks   10
I see the origin of this infection,
and trace the destiny of this obsession.

The mighty horses have worn down to tatters.
The knights are not the boys of the old days:
subject to serious infirmity,   15
terror of honesty, terror of battle.

—*Yevgeny Yevtushenko*
(translated by Robin Milner-
Gulland and Peter Levi)

Dulce et Decorum Est

Bent double, like old beggars under sacks,
Knock-kneed, coughing like hags, we cursed through sludge,
Till on the haunting flares we turned our backs,
And towards our distant rest began to trudge.
Men marched asleep. Many had lost their boots,   5
But limped on, blood-shod. All went lame, all blind;
Drunk with fatigue; deaf even to the hoots
Of gas-shells dropping softly behind.

Gas! Gas! Quick, boys—An ecstasy of fumbling,
Fitting the clumsy helmets just in time,   10
But someone still was yelling out and stumbling
And floundering like a man in fire or lime.—
Dim through the misty panes and thick green light,
As under a green sea, I saw him drowning.
In all my dreams before my helpless sight   15
He plunges at me, guttering, choking, drowning.

If in some smothering dreams, you too could pace
Behind the wagon that we flung him in,
And watch the white eyes writhing in his face,
His hanging face, like a devil's sick of sin;   20
If you could hear, at every jolt, the blood
Come gargling from the froth-corrupted lungs,
Bitter as the cud
Of vile, incurable sores on innocent tongues,
My friend, you would not tell with such high zest   25

To children ardent for some desperate glory,
The old Lie: Dulce et decorum est
Pro patria mori.

—Wilfred Owen

27–28. *Dulce . . . mori*: "It is fit and pleasing to die for the fatherland."
Horace, *Odes.* Book 3, ode 3, l. 13.

Channel Firing

That night your great guns, unawares,
Shook all our coffins as we lay,
And broke the chancel window-squares,
We thought it was the Judgment-day

And sat upright. While drearisome   5
Arose the howl of wakened hounds:
The mouse let fall the altar-crumb,
The worms drew back into the mounds,

The glebe cow drooled. Till God called, "No
It's gunnery practice out at sea   10
Just as before you went below;
The world is as it used to be:

"All nations striving strong to make
Red war yet redder. Mad as hatters
They do no more for Christès sake   15
Than you who are helpless in such matters.

"That this is not the judgment-hour
For some of them's a blessed thing,
For if it were they'd have to scour
Hell's floor for so much threatening . . .   20

"Ha, ha. It will be warmer when
I blow the trumpet (if indeed
I ever do; for you are men,
And rest eternal sorely need)."

So down we lay again. "I wonder,   25
Will the world ever saner be,"
Said one, "than when He sent us under
In our indifferent century!"

And many a skeleton shook his head.
"Instead of preaching forty year,"   30
My neighbor Parson Thirdly said,
"I wish I had stuck to pipes and beer."

Again the guns disturbed the hour,
Roaring their readiness to avenge,
As far inland as Stourton Tower,   35
And Camelot, and starlit Stonehenge.

                                                   —*Thomas Hardy*

9. *glebe*: ecclesiastical pasture lands. 14. *hatters*: Cf. *Alice in Wonderland*.
35. *Stourton Tower*: an ancient tower in Dorsetshire. 36. *Camelot*: the mythical
seat of Arthur's kingdom; *Stonehenge*: a prehistoric temple on Salisbury Plain.

Bombing Casualties in Spain

Doll's faces are rosier but these were children
their eyes not glass but gleaming gristle
dark lenses in whose quicksilvery glances
the sunlight quivered. These blanched lips
were warm once and bright with blood   5
but blood
held in a moist blob of flesh
not split and spatter'd in tousled hair.

In these shadowy tresses
red petals did not always   10
thus clot and blacken to a scar.

These are dead faces:
wasps' nests are not more wanly waxen
wood embers not so greyly ashen.
They are laid out in ranks   15

like paper lanterns that have fallen
after a night of riot
extinct in the dry morning air.

                                        —*Herbert Read*

FAITH AND DOUBT,
DENIAL AND AFFIRMATION

Faith: confidence, reliance, trust (in the ability, goodness, etc. of a person; in the efficacy or worth of a thing; or in the truth of a statement or doctrine). In early use, only with reference to religious objects; this is still the prevelant application and often colors the wider use.

Apparently with no surprise

Apparently with no surprise
To any happy flower,
The frost beheads it at its play
In accidental power.
The blond assassin passes on,   5
The sun proceeds unmoved
To measure off another day
For an approving God.

                                        —*Emily Dickinson*

Design

I found a dimpled spider, fat and white,
On a white heal-all, holding up a moth
Like a white piece of rigid satin cloth—
Assorted characters of death and blight
Mixed ready to begin the morning right,   5
Like the ingredients of a witches' broth—

A snow-drop spider, a flower like froth,
And dead wings carried like a paper kite.

What had that flower to do with being white,
The wayside blue and innocent heal-all?   10
What brought the kindred spider to that height,
Then steered the white moth thither in the night?
What but design of darkness to appall?—
If design govern in a thing so small.

                                        —*Robert Frost*

Angel and Stone

In the world are millions and millions of men, and each man,
With a few exceptions, believes himself to be at the center,
A small number of his more or less necessary planets careering
Around him in an orderly manner, some morning stars singing
     together,
More distant galaxies shining like dust in any stray sunbeam   5
Of his attention. Since this is true not of one man or of two,
But of ever so many, it is hard to imagine what life must be like.
But if you drop a stone into a pool, and observe the ripples
Moving in circles successively out to the edges of the pool and
     then
Reflecting back and passing through the ones which continue to
     come   10
Out of the center over the sunken stone, you observe it is pleasing.
And if you drop two stones it will still be pleasing, because now
The angular intersections of the two sets form a more complicated
Pattern, a kind of reticulation regular and of simple origins.
But if you throw a handful of sand into the water, it is confusion, 15
Not because the same laws have ceased to obtain, but only
     because
The limits of your vision in time and number forbid you to
     discriminate
Such fine, quick, myriad events as the angels and archangels,
     thrones

And dominations, principalities and powers, are delegated to
   witness
And declare the glory of before the Lord of everything that is.   20

Of these great beings and mirrors of being, little at present is
   known,
And of the manner of their perceiving not much more. We
   imagine them
As benign, as pensively smiling and somewhat coldly smiling, but
They may not be as we imagine them. Among them there are
   some who count
The grassblades and the grains of sand by one and one and one   25
And number the raindrops and memorize the eccentricities of
   snowflakes.
One of the greater ones reckons and records the tides of time,
Distinguishing the dynasties of mountains, races, cities,
As they rise, flower and fall, to whom an age is as a wave,
A nation the spray thrown from its crest; and one, being charged   30
With all the crossing moments, the comings-together and drivings-
   apart,
Reads in the chromatin its cryptic scripture as the cell divides;
And one is the watcher over chance events and the guardian of
   disorder
According to the law of the square root of n, so that a certain
   number
Of angels or molecules shall fall in irrelevance and be retrograde.   35

So do they go, those shining creatures, counting without confusion
And holding in their slow immeasurable gaze all the transactions
Of all the particles, item by atom, while the pyramids stand still
In the desert and the deermouse huddles in his hole and the rain
   falls
Piercing the skin of the pool with water in water and making a
   million
   40
And a million designs to be pleasingly latticed and laced and
   interfused
And mirrored to the Lord of everything that is by one and one
   and one.

                                          —Howard Nemerov

Stories of the Street

The stories of the street are mine
The Spanish voices laugh
The Cadillacs go creeping down
Through the night and the poison gas.
I lean from my window sill   5
In this old hotel I chose
One hand on my suicide
One hand on the rose.

I know you've heard it's over now
And war must surely come   10
The cities they are broke in half
And the middle men are gone.
But let me ask you one more time
O, children of the dust,
All these hunters who are shrieking now   15
Do they speak for us?

And where do all these highways go
Now that we are free?
Why are the armies marching still
That were coming home to me?   20
O, lady with your legs so fine
O, stranger at your wheel
You are locked into your suffering
And your pleasures are the seal.

The age of lust is giving birth   25
And both the parents ask
The nurse to tell them fairy tales
On both sides of the glass
Now the infant with his cord
Is hauled in like a kite   30

And one eye filled with blueprints
One eye filled with night.

O, come with me my little one
And we will find that farm
And grow us grass and apples there   35
And keep all the animals warm.
And if by chance I wake at night
And I ask you who I am
O, take me to the slaughter house
I will wait there with the lamb.   40

With one hand on a hexagram
And one hand on a girl
I balance on a wishing well
That all men call the world.
We are so small between the stars   45
So large against the sky
And lost among the subway crowds
I try to catch your eye.

                                        —*Leonard Cohen*

anyone lived in a pretty how town

anyone lived in a pretty how town
(with up so floating many bells down)
spring summer autumn winter
he sang his didn't he danced his did.

Women and men (both little and small)   5
cared for anyone not at all
they sowed their isn't they reaped their same
sun moon stars rain

children guessed (but only a few
and down they forgot as up they grew   10
autumn winter spring summer)
that noone loved him more by more

when by now and tree by leaf
she laughed his joy she cried his grief
bird by snow and stir by still   15
anyone's any was all to her

someones married their everyones
laughed their cryings and did their dance
(sleep wake hope and then) they
said their nevers they slept their dream   20

stars rain sun moon
(and only the snow can begin to explain
how children are apt to forget to remember
with up so floating many bells down)

one day anyone died i guess   25
(and noone stooped to kiss his face)
busy folk buried them side by side
little by little and was by was

all by all and deep by deep
and more by more they dream their sleep   30
noone and anyone earth by april
wish by spirit and if by yes.

Women and men (both dong and ding)
summer autumn winter spring
reaped their sowing and went their came   35
sun moon stars rain

—e. e. cummings

Along Comes Mary

Everytime I think that I'm the only one who's lonely
Someone calls on me
And every now and then, I spend my time at rhyme and verse
And curse the faults in me
But then, along comes Mary   5

And does she wanna give me kicks
And be my steady chick and give me
Pick of memories?
Or maybe rather gather tales
From all the fails and tribulations   10
No one ever sees?

When we met
I was out to lunch
Now my empty cup tastes
As sweet as the punch   15

When vague desire is the fire in the eyes of chicks
Whose sickness is the games they play
And when the masquerade is played and neighbor folks
Make jokes at who is most to blame today
Then along comes Mary   20
And does she wanna set them free
And make them see the realities in which
She got her name?
And will they struggle much when told that such
A tender touch of hers will make them   25
Not the same?

When we met
I was sure out to lunch
Now my empty cup tastes
As sweet as the punch.   30

Then when the morning of the warning's passed,
The gassed and flaccid kids are flung across the stars
The psychodramas and the traumas gone, the songs are left
    unsung
And hung upon the scars
And then along comes Mary   35
And does she wanna see the stains
The dead remains of all the pains
She sent the night before?
Or will their waking eyes reflect the lies

And realize their urgent cry 40
For sight no more?

When we met
I was sure out to lunch
Now my empty cup tastes
As sweet as the punch. 45

—Tandyn Almer

Journey of the Magi

"A cold coming we had of it,
Just the worst time of the year
For a journey, and such a long journey:
The ways deep and the weather sharp,
The very dead of winter." 5
And the camels galled, sore-footed, refractory,
Lying down in the melting snow.
There were times we regretted
The summer palaces on slopes, the terraces,
And the silken girls bringing sherbet. 10
Then the camel men cursing and grumbling
And running away, and wanting their liquor and women,
And the night-fires going out, and the lack of shelters,
And the cities hostile and the towns unfriendly
And the villages dirty and charging high prices: 15
A hard time we had of it.
At the end we preferred to travel all night,
Sleeping in snatches,
With the voices singing in our ears, saying
That this was all folly. 20

Then at dawn we came down to a temperate valley,
Wet, below the snow line, smelling of vegetation;
With a running stream and a water-mill beating the darkness,
And three trees on the low sky,
And an old white horse galloped away in the meadow. 25

Then we came to a tavern with vine-leaves over the lintel,
Six hands at an open door dicing for pieces of silver,
And feet kicking the empty wine-skins.
But there was no information, and so we continued
And arrived at evening, not a moment too soon   30
Finding the place; it was (you may say) satisfactory.

All this was a long time ago, I remember,
And I would do it again, but set down
This set down
This: were we led all that way for   35
Birth or Death? There was a Birth, certainly
We had evidence and no doubt. I had seen birth and death,
But had thought they were different; this Birth was
Hard and bitter agony for us, like Death, our death.
We returned to our places, these Kingdoms,   40
But no longer at ease here, in the old dispensation,
With an alien people clutching their gods.
I should be glad of another death.

          —*T. S. Eliot*

 1–5. The first five lines are quoted from a sermon on the nativity by Lancelot Andrewes (1555–1626). 25. *white horse*: Cf. Revelation 6:2 and 19:11.

God's Grandeur

The world is charged with the grandeur of God.
 It will flame out, like shining from shook foil;
 It gathers to a greatness, like the ooze of oil
Crushed. Why do men then now not reck his rod?
Generations have trod, have trod, have trod;   5
 And all is seared with trade; bleared, smeared with toil;
 And wears man's smudge and shares man's smell: the soil
Is bare now, nor can foot feel, being shod.

And for all this, nature is never spent;
 There lives the dearest freshness deep down things;   10
And though the last lights off the black West went

Oh morning, at the brown brink eastward, springs—
Because the Holy Ghost over the bent
World broods with warm breast and with ah! bright wings.
                                    —*Gerard Manley Hopkins*

4. *reck*: heed.

MAN AND THE HUMAN CONDITION

Humanity: the quality or condition of being human, manhood; the
human faculties collectively; human nature; man in the abstract.

Eleanor Rigby

Ah, look at all the lonely people!
Ah, look at all the lonely people!

Eleanor Rigby
Picks up the rice in the church where a wedding has been
Lives in a dream   5
Waits at the window
Wearing the face that she keeps in a jar by the door.
Who is it for?

All the lonely people,
Where do they all come from?   10
All the lonely people,
Where do they all belong?

Father McKenzie,
Writing the words of a sermon that no one will hear,
No one comes near   15
Look at him working,
Darning his socks in the night when there's nobody there
What does he care?

All the lonely people,
Where do they all come from?   20

All the lonely people,
Where do they all belong?

Ah, look at all the lonely people!
Ah, look at all the lonely people!

Eleanor Rigby,   25
Died in the church and was buried along with her name
Nobody came
Father McKenzie,
Wiping the dirt from his hands as he walks from the grave,
No one was saved.   30

All the lonely people,
Where do they all come from?
All the lonely people,
Where do they all belong?

Ah, look at all the lonely people!   35
Ah, look at all the lonely people!
                              —*John Lennon–Paul McCartney*

Poetry of Departures

Sometimes you hear, fifth-hand,
As epitaph:
He chucked up everything
And just cleared off,
And always the voice will sound   5
Certain you approve
This audacious, purifying,
Elemental move.

And they are right, I think.
We all hate home   10
And having to be there:
I detest my room.
Its specially-chosen junk,

The good books, the good bed,
And my life, in perfect order: 15
So to hear it said

He walked out on the whole crowd
Leaves me flushed and stirred,
Like *Then she undid her dress*
Or *Take that you bastard;* 20
Surely I can, if he did?
And that helps me stay
Sober and industrious.
But I'd go today,

Yes, swagger the nut-strewn roads, 25
Crouch in the fo'c'sle
Stubbly with goodness, if
It weren't so artificial,
Such a deliberate step backwards
To create an object: 30
Books; china; a life
Reprehensibly perfect.

—*Philip Larkin*

Thank You

Lookin' at the devil grinnin' at the gun
Fingers start shakin' I begin to run
Bullets start chasin' I begin to stop
We begin to wrestle I was on the top.
I want to thank you falettin' me be mice elf agin. 5
Thank you falettin' me be mice elf agin.

Stiff all in the collar fluffy in the face
Chit chat chatter tryin' stuffy in the place
Thank you for the party I could never stay
Many things is on my mind words in the way. 10
I want to thank you falettin' me be mice elf agin.
Thank you falettin' me be mice elf agin.

Ev'ryday people sing a simple song
Mama's so happy Mama start to cry
Papa still singin' you can make it if you try. 15
I want to thank you falettin' me be mice elf agin.
Thank you falettin' me be mice elf agin.

Flamin' eyes of people fear burnin' into you
Many men are missin' much hatin' what they do
Youth and Truth are makin' love dig it for a starter 20
Dyin' young is hard to take sellin' out is harder.
Thank you falettin' me be mice elf agin.
Thank you falettin' me be mice elf agin.

—Sylvester Stewart

Sailing to Byzantium

That is no country for old men. The young
In one another's arms, birds in the trees
—Those dying generations—at their song,
The salmon-falls, the mackerel-crowded seas,
Fish, flesh, or fowl, commend all summer long 5
Whatever is begotten, born, and dies.
Caught in that sensual music all neglect
Monuments of unaging intellect.

An aged man is but a paltry thing,
A tattered coat upon a stick, unless 10
Soul clap its hands and sing, and louder sing
For every tatter in its mortal dress,
Nor is there singing school but studying
Monuments of its own magnificence;
And therefore I have sailed the seas and come 15
To the holy city of Byzantium.

O sages standing in God's holy fire
As in the gold mosaic of a wall,
Come from the holy fire, perne in a gyre,

And be the singing-masters of my soul. 20
Consume my heart away; sick with desire
And fastened to a dying animal
It knows not what it is, and gather me
Into the artifice of eternity.

Once out of nature I shall never take 25
My bodily form from any natural thing,
But such a form as Grecian goldsmiths make
Of hammered gold and gold enameling
To keep a drowsy Emperor awake;
Or set upon a golden bough to sing 30
To lords and ladies of Byzantium
Of what is past, or passing, or to come.

—*William Butler Yeats*

18. *gold mosaic*: in Byzantine art, figures of saints and apostles are surrounded by gold tiles that form a golden background. 29. *drowsy Emperor*: Yeats' note indicates that he had read somewhere that in the emperor's palace in Byzantium was a tree made of silver and gold, containing mechanical birds that really sang.

The Crucifixion

And the night comes again to the circle-studded sky,
The stars settle slowly, in loneliness they lie.
Till the universe explodes as a falling star is raised;
The planets are paralyzed, the mountains are amazed;
But they all glow brighter from the brilliance of the blaze; 5
With the speed of insanity, then, he dies!

In the green fields of turning, a baby is born;
His cries crease the wind, and mingle with the morn;
An assault upon the order, the changing of the guard;
Chosen for a challenge that's hopelessly hard; 10
And the only single sign is the sighing of the stars;
But to the silence of distance they're sworn!

So dance, dance, dance
Teach us to be true;

Come dance, dance, dance;   15
'Cause we love you.

Images of innocence charge him to go on,
But the decadence of history is looking for a pawn,
To a nightmare of knowledge he opens up the gate;
A blinding revelation is served upon his plate,   20
That beneath the greatest love is a hurricane of hate,
And God help the critic of the dawn.

So he stands on the sea and he shouts to the shore
But the louder that he screams the longer he's ignored.
For the wine of oblivion is drunk to the dregs,   25
And the merchants of the masses almost have to be begged
Till the giant is aware that someone's pulling at his leg,
And someone is tapping at the door.

So dance, dance, dance
Teach us to be true;   30
Come dance, dance, dance;
'Cause we love you.

Then his message gathers meaning and it spreads across the land.
The rewarding of the fame is the following of the man.
But ignorance is everywhere and people have their way,   35
And success is an enemy to the losers of the day.
In the shadows of the churches who knows what they pray.
And blood is the language of the band.

The Spanish bulls are beaten, the crowd is soon beguiled,
The matador is beautiful, a symphony of style.   40
Excitement is ecstatic, passion places bets,
Gracefully he bows to ovations that he gets;
But the hands that are applauding are slippery with sweat,
And saliva is falling from their smiles.

So dance, dance, dance   45
Teach us to be true;
Come dance, dance, dance;
'Cause we love you.

Then this overflow of life is crushed into a liar.
The gentle soul is ripped apart and tossed into the fire.   50
It's the burial of beauty, it's the victory of night.
Truth becomes a tragedy limping from the light.
The heavens are horrified, they stagger from the sight,
And the cross is trembling with desire.

They say they can't believe it, "It's a sacrilegious shame.   55
Now who would want to hurt such a hero of the game.
But you know I predicted it; I knew he had to fall.
How did it happen? I hope his suffering was small.
Tell me every detail, I've got to know it all,
And do you have a picture of the pain?"   60

So dance, dance, dance
Teach us to be true;
Come dance, dance, dance;
'Cause we love you.

Time takes her toll and the memory fades,   65
But his glory is growing in the magic that he made.
Reality is ruined there is nothing more to fear.
The drama is distorted to what they want to hear.
Swimming in their sorrow in the twisting of a tear
As they wait for the new thrill parade.   70

The eyes of the rebel have been branded by the blind.
To the safety of sterility the threat has been refined.
The child was created to the slaughter house he's led.
So good to be alive when the eulogies are read.
The climax of emotion, the worship of the dead   75
As the cycle of sacrifice unwinds.

So dance, dance, dance
Teach us to be true;
Come dance, dance, dance;
'Cause we love you.   80

And the night comes again to the circle-studded sky,
The stars settle slowly, in loneliness they lie.

Till the universe explodes as a falling star is raised;
The planets are paralyzed, the mountains are amazed;
But they all glow brighter from the brilliance of the blaze;   85
With the speed of insanity, then, he dies!

                                                    —*Phil Ochs*

Mr. Flood's Party

Old Eben Flood, climbing alone one night
Over the hill between the town below
And the forsaken upland hermitage
That held as much as he should ever know
On earth again of home, paused warily.   5
The road was his with not a native near;
And Eben, having leisure, said aloud,
For no man else in Tilbury Town to hear:

"Well, Mr. Flood, we have the harvest moon
Again, and we may not have many more;   10
The bird is on the wing, the poet says,
And you and I have said it here before.
Drink to the bird." He raised up to the light
The jug that he had gone so far to fill,
And answered huskily: "Well, Mr. Flood;   15
Since you propose it, I believe I will."

Alone, as if enduring to the end
A valiant armor of scarred hopes outworn,
He stood there in the middle of the road
Like Roland's ghost winding a silent horn.   20
Below him, in the town among the trees,
Where friends of other days had honored him,
A phantom salutation of the dead
Rang thinly till old Eben's eyes were dim.

Then, as a mother lays her sleeping child   25
Down tenderly, fearing it may awake,
He set the jug down slowly at his feet

With trembling care, knowing that most things break;
And only when assured that on firm earth
It stood, as the uncertain lives of men   30
Assuredly did not, he paced away,
And with his hand extended paused again:

"Well, Mr. Flood, we have not met like this
In a long time; and many a change has come
To both of us, I fear, since last it was   35
We had a drop together. Welcome home!"
Convivially returning with himself,
Again he raised the jug up to the light;
And with an acquiescent quaver said:
"Well, Mr. Flood, if you insist, I might.   40

"Only a very little, Mr. Flood—
For auld lang syne. No more, sir; that will do."
So, for the time, apparently it did,
And Eben evidently thought so too;
For soon amid the silver loneliness   45
Of night he lifted up his voice and sang,
Secure, with only two moons listening,
Until the whole harmonious landscape rang—

"For auld lang syne." The weary throat gave out,
The last word wavered; and the song being done,   50
He raised again the jug regretfully
And shook his head, and was again alone.
There was not much that was ahead of him,
And there was nothing in the town below—
Where strangers would have shut the many doors   55
That many friends had opened long ago.
                                        —*Edwin Arlington Robinson*

Spring and Fall: To a Young Child

Márgarét, are you griéving
Over Goldengrove unleaving?

Leáves, líke the things of man, you
With your fresh thoughts care for, can you?
Áh! ás the heart grows older   5
It will come to such sights colder
By and by, nor spare a sigh
Though worlds of wanwood leafmeal lie;
And yet you wíll weep and know why.
Now no matter, child, the name: 10
Sórrow's spríngs áre the same,
Nor mouth had, no nor mind, expressed
What heart heard of, ghost guessed:
It is the blight man was born for,
It is Margaret you mourn for.   15

                               —Gerard Manley Hopkins

On Wenlock Edge the Wood's in Trouble

On Wenlock Edge the wood's in trouble;
   His forest fleece the Wrekin heaves;
The gale, it plies the saplings double,
   And thick on Severn snow the leaves.

'Twould blow like this through holt and hanger   5
   When Uricon the city stood:
'Tis the old wind in the old anger,
   But then it threshed another wood.

Then, 'twas before my time, the Roman
   At yonder heaving hill would stare: 10
The blood that warms an English yeoman,
   The thoughts that hurt him, they were there.

There, like the wind through woods in riot,
   Through him the gale of life blew high;
The tree of man was never quiet: 15
   Then 'twas the Roman, now 'tis I.

The gale, it plies the saplings double,
   It blows so hard, 'twill soon be gone:
To-day the Roman and his trouble
   Are ashes under Uricon.   20

                                 —A. E. Housman

1. *Wenlock Edge*: a range of mountains in Shropshire, England. 2. *the Wrekin*: a hill in Shropshire. 4. *Severn*: a river in western England. 6. *Uricon*: a Roman town on the site of Wroxeter, Shropshire.

I Dreamed I Saw St. Augustine

I dreamed I saw St. Augustine
Alive as you or me,
Tearing through these quarters
In the utmost misery,
With a blanket underneath his arm   5
And a coat of solid gold
Searching for the very souls
Whom already have been sold.

"Arise, arise," he cried so loud
In a voice without restraint,   10
"Come out, ye gifted kings and queens
And hear my sad complaint.
No martyr is among you now
Whom you can call your own.
So go on your way accordingly   15
But know you're not alone."

I dreamed I saw St. Augustine
Alive with fiery breath,
And I dreamed I was amongst the ones
That put him out to death.   20
Oh, I awoke in anger
So alone and terrified
I put my fingers against the glass
And bowed my head and cried.

                                  —Bob Dylan

A Dialogue of Self and Soul

I

My Soul. I summon to the winding ancient stair;
    Set all your mind upon the steep ascent,
    Upon the broken, crumbling battlement,
    Upon the breathless starlit air,
    Upon the star that marks the hidden pole;   5
    Fix every wandering thought upon
    That quarter where all thought is done:
    Who can distinguish darkness from the soul?

My Self. The consecrated blade upon my knees
    Is Sato's ancient blade, still as it was,   10
    Still razor-keen, still like a looking-glass
    Unspotted by the centuries;
    That flowering, silken, old embroidery, torn
    From some court-lady's dress and round
    The wooden scabbard bound and wound,   15
    Can, tattered, still protect, faded adorn.

My Soul. Why should the imagination of a man
    Long past his prime remember things that are
    Emblematical of love and war?
    Think of ancestral night that can,   20
    If but imagination scorn the earth
    And intellect its wandering
    To this and that and t'other thing,
    Deliver from the crime of death and birth.

My Self. Montashigi, third of his family, fashioned it   25
    Five hundred years ago, about it lie
    Flowers from I know not what embroidery—
    Heart's purple—and all these I set
    For emblems of the day against the tower
    Emblematical of the night,   30
    And claim as by a soldier's right
    A charter to commit the crime once more.

My Soul. Such fullness in that quarter overflows
 And falls into the basin of the mind
 That man is stricken deaf and dumb and blind,   35
 For intellect no longer knows
 Is from the *Ought,* or *Knower* from the *Known*—
 That is to say, ascends to Heaven;
 Only the dead can be forgiven;
 But when I think of that my tongue's a stone.   40

II

My Self. A living man is blind and drinks his drop.
 What matter if the ditches are impure?
 What matter if I live it all once more?
 Endure that toil of growing up;
 The ignominy of boyhood; the distress   45
 Of boyhood changing into man;
 The unfinished man and his pain
 Brought face to face with his own clumsiness;

 The finished man among his enemies?—
 How in the name of Heaven can he escape   50
 That defiling and disfigured shape
 The mirror of malicious eyes
 Casts upon his eyes until at last
 He thinks that shape must be in his shape?
 And what's the good of an escape   55
 If honour find him in the wintry blast?

 I am content to live it all again
 And yet again, if it be life to pitch
 Into the frog-spawn of a blind man's ditch,
 A blind man battering blind men;   60
 Or into that most fecund ditch of all,
 The folly that man does
 Or must suffer, if he woos
 A proud woman not kindred of his soul.

 I am content to follow to its source   65
 Every event in action or in thought;

Measure the lot; forgive myself the lot!
When such as I cast out remorse
So great a sweetness flows into the breast
We must laugh and we must sing,   70
We are blest by everything,
Everything we look upon is blest.

—*William Butler Yeats*

Musée des Beaux Arts

About suffering they were never wrong,
The Old Masters: how well they understood
Its human position; how it takes place
While someone else is eating or opening a window or just
     walking dully along;
How, when the aged are reverently, passionately waiting   5
For the miraculous birth, there always must be
Children who did not specially want it to happen, skating
On a pond at the edge of the wood:
They never forgot
That even the dreadful martyrdom must run its course   10
Anyhow in a corner, some untidy spot
Where the dogs go on with their doggy life and the torturer's
     horse
Scratches its innocent behind on a tree.

In Brueghel's *Icarus*, for instance: how everything turns away
Quite leisurely from the disaster; the ploughman may   15
Have heard the splash, the forsaken cry,
But for him it was not an important failure; the sun shone
As it had to on the white legs disappearing into the green
Water; and the expensive delicate ship that must have seen
Something amazing, a boy falling out of the sky,   20
Had somewhere to get to and sailed calmly on.

—*W. H. Auden*

Title: Museum of the Fine Arts.

Letter from Maine

Dear breathing planet-brother: softly on me
An island's green push in the fog and roped by
Tides I go to hear with my eyes and see with my
Feet the plunging wrestle of rocks decisioning
A wave a tug of the fishhawk on a tipping   5
Plank of air the raspberries, firs, Indian paint-
Brush, lobster pots, salt smell, kelp, rockweeds,
Snails, driftwood, white-throated sparrows, sail-fog,
Buoys, sea-urchins, jellyfish, lighthouse . . . all
In a batter mixed on this island bowl so that   10
On skies of brain and dawn there are italicized
The firs of time and I in a rock firmament's
Excitation put feet and eyes down on the equations
Of ocean and I learn my lines island-drenched
Forever stitched on the quilts of states of   15
Being—song, water, sun-jewels, the contour and
Peninsular . . . how vast the durance of the proffered
Surface of stars and other night neighbors and
I bend down to tie a knot around an evening or
A sunset season . . . and still the amplitudes cry in   20
The day and to the receptors of your friend.

—Daniel Smythe

Acquainted with the Night

I have been one acquainted with the night.
I have walked out in rain—and back in rain.
I have outwalked the furthest city light.

I have looked down the saddest city lane.
I have passed by the watchman on his beat   5
And dropped my eyes, unwilling to explain.

I have stood still and stopped the sound of feet
When far away an interrupted cry
Came over houses from another street,

But not to call me back or say good-by; 10
And further still at an unearthly height,
One luminary clock against the sky

Proclaimed the time was neither wrong nor right.
I have been one acquainted with the night.

—*Robert Frost*

DISCONTENT AND SOCIAL PROTEST

Protest: A formal statement or declaration of disapproval of or dissent from, or of consent under certain conditions only to, some action or proceeding; a remonstrance.

Blowin' in the Wind

How many roads must a man walk down before you call him a
man?
Yes, 'n' How many seas must a white dove sail before she sleeps in
the sand?
Yes, 'n' How many times must the cannon balls fly before they're
forever banned?
The answer, my friend, is blowin' in the wind,
The answer is blowin' in the wind. 5

How many times must a man look up before he can see the sky?
Yes, 'n' How many ears must one man have before he can hear
people cry?
Yes, 'n' How many deaths does it take 'till he knows that too
many people have died?
The answer, my friend, is blowin' in the wind,
The answer is blowin' in the wind. 10

How many years can a mountain exist before it is washed to the sea?
Yes, 'n' How many years can a people exist before they're allowed
    to be free?
Yes, 'n' How many times can a man turn his head pretending he
    just doesn't see?
The answer, my friend, is blowin' in the wind,
The answer is blowin' in the wind.   15

                                         —Bob Dylan

The Harder They Fall

London Bridge is falling down,
and the people want their crown.
They are not fooling around.
Gimme my crown, gimme my crown, gimme my crown.
So I say these words to you,   5
Though you won't believe a word I say . . .
Gonna say the words any way.

The poems are pretty; the tales are tall.
Only the witches recall:
The bigger they are; the harder they fall.   10

Jack and Jill went up the hill.
They were looking for a thrill,
But she forgot to take her pill.
Gimme my pill, gimme my pill, gimme my pill.
Through our fantasies we fly.   15
In the prison of our dreams we die.
Praying in an apple pie.

The poems are pretty; the tales are tall.
Only the witches recall:
The bigger they are; the harder they fall.   20

Mary had a little lamb.
Couldn't make it with a man.
She buried babies in the sand.

Gimme my sand, gimme my sand, gimme my sand.
And her visions came to stay.   25
She was beheaded on a holiday.
That's the price you have to pay.

The poems are pretty; the tales are tall.
Only the witches recall:
The bigger they are; the harder they fall.   30

Yes, Mother Goose is on the loose,
Stealing lines from Lenny Bruce,
Drinking booze and killing Jews.
Gimme my Jews, Gimme my booze, gimme my Jews.
Six million jingles can't be wrong.   35
From the dragon to the Viet Cong,
Fairy tales have come along.

The poems are pretty; the tales are tall.
Only the witches recall:
The bigger they are; the harder they fall.   40

—*Phil Ochs*

The Flower Market

In the Royal City spring is almost over:
Tinkle, tinkle—the coaches and the horsemen pass.
We tell each other "This is the peony season":
And follow with the crowd that goes to the Flower Market.
"Cheap and dear—no uniform price: 5
The cost of the plant depends on the number of blossoms.
For the fine flower,—a hundred pieces of damask:
For the cheap flower,—five bits of silk.
Above is spread an awning to protect them;
Around is woven a wattle fence to screen them.   10
When they are transplanted, they will not lose their beauty."
Each household thoughtlessly follows the custom,
Man by man, no one realizing.
There happened to be an old farm labourer

Who came by chance that way. 15
He bowed his head and sighed a deep sigh:
But this sigh nobody understood.
He was thinking, "A cluster of deep-red flowers
Would pay the taxes of ten poor houses."
—*Po Chu-I* (translated by Arthur Waley)

Five Ways To Kill a Man

There are many cumbersome ways to kill a man:
you can make him carry a plank of wood
to the top of a hill and nail him to it. To do this
properly you require a crowd of people
wearing sandals, a cock that crows, a cloak 5
to dissect, a sponge, some vinegar and one
man to hammer the nails home.

Or you can take a length of steel,
shaped and chased in a traditional way,
and attempt to pierce the metal cage he wears. 10
But for this you need white horses,
English trees, men with bows and arrows,
at least two flags, a prince and a
castle to hold your banquet in.

Dispensing with nobility, you may, if the wind 15
allows, blow gas at him. But then you need
a mile of mud sliced through with ditches,
not to mention black boots, bomb craters,
more mud, a plague of rats, a dozen songs
and some round hats made of steel. 20

In an age of aeroplanes, you may fly
miles above your victim and dispose of him by
pressing one small switch. All you then
require is an ocean to separate you, two
systems of government, a nation's scientists, 25
several factories, a psychopath and
land that no one needs for several years.

These are, as I began, cumbersome ways
to kill a man. Simpler, direct, and much more neat
is to see that he is living somewhere in the middle   30
of the twentieth century, and leave him there.

—*Edwin Brock*

Karma

Christmas was in the air and all was well
With him, but for a few confusing flaws
In divers of God's images. Because
A friend of his would neither buy nor sell,
Was he to answer for the axe that fell?   5
He pondered; and the reason for it was,
Partly, a slowly freezing Santa Claus
Upon the corner, with his beard and bell.
Acknowledging an improvident surprise,
He magnified a fancy that he wished   10
The friend whom he had wrecked were here again.
Not sure of that, he found a compromise;
And from the fullness of his heart he fished
A dime for Jesus who had died for man.

—*Edwin Arlington Robinson*

Shine, Perishing Republic

While this America settles in the mold of its vulgarity, heavily
    thickening to empire,
And protest, only a bubble in the molten mass, pops and sighs out,
    and the mass hardens,

I sadly smiling remember that the flower fades to make fruit, the
    fruit rots to make earth.
Out of the mother; and through the spring exultances, ripeness and
    decadence; and home to the mother.

You make haste on decay: not blameworthy; life is good, be it
    stubbornly long or suddenly   5

A mortal splendor: meteors are not needed less than mountains:
  shine, perishing republic.

But for my children, I would rather have them keep their distance
    from the thickening center; corruption
Never has been compulsory, when the cities lie at the monster's
  feet there are left the mountains.

And boys, be in nothing so moderate as in love of man, a clever
  servant, insufferable master.
There is the trap that catches noblest spirits, that caught—they
  say—God, when he walked on earth.   10

                                        —*Robinson Jeffers*

On King Charles

                                *For which he was banish'd the Court
                                and turn'd* Mountebank

In the Isle of Great *Britain* long since famous known,
For breeding the best C[ully] in *Christendom;*
There reigns, and long may he reign and thrive,
The easiest Prince and best bred Man alive:
Him no ambition moves to seek Renown,   5
Like the *French* Fool to wander up and down,
Starving his Subjects, hazarding his Crown.
Nor are his high desires above his strength,
His Scepter and his P—— are of a length,
And she that plays with one may sway the other,   10
And make him little wiser than his Brother.
I hate all Monarchs and the Thrones they sit on,
From the Hector of *France* to the Cully of *Britain.*
Poor Prince, thy P—— like the Buffoons at Court,
It governs thee, because it makes thee sport;   15
Tho' Safety, Law, Religion, Life lay on't,
'Twill break through all to its way to C——.
Restless he rolls about from Whore to Whore,
A merry Monarch, scandalous and poor.
To *Carewell* the most Dear of all thy Dears,   20
The sure relief of thy declining Years;

Oft he bewails his fortune and her fate,
To love so well, and to be lov'd so late;
For when in her he settles well his T——,
Yet his dull graceless Buttocks hang an Arse.   25
This you'd believe, had I but time to tell you,
The pain it costs to poor laborious *Nelly*,
While she employs Hands, Fingers, Lips and thighs,
E'er she can raise the Member she enjoys.

—John Wilmot, Earl of Rochester

  13. *Cully*: fool.

London

I wander through each charter'd street,
Near where the charter'd Thames does flow,
And mark in every face I meet
Marks of weakness, marks of woe.

In every cry of every Man,   5
In every Infant's cry of fear,
In every voice, in every ban
The mind-forg'd manacles I hear.

How the chimney-sweeper's cry
Every black'ning church appals;   10
And the hapless soldier's sigh
Runs in blood down palace walls.

But most through midnight streets I hear
How the youthful harlot's curse
Blasts the new-born infant's tear,   15
And blights with plagues the marriage hearse.

—William Blake

For What It's Worth

There's something happening here
What it is ain't exactly clear

There's a man with a gun over there
Tellin' me I've got to beware
I think it's time we stop, children,   5
What's that sound?
Everybody look what's goin' down.

There's battle lines bein' drawn
Nobody's right if everybody's wrong
Young people speakin' their minds   10
Gettin' so much resistance from behind
I think it's time we stop, children,
What's that sound?
Everybody look what's goin' down.

What a field day for the heat   15
A thousand people in the street
Singin' songs and carryin' signs
Mostly say "Hooray for our side"
I think it's time we stop, children,
What's that sound?   20
Everybody look what's goin'down.

Paranoia strikes deep
Into your life it will creep
It starts when you're always afraid
Step out of line, the man come and take you away   25
I think it's time we stop, children,
What's that sound?
Everybody look what's goin' down.

                                                        —*Stephen Stills*

15. *heat*: police.

Christ climbed down

Christ climbed down
from His bare Tree
this year
and ran away to where

there were no rootless Christmas trees   5
hung with candycanes and breakable stars

Christ climbed down
from His bare Tree
this year
and ran away to where   10
there were no gilded Christmas trees
and no tinsel Christmas trees
and no tinfoil Christmas trees
and no pink plastic Christmas trees
and no gold Christmas trees   15
and no black Christmas trees
and no powderblue Christmas trees
hung with electric candles
and encircled by tin electric trains
and clever cornball relatives   20

Christ climbed down
from His bare Tree
this year
and ran away to where
no intrepid Bible salesmen   25
covered the territory
in two-tone cadillacs
and where no Sears Roebuck creches
complete with plastic babe in manger
arrived by parcel post   30
the babe by special delivery
and where no televised Wise Men
praised the Lord Calvert Whiskey

Christ climbed down
from His bare Tree   35
this year
and ran away to where
no fat handshaking stranger
in a red flannel suit
and a fake white beard   40

went around passing himself off
as some sort of North Pole saint
crossing the desert to Bethlehem
Pennsylvania
in a Volkswagon sled   45
drawn by rollicking Adirondack reindeer
with German names
and bearing sacks of Humble Gifts
from Saks Fifth Avenue
for everybody's imagined Christ child   50

Christ climbed down
from His bare Tree
this year
and ran away to where
no Bing Crosby carollers   55
groaned of a tight Christmas
and where no Radio City angels
iceskated wingless
thru a winter wonderland
into a jinglebell heaven   60
daily at 8:30
with Midnight Mass matinees

Christ climbed down
from His bare Tree
this year   65
and softly stole away into
some anonymous Mary's womb again
where in the darkest night
of everybody's anonymous soul
He awaits again   70
an unimaginable
and impossibly
Immaculate Reconception
the very craziest
of Second Comings   75

                                        —*Lawrence Ferlinghetti*

Dock of the Bay

Sittin' in the morning sun
I'll be sittin' when the evening comes
Watching the ships roll in
Then I watch 'em roll away again, yeah
I'm sittin' on the dock of the bay   5
Watching that tide roll in
Just sittin' on the dock of the bay
   wastin' time.

I left my home in Georgia
Headed for the Frisco Bay   10
I had nothing to live for
Looks like nothing's gonna come my way
So I'm just sittin' on the dock of the bay
Watching the tide roll in
I'm sittin' on the dock of the bay   15
   wastin' time.

Looks like nothing's gonna change
Everything still remains the same
I can't do what ten people tell me to do
So I guess I'll remain the same   20
Just sittin' here resting my bones
And this loneliness won't leave me alone
This 2,000 miles I roamed just to make this dock my home
Now I'm sittin' on the dock of the bay
Watching the tide roll in   25
Sittin' on the dock of the bay
   wastin' time.

—*Otis Redding–Steve Cropper*

A Select List
of Recordings

For obvious reasons, this list is far from complete. For both songs and poems, I have given preference to recordings by author and composer whenever possible. For poets no longer living and traditional songs, I have tried to find the best recordings around or, for songs, the recording that made the song popular.

Almer, Tandyn. Along Comes Mary. Association: Warner Brothers (S) 1702, *Along Comes Mary*.

anonymous. Barbara Allan. Kathleen Danson: Folkways/Scholastic LC R-59-64, *Early English Ballads*.

————. Come All You Fair and Tender Ladies. Peter, Paul, and Mary: Warner Brothers 1473, *Moving*. Buffy Sainte-Marie: Vanguard (S) 79171, *Many a Mile*.

————. Edward, Edward. F. Worlock: Caedmon TC 1103, *Poetry of Robert Burns and Border Ballads*.

————. The House of the Rising Sun. Animals: MGM (S) 4324, *Best of the Animals*. Bob Dylan: Columbia (S) CS-8579, *Bob Dylan*. Tim Hardin: V.R.F. (S) 3064, *Tim Hardin*. Chambers Brothers: Vanguard (S) 128, *Feelin' the Blues*.

————. Lord Randall. Buffy Sainte-Marie: Vanguard (S) 79250, *Fire and Fleet and Candlelight*. Kathleen Danson: Folkways/Scholastic LC R-59-64, *Early English Ballads*.

————. A Man Come into Egypt. Peter, Paul, and Mary: Warner Brothers 1473, *Moving*.

————. Pretty Polly. Judy Collins: Elektra EKS-74033, *Who Knows Where the Time Goes?*

————. Sir Patrick Spence. F. Worlock: Caedmon TC 1103, *Poetry of Robert Burns and Border Ballads*.

————. The Wife of Usher's Well. F. Worlock: Caedmon TC 1103, *Poetry of Robert Burns and Border Ballads*.

Arnold, Matthew. Dover Beach. John Neville: Caedmon TC 2011, *Golden Treasury of English Poetry.* Argo RG 521, *Poems of Arnold, Clough, and Fitzgerald.*

Auden, W. H. In Memory of W. B. Yeats. W. H. Auden: Caedmon TC 2006, *The Caedmon Treasury of Modern Poets Reading Their Own Poetry.*

Beatles, The. Sergeant Pepper's Lonely Hearts Club Band. Beatles: Capitol (S) SMAS-2653, *Sergeant Pepper's Lonely Hearts Club Band.*

Blake, William. The Lamb. Jo Van Fleet: Caedmon TC 1022, *Hearing Poetry, Vol. II.* Caedmon TC 1101, *Poetry of Blake.*

———. A Poison Tree. Jo Van Fleet: Caedmon TC 1022, *Hearing Poetry, Vol. II.* Caedmon TC 1101, *Poetry of Blake.*

———. The Sick Rose. Ralph Richardson: Caedmon TC 1101, *Poetry of Blake.* Argo RG 428, *Poems of William Blake.*

———. The Tyger. Jo Van Fleet: Caedmon TC 1022, *Hearing Poetry, Vol. II.* Caedmon TC 1101, *Poetry of Blake.* Argo RG 428, *Poems of William Blake.*

Browning, Robert. The Bishop Orders His Tomb at Saint Praxed's Church. Argo RG 346, *Poems of Robert Browning.*

———. My Last Duchess. Frank Silvera: Caedmon TC 1022, *Hearing Poetry, Vol. II.* James Mason: Caedmon TC 1201, *My Last Duchess and Other Poems, Vol. II.* Argo RG 346, *Poems of Robert Browning.*

Bryant, Felice and Boudleaux. Bye Bye, Love. Everly Brothers: Warner Brothers (S) 1554, *The Very Best of the Everly Brothers.* Simon and Garfunkel: Columbia (S) KCS-9914, *Bridge over Troubled Water.*

Cohen, Leonard. Bird on the Wire. Leonard Cohen: Columbia (S) CS-9767, *Songs from a Room.* Judy Collins: Elektra EKS-74033, *Who Knows Where the Time Goes?*

———. Sisters of Mercy. Leonard Cohen: Columbia (S) CS-9533, *Leonard Cohen.* Judy Collins: Elektra (S) 74012, *Wildflowers.*

———. Stories of the Street. Leonard Cohen: Columbia (S) CS-9533, *Leonard Cohen.*

———. The Story of Isaac. Leonard Cohen: Columbia (S) CS-9767, *Songs from a Room.* Judy Collins: Elektra EKS-74033, *Who Knows Where the Time Goes?*

———. Suzanne. Leonard Cohen: Columbia (S) CS-9533, *Leonard Cohen.* Judy Collins: Elektra (S) 74027, *In My Life.* Noel Harrison: Reprise (S) 6263, *Collage.*

———. Tonight Will Be Fine. Leonard Cohen: Columbia (S) CS-9767, *Songs from a Room.*

Coleridge, Samuel Taylor. Kubla Khan. Ralph Richardson: Caedmon

TC 1092, *Poetry of Samuel T. Coleridge*. John Neville: Caedmon
TC 2011, *Golden Treasury of English Poetry*.

Collins, Judy. My Father. Judy Collins: Elektra EKS-7403, *Who
Knows Where the Time Goes?*

cummings, e. e. next to of course god. e. e. cummings: Caedmon TC
1017, *E. E. Cummings Reads His Poetry*.

Denny, Sandy. Who Knows Where the Time Goes? Judy Collins:
Elektra EKS-74033, *Who Knows Where the Time Goes?* Fairport
Convention: A&M (S) 4206, *Unhalfbricking*.

Dickinson, Emily. Hope is the thing with feathers. Caedmon TC 2009,
Great American Poetry. Julie Harris: Caedmon TC 1119, *Dickinson's Poems and Letters*.

Donne, John. Death Be Not Proud. Caedmon TC 1021, *Hearing
Poetry, Vol. I*. Argo 404, *Religious Metaphysical Poetry*.

———. A Valediction: Forbidding Morning. Argo RG 403, *Love Poems
of John Donne*.

Dylan, Bob. All Along the Watchtower. Bob Dylan: Columbia (S)
CS-9604, *John Wesley Harding*. Jimi Hendrix: Reprise (S) 2025,
Smash Hits.

———. Blowin' in the Wind. Bob Dylan: Columbia (S) CS-8786, *Free
Wheelin' Bob Dylan*. Peter, Paul, and Mary: Warner Brothers (S)
1507, *In the Wind*.

———. I Dreamed I Saw St. Augustine. Bob Dylan: Columbia (S)
CS-9604, *John Wesley Harding*. Joan Baez: Vanguard (S) 79306-7,
Any Day Now.

———. I Pity the Poor Immigrant. Bob Dylan: Columbia (S) CS-9604,
John Wesley Harding. Joan Baez: Vanguard (S) 79306-7, *Any
Day Now*.

———. Lay, Lady, Lay. Bob Dylan: Columbia KCS-9825, *Nashville
Skyline*.

———. Love Minus Zero/No Limit. Bob Dylan: Columbia CS-9128,
Bringing It All Back Home. Joan Baez: Vanguard (S) 79306-7, *Any
Day Now*.

———. Mister Tambourine Man. Bob Dylan: Columbia (S) CS-9128,
Bringin' It All Back Home. Byrds: Columbia (S) CS-9172, *Mr.
Tambourine Man*.

———. Sad-Eyed Lady of the Lowlands. Bob Dylan: Columbia (S)
C2S-2841, *Blonde on Blonde*. Joan Baez: Vanguard (S) 79306-7,
Any Day Now.

———. She Belongs to Me. Bob Dylan: Columbia (S) CS-9128, *Bringin' It All Back Home*. Bob Dylan: Columbia CS C2X-30050, *Self
Portrait*.

———. Subterranean Homesick Blues. Bob Dylan: Columbia (S) CS-9128, *Bringin' It All Back Home*.

Frost, Robert. After Apple-Picking. Robert Frost: Caedmon TC 2006, *The Caedmon Treasury of Modern Poets Reading Their Own Poetry* Robert Frost: Caedmon TC 1060, *Robert Frost Reading*.

———. Departmental. Robert Frost: Caedmon TC 1060, *Robert Frost Reading*.

———. Provide, Provide. Robert Frost: Caedmon TC 1060, *Robert Frost Reading*.

Hardin, Tim. If I Were a Carpenter. Tim Hardin: V.R.F. (S) 3064, *Tim Hardin*. Joan Baez: Vanguard (S) 79240, *Joan*.

Hardy, Thomas. Channel Firing. Richard Burton: Caedmon TC 1140, *Poetry of Thomas Hardy*.

Harrison, George. While My Guitar Gently Weeps. Beatles: Apple SWBO-101, *Beatles*.

Hopkins, Gerard Manley. Carrion Comfort. Cyril Cusack: Caedmon TC 1111, *Poetry of Gerard Manley Hopkins*.

———. God's Grandeur. Cyril Cusack: Caedmon TC 1111, *Poetry of Gerard Manley Hopkins*.

———. Pied Beauty. Cyril Cusack: Caedmon TC 1111, *Poetry of Gerard Manley Hopkins*.

———. Spring and Fall: To a Young Child. Cyril Cusack: Caedmon TC 1111, *Poetry of Gerard Manley Hopkins*.

———. The Windhover. Cyril Cusack: Caedmon TC 1111, *Poetry of Gerard Manley Hopkins*.

Housman, A. E. Eight O'Clock. James Mason: Caedmon TC 1203, *A Shropshire Lad and Other Poetry*.

———. 1887. James Mason: Caedmon TC 1203, *A Shropshire Lad and Other Poetry*.

———. Loveliest of Trees. James Mason: Caedmon TC 1203, *A Shropshire Lad and Other Poetry*.

———. On Wenlock Edge the Wood's in Trouble. James Mason: Caedmon TC 1203, *A Shropshire Lad and Other Poetry*. Robert Donat: Argo RG 437, *Robert Donat Reads Selected Poetry*.

———. Terence, This Is Stupid Stuff. James Mason: Caedmon TC 1203, *A Shropshire Lad and Other Poetry*.

———. To an Athlete Dying Young. James Mason: Caedmon TC 1203, *A Shropshire Lad and Other Poetry*.

Hughes, Langston. Ballad of the Landlord. Ruby Dee: Caedmon TC 1272, *Poetry of Langston Hughes*.

Jagger–Richards. Honky Tonk Women. Rolling Stones: London NPS5, *Get Yer YaYa's Out!*

——. No Expectations. Rolling Stones: London PS-539, *Beggar's Banquet*. Joan Baez: Vanguard (S) 79310, *One Day at a Time*.

Jeffers, Robinson. Shine, Perishing Republic. Judith Anderson: Caedmon TC 1297, *The Poetry of Robinson Jeffers*.

Johnson, James Weldon. The Creation. Bryce Bond: Scholastic/Folkways LC R-65-1755, *God's Trombones*.

Keats, John. La Belle Dame Sans Merci. Caedmon TC 2011, *Golden Treasury of English Literature*. Argo RG 341, *Poems of John Keats*.

Kilmer, Joyce. Trees. Caedmon TC 1207, *Favorite American Poems*.

Kirkman, Terry. Requiem for the Masses. Association: Warner Brothers (S) 1696, *Insight Out*.

Kupferberg, Tuli. Morning, Morning. Richie Havens: MGM (S) 4698, *Mixed Bag*. Syder Turner: MGM (S) 4450, *Stand By Me*.

Lee, Don L. But He Was Cool. (Tape available from Broadside Press, 12651 Old Mill Place, Detroit, Michigan, 48238, *Don't Cry, Scream*.)

Lennon, John. Eleanor Rigby. Beatles: Capitol (S) ST-2576, *Revolver*.

——. Norwegian Wood. Beatles: Capitol (S) ST-2442, *Rubber Soul*.

Lennon-McCartney. I Am the Walrus. Beatles: Capitol (S) SMAL-2835, *Magical Mystery Tour*.

——. Let It Be. Beatles: Apple (S) AR-34001, *Let It Be*.

Lind, Bob. Elusive Butterfly. Bob Lind: World Pacific (S) 21841, *Don't Be Concerned*.

Lindsay, Vachel. General William Booth Enters into Heaven. Vachel Lindsay: Caedmon TC 1041, *Vachel Lindsay Reading*.

MacLeish, Archibald. You, Andrew Marvell. Argo RG 245/6, *An Historical Anthology of American Poetry*.

Marvell, Andrew. To His Coy Mistress. Caedmon TC 1049, *Seventeenth Century Poetry*. Argo 427, *Secular Metaphysical Poetry*.

Mayfield, Curtis. Isle of Sirens. Impressions: ABC ABCS-606, *The Fabulous Impressions*.

Milton, John. On the Late Massacre in Piedmont. Argo 433, *Milton's Shorter Poems*.

Mitchell, Joni. Woodstock. Joni Mitchell: Reprise (S) 6376, *Ladies of the Canyon*. Crosby, Stills, Nash, and Young: Atco (S) 7200, *Déjà Vu*.

Morrison, Jim. Horse Latitudes. Doors: Elektra (S) 74007, *The Doors*.

——. Moonlight Drive. Doors: Elektra (S) 74014, *Strange Days*.

——. Twentieth Century Fox. Doors: Elektra (S) 74007, *The Doors*.

Nelson, Willie. One Day at a Time. Willie Nelson: Victor (S) LSP-3418, *Country Willie—His Own Songs*. Joan Baez: Vanguard VSD-79310, *One Day at a Time*.

Ochs, Phil. The Crucifixion. Phil Ochs: A&M (S) 4133, *Pleasures Of the Harbor*.

————. The Flower Lady. Phil Ochs: A&M (S) 4133, *Pleasures of the Harbor*.

————. The Harder They Fall. Phil Ochs: A&M (S) 4148, *Tape from California*.

————. I Kill Therefore I Am. Phil Ochs: A&M (S) 4181, *Rehearsals for Retirement*.

————. Joe Hill. Phil Ochs: A&M (S) 4133, *Pleasures of the Harbor*.

————. Pleasures of the Harbor. Phil Ochs: A&M (S) 4133, *Pleasures of the Harbor*.

————. Where Were You in Chicago? Phil Ochs: A&M (S) 4181, *Rehearsals for Retirement*.

————. White Boots Marching in a Yellow Land. Phil Ochs: A&M (S) 4148, *Tape from California*.

————. William Butler Yeats Visits Lincoln Park and Escapes Unscathed. Phil Ochs: A&M (S) 4181, *Rehearsals for Retirement*.

Phillips, John. 'California Dreamin'. Mamas and the Papas: Dunhill (S) 50006, *The Mamas and the Papas*.

Putnam, Curly. Green, Green Grass of Home. Curly Putnam: ABC (S) 618, *Lonely Country of Curly Putnam*. Johnny Cash: Columbia (S) CS-9639, *Johnny Cash at Folsom Prison*. Joan Baez: Vanguard VSD-79308, *David's Album*.

Ransom, John Crowe. Bells for John Whiteside's Daughter. Argo RG 245/6, *An Historical Anthology of American Literature*.

Redding–Cropper. Dock of the Bay. Otis Redding: Volt (S) 419, *Dock of the Bay*.

Reid–Brooker. A Whiter Shade of Pale. Procol Harum: Deram (S) 18008, *Procol Harum*.

Robinson–Hayes. Joe Hill. Joan Baez: Cotillion (S) 3-500, *Woodstock*. Joan Baez: Vanguard (S) VSD-79310, *One Day at a Time*.

Russell, Bobby. Honey. Bobby Russell: Elf (S) 9500, *Words, Music, Laughter, and Tears*. Bobby Goldsboro: UAR (S) 6642, *Honey*.

Shakespeare, William. Winter. Claire Bloom: Caedmon TC 2011, *Golden Treasury of English Poetry*.

Shelley, Percy Bysshe. Ode to the West Wind. Argo RG 380, *Poems of Percy Bysshe Shelley*.

Simon, Paul. Bleecker Street. Simon and Garfunkel: Columbia (S) CS-9049, *Wednesday Morning, 3 A.M.*

————. Sparrow. Simon and Garfunkel: Columbia (S) CS-9049, *Wednesday Morning, 3 A.M.*

Slick, Grace. White Rabbit. Great Society/Grace Slick: Columbia (S) CS-9624, *Conspicuous Only in Its Absence*. Jefferson Airplane: Victor (S) LSP-3766, *Surrealistic Pillow*.

Stevens, Wallace. The Idea of Order at Key West. Wallace Stevens: Caedmon TC 1068, *Wallace Stevens Reading His Poems.* Wallace Stevens: Caedmon TC 2006, *The Caedmon Treasury of Modern Poets Reading Their Own Poetry.*

Stewart, Sylvester. Thank You. Sly and the Family Stone: Epic KE30325, *Greatest Hits.*

Stills, Stephen. For What It's Worth. Buffalo Springfield: Atco SD 33-283, *Retrospective.*

Thomas, Dylan. Fern Hill. Dylan Thomas: Caedmon TC 2014, *Dylan Thomas Reading His Complete Recorded Poetry, Vol. I.* Louis Mac-Niece: Argo RG 29, *Homage to Dylan Thomas.* Richard Burton: Argo RG 43, *Poems of Dylan Thomas.*

Whitman, Walt. When Lilacs Last in the Dooryard Bloom'd. Ed Begley: Caedmon TC 1154, *Leaves of Grass, Vol. II.*

Williams, Mason. You Done Stompt on My Heart. John Denver: RCA (S) LSP-4207, *Rhymes and Reasons.*

Wordsworth, William. London, 1802. Eric Portman: Caedmon TC 2011, *Golden Treasury of English Poetry.* Argo RG 347, *Poems of Wordsworth, Vol. II.*

———. Ode: Intimations of Immortality from Recollections of Early Childhood. Argo RG 347, *Poems of William Wordsworth, Vol. II.*

———. The World Is Too Much with Us. Eric Portman: Caedmon TC 2011, *Golden Treasury of English Poetry.* Argo RG 347, *Poems of Wordsworth, Vol. II.* Sir Cedric Hardwicke: Caedmon TC 1026, *Poetry of William Wordsworth.*

Wyatt, Sir Thomas. They Flee from Me. Argo RG 484, *Elizabethan and Jacobean Lyric.*

Yarrow, Peter. The Great Mandella. Peter, Paul, and Mary: Warner Brothers WS 1700, *Album 1700.*

———. Puff. Peter, Paul, and Mary: Warner Brothers W 1473, *Moving;* Warner Brothers (S) BS-2552, *Ten Years After;* Warner Brothers (S) 1473, *Peter, Paul, and Mary.*

Yeats, William Butler. Crazy Jane Talks with the Bishop. Argo RG 449, *Poems of W. B. Yeats.*

———. A Dialogue of Self and Soul. Cyril Cusack: Caedmon TC 1081, *Poetry of W. B. Yeats.* Argo RG 449, *Poems of W. B. Yeats.*

———. Leda and the Swan. Argo RG 449, *Poems of W. B. Yeats.*

———. Sailing to Byzantium. Argo RG 449, *Poems of W. B. Yeats.* Siobhan McKenna: Caedmon TC 1081, *Poetry of W. B .Yeats.*

———. The Second Coming. Siobhan McKenna: Caedmon TC 1081, *Poetry of W. B. Yeats.* Argo RG 449, *Poems of W. B. Yeats.*

———. When You Are Old. Argo RG 370, *Now, What Is Love.*

Selected Bibliography

The items contained in this bibliography are *selected* only in the sense that they should prove useful in treating the lyrics printed in the text of this anthology, either in the general background they provide, or in the insights they offer into particular lyrics. Obviously, many good pieces on rock are not included because they are irrevelant for these purposes; equally obviously, some of the items included are useful but by no means the best-written pieces of prose in the language. Those marked with an asterisk are items which are especially pertinent; items marked with a (†) are items included in Jonathan Eisen's first-rate anthology, *The Age of Rock,* which I strongly recommend.

Anon. "Beat in the Classroom." *Melody Maker,* 39 (April 25, 1964):3.
———. "Children of Bobby Dylan: Boom in Protest Songs with a Rock Beat." *Life,* 59 (Nov. 5, 1965):43–4.
———. "Great Rock Conspiracy: Theories of Gary Allen." *National Review,* 21 (Sept. 23, 1969):959.
———. "Purge: Morality Campaign Against Dirty Lyrics." *Newsweek,* 69 (May 8, 1967):114.
———. "Youth Music—A Special Report." *Music Educator's Journal,* LVI, iii (Nov., 1969), 43–73.
†*Aldridge, Alan. "Beatles Not All That Turned On." *Washington Post.*
*———, ed. *Beatles Illustrated Lyrics.* 2 vols. Delacorte Press, 1969, 1971.
Alterman, Loraine. "Paul Simon." *Rolling Stone,* No. 59 (May 28, 1970).
*Belz, Carl. *The Story of Rock.* New York: Oxford U. Press, 1969.
†Birchall, Ian. "The Decline and Fall of British Rhythm and Blues."
†*Christgau, Robert. "Rock Lyrics Are Poetry (Maybe)." *Cheetah* (Dec. 1967).
———. "Secular Music." *Esquire,* 71 (April, 1969):62ff.
Corliss, R. "Pop Music: What's Been Happening." *National Review,* 19 (April 4, 1967):371–4.
Cott, Jonathan and Dalton, David. "Let It Be." *Rolling Stone,* No. 62 (July 9, 1970).
Davies, Hunter. *The Beatles.* New York: Dell, 1968.
DeMorse, D. E. "Avant-Rock in the Classroom." *English Journal,* 58 (Feb., 1969):196–200.

DeMott, R. "Rock as Salvation." *New York Times Magazine* (Aug. 25, 1969):49.

*Eisen, Jonathan, ed. *The Age of Rock*. New York: Random House (Vintage), 2 vols., 1969, 1970.

English, Helen W. "Rock Poetry, Relevance, and Revelation," *English Journal*, LIX (Nov., 1970), 1122–27.

Etzkon, K. P. "The Relationship Between Musical and Social Patterns in American Pop Music." *Journal of Research in Music Education*, 12 (Nov. 4, 1964):279–86.

Gabree, J. "Rock: Art Revolution, or Sell-out?" *Hi Fi*, 19 (Aug., 1969):10–11.

———. *The World of Rock*. Greenwich: Fawcett Publications, 1968.

Gannon, F. "London Scene: Pop Music." *National Review*, 17 (Sept. 21, 1965):838–40.

Gillett, Charlie. *The Sound of the City*. New York: E. P. Dutton, 1970.

*Goldberg, Steven. "Bob Dylan and the Poetry of Salvation." *Saturday Review*, 53 (May 30, 1970):43–46.

———. "That Angry Kid Has Gone All Over Romantic: About the New Dylan Album." *Life*, 66 (May 23, 1969):18.

*Goldstein, R. *The Poetry of Rock*. New York: Bantam Books, 1969.

*Greenfield, J. "For Simon and Garfunkel, All Is Groovy." *New York Times Magazine* (Oct. 13, 1968):48–9.

Hafferkamp, Jack. "Ladies and Gents, Leonard Cohen." *Rolling Stone*, No. 75 (Feb. 4, 1971):26.

Hopkins, Jerry. *The Rock Story*. New York: Signet, 1970.

Kanfer, S. "Two Fine Rockers Roll Their Own: Simon and Garfunkel." *Life*, 62 (April 21, 1967):18.

Kermode, Frank, Stephen Spender, and Art Kane, "Bob Dylan: The Metaphor at the End of the Funnel," *Esquire*, LXXVII (May, 1972), 109–18ff.

Korall, B. "Music of Protest." *Saturday Review*, 51 (Nov. 16, 1968):26ff.

Kramer, Daniel. *Bob Dylan*. New York: Simon & Schuster, 1967.

Kramer, Rita. "It's Time to Start Listening." *New York Times Magazine* (Sept. 17, 1967):180ff.

†*Landau, Jon. "John Wesley Harding." *Crawdaddy*.

MacCluskey, T. "Musical Events: Musicology of Rock." *New Yorker*, 45 (Nov. 15, 1969):211–13.

Marcus, Greil, ed. *Rock and Roll Will Stand*. Boston: Beacon Press, 1969.

Marks, J. *Rock and Other Four Letter Words*. New York: Bantam Books, 1968.

†Meltzer, Richard. "The Aesthetics of Rock," New York: Something Else Press, 1971.

Nicholas, A. X. *The Poetry of Soul*. New York: Bantam Books, 1971.

†*Peyser, Joan. "The Music of Sound." *Columbia University Forum*, 10 (Fall, 1967).

Philips, T. "Vietnam Blues: Protest Songs." *New York Times Magazine* (Oct. 8, 1967):12ff.

†*Poirier, Richard. "Learning from the Beatles." *Partisan Review*, Fall, 1967, 526–46.

Rohde, A. Kandy. *The Gold of Rock and Roll, 1955–1967*. New York: Arbor House, 1970.

Rolling Stone. *The Rolling Stone Interviews*. Simon & Schuster (Pocket Book 68546), 1971.

———. *The Rolling Stone Record Review*. Simon & Schuster (Pocket Book 78531), 1971.

Rosenstome, R. A. "Times They Are A-Changin': the Music of Protest." *Annals of the American Academy of Political & Social Sciences,* 382 (March, 1969): 131–44.

Roxon, Lillian. *Rock Encyclopedia.* New York: Grosset & Dunlap, 1969.

Sadek, E. "Simon and Garfunkel: The Singers and the Songs." *Saturday Review,* 53 (Feb. 28, 1970):91.

*Scaduto, Anthony. *Bob Dylan.* Grosset & Dunlap, 1972.

Simon, Paul and Garfunkel, Art. "Simon and Garfunkel: Interview." *New Yorker,* 43 (Sept. 2, 1967): 24–7.

Smith, Jack E. Jr. "Turning On: The Selling Of the Present, 1970," *College English,* LX, iii (March, 1971), 333–8.

*Spinner, Stephanie. *Rock Is Beautiful.* New York: Dell, 1970.

Stafford, Jo and Greeley, B. "A Great Thing's Been Lost to Rock and Roll—the American Pop Song." *Variety,* 233 (Jan. 29, 1964):57.

Wenner, Jann. "John Lennon." *Rolling Stone,* No. 74 (Jan.-Feb., 1971):75.

———, ed. *Lennon Remembers.* Straight Arrow Books, 1971.

———. "Paul McCartney." *Rolling Stone,* No. 57 (April 30, 1970).

*———. "The Rolling Stone Interview: Dylan." *Rolling Stone,* No. 47 (Nov. 29, 1969).

Whittemore, Reed. "Review: *Beatles Illustrated Lyrics.*" *New Republic,* 161 (Nov. 8, 1969):25.

Williams, Paul. *Outlaw Blues.* New York: Pocket Books, 1969.

*Willis, Ellen. "The Sound of Dylan." *Commentary* 44 (Nov., 1968):71–8. Reprinted in *Representative Men* (New York: The Free Press, 1970).

Zappa, Frank. "Oracle Has It All Psyched Out: Rock Music and Its Relationship to Society." *Life,* 64 (June 28, 1968):82–4.

Index:
Titles and Authors